Portrait of a Port: Boston, 1852–1914

Portrait of a Port: Boston, 1852–1914   *W. H. Bunting, Compiler and Annotator*

The Belknap Press of Harvard University Press
Cambridge, Massachusetts, and London, England

First Harvard University Press paperback edition, 1994

Library of Congress Catalog Card Number 77–145893
ISBN 0-674-69076-1 (pbk.)
Book design by David Ford
Printed in the United States of America

Preface

This is a book of photographs. The photographs are concerned with the port of Boston, 1852–1914. Nevertheless, this is not a photographic *history* of the port of Boston during that period. A major port is a far-reaching social and economic phenomenon that defies photographic capture. Like most ports, Boston was primarily a point of converging transportation systems involved in the carriage of particular freights. It both fostered and served a great city and an important industrial hinterland. It was a small part of the tremendous, ever-changing, seemingly amorphous network of world commerce. An adequate overview of Boston's position in the system during the last half of the nineteenth century would have to include the *pampas* of Argentina, the timberlands of Canada, Maine, and Georgia, the wheatlands of Kansas, the canefields of Java, and the coalfields of West Virginia—not to mention the shoe factories of Lynn, the textile mills on the Merrimac, and the magnificent harbor of the great domineering rival to the west, New York. It would have to rank locomotives with vessels, rail founders with shipbuilders.

Nor is it even entirely accurate to call this book a photographic *maritime* history of the port of Boston since it cannot be fully comprehensive. Nevertheless, the book's treatment of that history is intended to be a fair representation of the whole.

Personal preferences have compromised the historical purity of this collection from its very beginning. The professional photographer primarily took those photographs that he was hired to take; the amateur usually pursued his own narrow interests with little peripheral vision. Technologically hampered, photographers were generally very discriminating. The ingrained habits of formalized picture-taking persisted long after more casual photography was possible. Thousands of commonplace scenes which would interest us greatly today were ignored (how many of us have recorded the interior of a supermarket for future historians?). There is a danger of accepting as commonplace particular scenes which were photographed precisely because of their novelty.

Only a very small percentage of the photographs taken survived. Of those that I was able to see I selected the pictures which I most enjoyed looking at, which would reproduce well, and which I judged to be of historical interest. The choices were often difficult, and I could have happily selected twice as many. If another person had compiled this collection the result would no doubt be very different.

The dates "1852–1914" in the subtitle are in one sense misleading, since the collection is of necessity chronologically unbalanced. Most of the photographs are from the twenty years between 1880 and 1900, and that is the only period that develops much of any horizontal identity. Very few of the photographs date from before the end of the Civil War. It has often been maintained that the nineteenth century lasted until 1914; certainly in America the century's mid-point was the Civil War. Therefore, this book is primarily concerned with the port of Boston during the last half of the nineteenth century.

Despite its limitations, I believe that the collection does draw together to form a visual maritime portrait of the port, as composed by the photographers and their clients. It is, perhaps, a reasonable representation of the port as they saw it. The contemporary image—be it of the shape of a ship or a concept of commerce—will always be crucial to the understanding of history.

The principal creators of this book were the photographers. Despite great handicaps, they produced works of artistry and quality. Necessarily men of great patience and perseverance, they succeeded in preserving frozen images of time—acts of magic not adequately explained by chemical formulas alone. They have greatly enriched my life, and I hope that this book succeeds in sharing some of the pleasure that I have been afforded.

A scholarly friend has accused me of unleashing yet another "'coffee-table book" on the world. Though I will be most pleased if anyone chooses to keep this book in so accessible a location, I disagree with the implication that "picture books" are not to be taken seriously. No doubt my friend would have been most impressed if I were publishing a collection of unearthed manuscripts, but—reflecting a widespread prejudice—considered a collection of photographs to be of interest only to hobbyists. I suspect that this common judgment is a reflection of an intellectual perversion of the Puritan ethic, and that historic photographs are scorned as valuable documents primarily because they are so very entertaining! I would maintain that not only are photographs extremely important historic records, but that in many specific instances they comprise the very best medium through which the past may be presented.

A viewer's interest in a photograph is in direct proportion to his comprehension of the depicted scene. It is the more usual custom to illustrate a text with entertaining pictures; in this case I have attempted to illustrate some entertaining photographs with an informative text.

Writing acknowledgments is at once a pleasant and a painful task. Although I have the opportunity to thank some of the individuals who helped me, there is not space to include the names of many others. I wonder if ever a book so modest depended so heavily upon the aid of so many. The complete list would include librarians by the score, curators, secretaries, photo processors, professors, editors, authors, interested friends, interested friends of friends, mariners, and a few original old-timers. To this wonderful group I extend my sincere thanks, and I prize the friendships which have developed. The vital individuals and institutions who so kindly allowed their photographs to be included are recognized in the appendix. I wish to cite the following individually.

Director Abbott Cummings, Mrs. Wallace Whitney, and other staff members of the Society for the Preservation of New England Antiquities. I doubt whether there exists anywhere a friendlier or more helpful organization.

Director Ernest Dodge and the staff of the Peabody Museum of Salem, for great assistance and many kindnesses.

Mrs. Paul Gring, of Cambridge, Massachusetts, a lovely and gracious lady for whom the *Helen Barnet Gring*, a four-masted schooner of Boston was named, and who provided many of the outstanding photographs in the collection.

Mr. Albert M. Barnes, of the Mariners Museum; Captain F. E. Bowker, of Mystic, Connecticut; Mr. Frank Kelly of South Boston; Mr. Andrew Nesdall of Waban, Massachusetts; Professor J. H. Parry of Harvard University; Mr. Fred Stone of Cambridge, and Walter Whitehill of the Boston Athenaeum, for their varied helpful deeds.

Professor Emeritus Edward C. Kirkland, of Bowdoin College (whom I have never met) for writing his magnificent *Men, Cities and Transportation*, upon which I have been heavily dependent. I hope that he may be able to recognize its effect upon this effort.

Captain W. J. L. Parker, U.S.C.G. (Ret.), for his many contributions and corrections. Captain Parker is an outstanding authority on shipping, specializing in the history of American East Coast schooners. He combines the perspectives of both seaman and historian with the memory of a computer and the dedication of a craftsman. Nevertheless, he has displayed remarkable patience toward one who stands at the outskirts of his domain. Had I not been able to rely upon Captain Parker's exacting criticism I would never have attempted this book.

And finally, my wife Lonna, for her great patience, sound criticism, and vital encouragement; and my sister-in-law Meredith, a generous soul, who lent me the typewriter with which I wrote the book.

Though many persons have been responsible for much that is right with this book by correcting or improving much that was wrong or weak, no one other than myself may be implicated in any way for the shortcomings that remain.

W. H. B.

For my friends

Contents

Illustrations

Some Preliminary Considerations

The lay of the land has never counted for less than it does today—Boston and Salt Lake City were never more alike, and the trend continues at an increasing rate. Today, persons traveling overland from Boston to Portland or New York commonly do not know what rivers they are passing over. This is quite a recent phenomenon. At one time the river crossings would have been major events of the journey. The travelers' dullness is abetted by modern highway bridges, which display little real interest or respect towards rivers. Structurally fascinating, they are not content simply to connect bank to bank, but must create such a show of their own that the spirituality of a river crossing is lost. These are our bridges, and they reflect our values. In order to understand past values—as well as our own—it is increasingly important (and increasingly difficult) to try to comprehend the geographic images and realities of the past.

Most of the great cities retain distinct geographic identities despite our efforts to the contrary. For example, it is possible to create a satisfactory mental image of New York before the Europeans arrived, when things were seemingly the way they always had been. Lined by eagle-topped Palisades, a confident river, draining the wilderness, flows into an exceptional bay rich with marshlands to the west, with wooded bluffs to the east, and the great and empty Atlantic to the south. To the northeast, out through a clean and swiftly flowing salt river—the route of the summer bluefish—lies the Sound, navigated solely by migrating Indian canoes.

It is harder to visualize Boston of old, for here the original geographical components have been effectively obliterated by massive cuts and fills. Few Bostonians today view the harbor as an integral geographical part of the city, or much less—as in the past—view the city as a component of the harbor. Where once streets led easily and naturally to the wharves, today the waterfront is fenced off by highways, and largely forgotten. Economically speaking, this is perhaps as it should be, but spiritually we are the poorer for having lost our sense of identity with our particular geographic situation.

In the seventeenth century, Thomas Morton, the celebrated extrovert of Merrymount, wrote "The Beare is a tyrant at a Lobster, and at low water will downe to the Rocks, and groape after them with great diligence." [1] The harbor must have been an admirable place then, rich in fish and wildlife, with vast areas of salt creeks and marshlands. The islands, wooded drumlins, lay at anchor on every hand.

Boston was precisely located on an oddly shaped island, attached to the great and dark continent by but a narrow neck. Settlement of the surrounding area occurred very quickly, but many Bostonians prominent in the mid-nineteenth century were heirs to colonial geographical conceptions. As students at Harvard, those so inclined could still amuse themselves hunting in the marshes of Cambridge. As boys, standing on a Boston height, looking beyond the harbor islands, they could see in their mind's eye the white and dangerous sands of Cape Cod; the cold, grey and dripping Gulf of Maine; and the Atlantic, highway to the world. Turning and watching the sun disappear behind the western hills they could experience the eerie sensation, no doubt strongly felt by their Puritan forebears, of watching the great wilderness continent of silent forests, cold mountains, winding rivers, and Indian fires, darkening slowly from east to west, from the ancient Atlantic to the far Pacific.

I mention these impressions because I think that one's obvious reaction when observing old photographs is simply to measure the scenes against the present. It is just as important to measure them against their own heritage. To the people in the photographs, and to the photographers, our present was an unimaginable abstraction. They thought that they understood their past. The changes occurring within the nineteenth century were sweeping and profound. We should bear in mind the spiritual and physical roots of the persons affecting and experiencing those changes. We should try to understand a little of what lay behind the faces which chanced to be frozen in photographs, be they Yankee, Irish, Negro, Italian, Provincial, or other. We should try to understand a little of what might have been in the photographer's mind, for a photograph is a record of what a person once saw. We should try to understand the depths of that vision.

Portrait of a Port: Boston, 1852–1914

[1] A Short History of the Port of Boston

Massachusetts Bay is located at the westernmost end of the Gulf of Maine. It is bordered on the east, beneath the cold water, by gravel-bottomed Stellwagen Bank, which attempts to connect the Bay's great capes, granite Cape Ann to the north, and sandy Race Point to the south. Boston Harbor, once—before its aesthetic destruction by industrialism and overpopulation—a grand collection of bays, rivers, islands, marshes, and deep thoroughfares, protected from the swells of the Atlantic by the breakwater of the Brewsters, lies in the Bay's westernmost indentation.

The watery territory of the harbor, behind the portals of Deer Island and Point Allerton, is divided by a spine of islands running east and west. South of Long Island is the outer harbor, which opens to the sea through Nantasket Roads, and contains shoal Hingham, Hull, and Quincy Bays, and three tidal rivers. The inner harbor is to the north and west of Long Island; it opens to Broad Sound on the east, and connects to Nantasket Roads through the Narrows Channel (east of Lovell's Island), long the main entrance to the port. Shoal Dorchester Bay and commodious President Roads lie alongside the western islands, while farther to the north, at the confluence of the Charles River, the Mystic River, and Chelsea Creek is the city of Boston and its waterfront neighbors.

In many respects, this has always been an admirable harbor. In the years before large-scale dredging was possible the deep natural channels and roadsteads were of inestimable value. The island breakwaters created nearly four thousand acres of sheltered anchorages only a few miles from the sea. Until they were altered and reduced by erosion, caused in many instances by the diggings of the ballast industry [1], bold and handsome headlands greatly aided the pilotage of vessels through the network of channels.

The harbor's relative geographic situation, however, has never been so fortunate. Before the opening of the Cape Cod Canal, in 1914, Boston was to a great extent barricaded from the waters and seaboard to the south by George's Bank, Nantucket Shoals, and the great sand Cape. Although the waters just east of the Cape saw the heaviest coastal traffic of the continent, every year a considerable toll was collected, paid in wrecked ships and drowned sailors. Southern New England and the rich valley of the Connecticut fell easily under the influence of New York. And to the very end of deep-water sail, vessels bound for Boston from the Caribbean or the South Atlantic often felt compelled to approach by way of Vineyard and Nantucket Sounds, where they were likely to be long embayed by foul winds and tides before getting a clear chance to gain lonely Monomoy and dangerous Pollock Rip—and all the while New York lay invitingly close at hand. Nor were the shoals and fogs of the Sounds, or the long and deadly curving beaches of Cape Cod the final hazards of the voyage. In the winter Massachusetts Bay can be a most unfriendly location. Soundings in the Bay are often deceptive, and many mariners guilty of only minor errors of navigation have ended their lives on the ledges of Cohasset, the Brewsters, or the Graves.

From ashore, the geographic situation of the port was even less encouraging. Boston lacked both a hinterland rich with agriculture or minerals and a natural highway to the interior, like the St. Lawrence, the Hudson, or the Mohawk Valley. Standing to the west was the barrier of the Berkshires; even worse, any route forced over or under those old hills entered the domain of the great port of New York, which enjoyed in abundance all the natural advantages which Boston lacked.

To be certain, Boston's location was not totally without advantage. It was well situated to fine fishing grounds—although other ports were closer to better ones. As generations of local boosters have parroted, Boston is closer to Europe than are any of her principal rivals. But this proximity is an advantage only in certain special shipping situations, and in general it has simply meant that Boston was farther by land from the centers of American population and production. The most basic principle of transportation is that carriage by water is more efficient than carriage by land. Hence, though it was true that Boston was assured leadership in trade to her east, all the spruce and lime of Maine, all the salt fish and coal of the Maritime Provinces, and all the money ever spent at Boston by the notoriously tight-fingered Down Easters counted for pathetically little against the vital cotton, the golden grain, and the expanding markets of the South and the West.

Despite these deterrents, Boston remained the nation's second most active port throughout most of the nineteenth century. Boston successfully made the crucial transition from being a port in the old mercantile tradition to becoming a port in the modern sense, occupying a position in extended large-scale transportation networks. It fostered and served a growing industrial hinterland of great importance. This considerable achievement resulted largely from the substitution of dynamic and flexible enterprise for missing natural advantages.

The story of the early growth of the port of Boston is best told in Samuel Eliot Morison's *The Maritime History of Massachusetts, 1783–1860*,[2] and the interested reader is advised to treat himself to that lively classic. Morison's opening sentence reads: "Massachusetts has a history of many moods, every one of which may be traced in the national character of America." I would suggest that this

observation could also apply to the history of the port of Boston, at least till the end of the nineteenth century. Every sailor knows that a distant light may best be discovered when the lookout is not concentrating directly upon it. Similarly, the student of the port of Boston is treated to unexpected glimpses of much larger historical processes, for by its very nature a port is like a magic lens and bends one's vision in a multitude of directions.

In 1630 the Shawmut peninsula—Boston proper—was settled by a company of Englishmen led by John Winthrop. Selected after several other sites had proved unsatisfactory, the peninsula provided good defenses, drinking water, good anchorages, and high ground close to the deep channel. Unlike the fishermen-settlers of Marblehead or Scituate, the Bostonians hoped to lead a pastoral existence. In 1641 civil war in England disrupted links with home, and, as Governor Winthrop later wrote:

. . . all foreign commodities grew scarce and our own of no price. Corn would buy nothing . . . These straits set our people on work to provide fish, clapboards, plank, etc. . . . and to look to the West Indies for a trade.[3]

By the mid-forties vessels from Boston were fishing on grounds as distant as the Grand Banks and trading salt fish at Mediterranean ports for European goods. Generally speaking, however, Boston fishermen were of little importance to the offshore fisheries, then or later; Bostonians seemed early to understand that wealth was made not through the production of a commodity, nor even through its simple carriage, but rather through its clever distribution.

The Massachusetts colony lacked a native commodity—other than ships—with which to trade with England. In order to acquire European goods and specie, colonial merchants engaged in offtimes illegal competition with English shipping. Edward Randolph, a crown agent investigating colonial infractions of English navigation laws, reported in 1676 that;

. . . it is the great care of merchants to keep their ships in constant imploy, which makes them trye all ports to force a trade, whereby they abound with all sorts of commodities, and Boston may be esteemed the mart town of the West Indies.[4]

By 1652 the colony was able to mint its own coins from silver acquired in the West Indies. To a great extent New England shipping supported the development of the West Indian sugar colonies, supplying foodstuffs, timber, and European goods in exchange for molasses and rum. Rum became the favorite American drink, and was the stock-in-trade on both the Guinea slave coast and the American frontier. As an indication of the size of the West Indian trade—and of the consequent closeness of West Indian and New England societies—Randolph recorded that of the 131 vessels that cleared Boston between March 25 and September 29, 1688, eighty-four were bound for West Indian ports. Eleven were bound for Spanish ports, and only seven were for England.[5]

By allowing colonial vessels to participate in the closed trades within the empire, the English Navigation Laws provided a measure of commercial protection for colonial shipbuilders and merchants. In 1702 the only English ports possessing more shipping tonnage than Boston were London and Bristol.[6] By 1760 probably one out of four vessels in the greatly expanded English merchant fleet were American-built.[7] Boston's vessels were overwhelmingly home-owned, and represented negligible English capital; vessel shares were owned by a large proportion of the town's inhabitants.[8] From 1690 to 1740 the population of Boston grew from seven thousand to seventeen thousand. Throughout New England the creation of the distinctive Yankee race, "a new Nordic amalgam on an English puritan base," [9] was well under way. According to Morison, it was the "Yankee middle class of the water-front, keen, ambitious, inventive, courageous, that produced the great merchants and shipmasters of later generations." [10] They also made no small contribution to the creation and successful execution of the curiously conservative American Revolution.

If an opinion taker had toured the colonies interviewing rebels during the War of Independence he could have discovered a variety of local grievances against English rule. The Dutch fur trader from New York would no doubt have bitterly protested English attempts to regulate his traffic with the Indians; a logger from New Hampshire might have expressed his disgust with the hopelessly unreasonable Royal timber laws, and their corrupt and selective enforcement; the planter from Virginia might not have discussed the great debt held by his tobacco factor in London, but he was probably thinking of it. There would have been much talk about "liberty," but little mention of "democracy" save, possibly, in frontier areas. Certainly there would have been scant discussion of "democracy" at Boston—Boston, the home of the Revolution, was above all a shipping town, and the quarterdeck was not the nursery of dangerous notions concerning the equal rights of man.[11] Rather, the treasonous talk in Boston concerned the rights of free traders and the ending of commercial restrictions conceived by politicians of a distant land who were serving their own parochial interests. Many Boston merchants supported the war with their wealth—Massachusetts raised its own state navy; many others combined rebellion with profit-seeking, and over sixteen hundred letters-of-marque were issued to Massachusetts privateers.[12]

The year 1783 and Peace found Boston and the Commonwealth facing severe depression. The war and its political consequences had greatly disrupted the shipping industry. The fishing and trading fleets had to be rebuilt; Britain would purchase no more American tonnage; and most of the ports of the Caribbean were legally closed to American shipping. Although France and Spain soon relaxed their West Indies prohibitions, the British islands remained legally closed to American traders until 1830. Trade to the West Indies never ceased, but it was seriously reduced, and all of Massachusetts suffered as a consequence.

Within half-a-dozen years the depression was broken as the innovative merchants and peerless mariners of Boston and Salem created a remarkable economic revival. Using small vessels, backed by no great capital resources, no diplomatic or naval power, and by no great central organization, sharp young Yankees forced an entry into the rich China, India, and spice island trades, and transformed Salem and Boston into great markets for oriental goods. In the Far East, American activity soon rivaled the English, while Chinese and East Indian goods landed at home fueled trades to other lands.

Salem was early the leader in the trade to East Africa, India, and the spice islands. Until 1811, when British law prohibited all but direct voyages between India and the United States, Salem vessels frequently called at many intermediate eastern ports, trading entire cargoes many times. A cargo of mixed Baltic, domestic, and West Indian oddments loaded in Salem had often turned to wine for the Indian market by the time the vessel arrived off the Hoogly.[13]

Boston was the undisputed leader in the Canton trade. Traditionally, the great problem that faced westerners who would trade with China was the task of supplying commodities which the Chinese desired. Only western specie and eastern oddities (sea cucumbers, opium, rhino horns, and so on) commanded a market in China. In general, western trading at Canton (the only port in China open to foreigners) was supported by the plunder of the West Indies. Even the lordly British East India Company, with access to the opium of India, dealt chiefly with silver.

Maritime Massachusetts hungered for trade, but was in no position to export specie. Instead, Boston merchants devised a clever new solution to the Chinese puzzle. Their ships cleared Boston (or, often, an English port) carrying trading stocks of cloth, garments, shoes, copper, iron chisels, nails, and other cheap goods, bound around Cape Horn for the wild coast of the Pacific Northwest. Once on the "Northwest Coast," the Bostonians trafficked with the dangerous local Indians for peltry—primarily for the exquisite black pelts of the sea otter, which were highly prized by the mandarins. Profits realized from the sale of the furs (and often Hawaiian sandlewood) at Canton were reinvested in Chinese goods—tea, silk, chinaware, nankeens, crepe—which would bring high prices at Boston.[14]

The special importance of the China trade cannot be understood within modern concepts of shipping. Boston vessels engaged in the China trade did not represent hired tonnage earning a margin on freight rates—rather, they were the particular tools with which their owners (and captains) engaged in the business of amassing great fortunes through a highly selective speculative commerce. Strictly speaking, Boston's China merchants were traders, not shippers. True to their bold spirits, China·trade fortunes, as a group, have been among

the most durable and influential sources of capital in American history.

As Massachusetts shipping revived, the old Mediterranean trades were renewed with vigor. New commerce was established with the Baltic, entailing the exchange of West Indian products for iron, flax, and hemp. Much of the trade between western Russia and the Far East was routed through Boston and Salem.[15] In November 1794 an observer reported that Boston possessed eighty wharves and quays, and that not less than 450 sail of ships (vessels square-rigged on all three masts), barks, brigs, schooners, sloops, and small craft were in the port.[16]

Continuing war in Europe created demands for foodstuffs, and great opportunities for "neutral traders," giving much encouragement to New England shipping. Vessels cleared with cargoes of salt fish, then traded about with Mediterranean and European goods. Often both vessel and cargo were disposed of in the final transaction of the venture. Specie acquired through European trading financed expansion of the China trade.[17]

In 1807 both France and England strengthened their regulations devised to drive neutral traders from the other's ports. Friction at sea and the threat of war persuaded President Jefferson (who was no great friend of the wealthy Federalist shipping interests) to declare an embargo on all foreign commerce, which remained in effect until 1809. In 1807 Massachusetts' registered tonnage engaged in foreign commerce was over twice that of her nearest rival, New York, and was 37 percent of the national total. Her fishing fleet, which was largely dependent upon foreign trade, was nearly 90 percent of the total. In 1806 Massachusetts' income from freight money alone was likely equal to the entire federal revenue.[18] The stunning effect of the embargo—which inexplicably included the East Indian and China trades as well—can thus be appreciated. The greatest long-term damage occurred in the smaller, less resilient ports, such as Salem, Newburyport, and Plymouth, and one result of the embargo was the further consolidation of shipping at Boston.[19]

The causes of the War of 1812 have been debated at length, to varied effect. Despite the beliefs of generations of schoolteachers, much evidence contradicts the old assumption that the war was declared in response to the pleas of aggrieved sailors and shipowners. Although the maritime issues were very real, maritime New England was thoroughly opposed to war. Support for the war came rather from southerners and westerners who had never seen a ship, but who—it has been suggested—were eager for territorial expansion.

In 1813 and 1814 a new embargo and the British naval blockade again throttled maritime commerce. So tightly were the nooses drawn that extended wagon trades commenced along the seaboard. Transportation by land was still fearfully inefficient, and the seventy-five-day passage from Worcester to Charleston, South Carolina, posted by a four-horsed wagon carrying cotton cards, was not unusual.[20] While newspapers reported wagon entries under "Horse-marine Intelligence," [21] maritime New England seethed with impotent anger. The treasonous suggestions forwarded by a minority of radicals at the Hartford Convention (convened in December 1814) typified the over-reaction which doomed the political future of Federalism.

The great expansion of New England shipping through the Federalist period established patterns of seafaring which were to persist generally until about 1840. Although Massachusetts possessed a great seafaring community, it never developed a "native deep-sea proletariat" of the English or European style.[22] The sailors of American ships were predominantly American-born and young. They went to sea as boys and returned to the farms of home when their appetites for travel and adventure had been satisfied. Those able boys who stayed at sea often won quick promotion to command, wealth, and retirement to concerns ashore. Many masters of deep-water traders were only in their twenties. A seaman over thirty was a rarity. In radical contrast to conditions later in the century, wages at sea were generally higher that those ashore, and Emerson observed that sailors were "the best dressed of mankind." [23] As a class, American shipmasters were undoubtedly the best educated in the world, partly because of the social prestige of the profession and partly because they were often engaged in mercantile speculation requiring diplomacy and intelligence. In England, by contrast, sea-minded young gentlemen joined the Navy, and the merchant shipmaster was more usually engaged in the simple carriage of commodities over established trading routes.

Ships were uniformly small. Navigation was often of a primitive character, despite the best efforts of Salem's true genius, Nathaniel Bowditch. Nevertheless, Massachusetts vesssels did not often go missing.[24] The standards of seamanship were very high. This was an era when even commonplace vessels engaged in trades of little note were fitted with studding sails, and carried them at every opportunity. In *Two Years Before the Mast,* Richard Henry Dana tells us that the Boston ship *Alert,* bound home from California with a cargo of hides in 1836, carried a *reefed* topmast studding sail in a gale off Cape Horn! [25]

The high standards and rare spirit which pervaded the merchant marine are apparent in Dana's description of the *Alert* getting underway from an anchorage on the desolate California coast under the eyes of a contemptible New Bedford whaler (whalers occupied a class of their own, and were strictly avoided by true merchant sailors).

Everything being now ready, and the passengers aboard, we ran up the ensign and broad pennant, (for there was no man-of-war, and we were the largest vessel on the coast,) and the other vessels ran up their ensigns. Having hove short, cast off the gaskets, and made the bunt of each sail fast by the jigger, with a man on each yard; at the word, the whole canvass of the ship was loosed, and with the greatest rapidity possible, everything was sheeted home and hoisted up, the anchor tripped and catheaded, and the ship under headway. We were determined to show the "spouter" how things could be done in a smart ship, with a good crew, though not more than half their number. The royal yards were all crossed at once, and royals and sky-sails set, and, as we had the wind free, the booms were run out, and every one was aloft, active as cats, laying out on the yards and booms, reeving the studdingsail gear; and sail after sail the captain piled upon her, until she was covered with canvass, her sails looking like a great white cloud resting upon a black speck. Before we doubled the point, we were going at a dashing rate, and leaving the shipping far astern.[26]

The revival of trade after 1814 was gradual but steady. Boston continued to own the greatest tonnage per capita of any American port, and only

New York had an absolute tonnage advantage. Innovative men, including many Boston merchants, began to develop New England industry, and by 1840 Massachusetts was predominantly a manufacturing state. The growth of the textile industry, in particular, had beneficial effects upon the port, as it greatly encouraged trade with southern cotton ports and South American wool ports. Similarly, the growth of the shoe industry fostered a tremendous traffic in hides from Argentina, Uruguay, and Chile. Other South American products exchanged for Yankee timber and manufactures were coffee from Brazil and copper and nitrates from Chile. The unusually low cost of hides from California made possible the trade so magnificently described by Dana.[27]

The old trade to China via the Northwest Coast died out around 1820; trade to China itself continued, although it was of decreasing importance. Boston ships arrived at Canton not with otter pelts and sandlewood, but with English and New England manufactures—including textiles!—often supplemented by opium. After about 1815 ships at Canton primarily loaded tea, and although most belonged to Boston, they sailed for New York in increasing numbers.

Boston's failing East India trade was saved by the imaginative enterprise of Frederick Tudor, who undertook shipping ice to southern and tropical ports. When he demonstrated that it was a profitable business, others joined, and by the mid-thirties ice from Boston-area ponds was melting in drinks from Rio to Calcutta. "East India goods" were no longer pepper, sugar, and cottons, but jute, linseed, hides, dyestuffs, and saltpetre.[28]

Despite the shift of the Canton trade to the New York market, Boston persisted as the principal American port of re-export for goods from Calcutta, the Mediterranean, the Near East, and the Baltic. Typically, of the one hundred American vessels that passed Elsinore (at the entrance to the Baltic) from January to August 1822, thirty-eight were from Boston, twelve were from Salem, and twelve were from other Massachusetts ports.[29]

In all of the early history of America there was probably no business of greater importance which has been so thoroughly ignored by posterity as coastal shipping. The logger, the trapper, the frontier scout, the farmer, the soldier, the rich merchant captain, the slave, and the financier have all been duly remembered; yet only rarely is the coastal seaman mentioned. Nevertheless, for hundreds of years the Atlantic coastal waters and the rivers that flow into them were the principal arteries of transportation and commerce; transportation is perhaps the basic foundation of the American story.

Yet it is not difficult to understand why the coasting trades have been so grievously ignored. To begin with, coasting so thoroughly pervaded life on the Atlantic seaboard that it was taken largely for granted. Few records of its extent were kept, or remain. Customs figures describe foreign shipping in great detail, yet generally ignore domestic shipping; private recorders often did not include heavy local or small vessel traffic. (At Boston the situation is further confused as both deep-water and coastal shipping figures are frequently distorted by the trades to the Canadian Maritime Provinces, which were officially "foreign," but practically were of domestic character.)

We do know that in 1828 America's "enrolled" tonnage—principally engaged coastwise—exceeded her foreign-going "registered" tonnage for the first time; ten years later it moved permanently ahead.[30] By contrast, in 1829 the total registered tonnage belonging to the port of Boston was nearly three times the total enrolled and licensed tonnage of the port.[31] In terms of traffic, however, domestic arrivals at Boston in 1835 were roughly three times the foreign entries.[32]

Coasters arrived at Boston from both near and far, from the coast of Maine, Cape Ann, the North Shore, the South Shore, Cape Cod, New York, Philadelphia, the near South, and the Deep South. From the eastward came timber, hay, lime, potatoes, shingles, staves, bedposts, axe handles, passengers, cattle, salt fish, potashes, cordwood, soft coal, gypsum, grindstones, and a multitude of related sea and country products.[33]

Great fleets of coasters, many of them square-rigged, rounded Race Point from the westward and the South. Carl Cutler has enumerated eighty sailing packet lines established between Boston and New York, Albany-Troy, Philadelphia, Baltimore, Charleston, Savannah, Mobile, and New Orleans from the twenties through the fifties.[34] Despite the barrier of Cape Cod, Boston and New York were each the greatest single factor in the other's trade.[35] In the thirties packets were the mainstay of Boston–New York commerce, carrying passengers, flour, rye, corn, and oats in addition to all manner of express freight. Baltimore, too, was a great grain port; a vast fleet of vessels carried anthracite coal from Philadelphia. From farther south came tobacco, rice, cotton, and naval stores.[36]

Boston, in return, filled the coasters with the manufactures of her hinterland (shoes, boots, textiles, carriages, and so on) and with the varied imports (West Indian, East Indian, Baltic, Mediterranean, and South American goods) gathered by her great fleet of deep-water traders.

Although many American coastwise passages were far longer than many European foreign voyages, the geography of the coast and the economics of most of the trades favored the use of small brigs, sloops, and ubiquitous schooners. (The cotton trade, to Mobile and New Orleans, was an exception and employed barks and ships). The coastwise arrivals at Boston in 1825 reportedly included 23 ships, 215 brigs, 977 sloops, and 1292 schooners.[37]

The coasting trades created no lordly merchant princes, and a coasting skipper could not retire after a particularly fortunate voyage. To a dreaming farm boy, Bangor, Portsmouth, or even Philadelphia, were hardly the equals of Calcutta, Whampoa, or Madagascar. Flood tide on the Penobscot was not the bore of the Hoogly, and who would load coal up the Delaware when he might load silks at the Pagoda Anchorage? Coastermen did not frolic with the amorous girls of Hawaii, or watch the great lacquered tea deckers standing down the river from forbidden China—and so, they have been forgotten. But the drowned coasterman cast up on a winter beach of old Cape Cod was surely just as dead as his roving brother stuck through the back by a China Sea pirate, and Massachusetts Bay engulfed by a winter hurricane was just as hazardous a location as the waters of Cape Horn or the treacherous Sunda Straits. And who would not say that the 100,000 cords of coaster-delivered wood required in 1829 to keep Boston warm and fed did not contribute more to health and happiness than all the silk and tea landed by the Canton fleet?[38]

After several false starts, regular steamboat service to Portland was established in the 1830s. Additionally, there were limited local steam services. In general, the development of steam navigation on Massachusetts Bay was very retarded, owing partly to the lack of sheltered waters and the relatively dependable prevailing southwesterlies.

The selection of Boston in 1840 as the western terminus for Cunard's pioneer transatlantic steamship service from Liverpool was considered a great coup by Bostonians and rivals alike. Although transatlantic steamship service was a spectacular novelty, many years passed before steam supplanted sail to any great degree. Until the establishment of Enoch Train's Line in 1844, however, Boston was unable to support a Liverpool sailing packet line of its own. Two previous attempts failed as a result of Boston's lack of sufficient export cargoes, which forced packets to load at southern cotton ports, and demolished any pretext of a schedule. By contrast, New York's Black Ball Line, established in 1818, maintained sailings for over sixty years. Most of the cotton arriving at Boston was delivered to New England textile manufacturers, whereas New York's highly developed southern trades transformed that city into a great cotton exporter.[39]

Of central importance to the phenomenal growth of the port of New York was the Erie Canal, completed from Albany to Buffalo in 1825. The Erie provided the first practical means for bulk transportation between the Atlantic seaboard and the agricultural New West. Previously, the Appalachian barrier had caused the West's produce to be floated down the rivers to New Orleans. Within a few years of its opening the canal made New York the flour market of the nation—and Boston was one of its best customers. Of more importance, the canal created vast new markets for imports, which directly benefited New York port. Habits, connections, and patterns of commerce established by canal trade persisted into the age of the railroad.[40] By 1840, except for the immediate hinterlands of Boston, Philadelphia, and Baltimore, most of the nation had become the hinterland of New York. By 1860 the foreign commerce of New York was nearly six times that of all New England.[41]

It is worth noting, however, that twenty years

earlier the commerce of New York had already been largely captured by aggressive Yankees who overpowered the easy-going Knickerbockers.[42] Although most of these sharp characters were migrants from Connecticut, many of New York's great shipbuilders and merchants were Massachusetts men. Additionally, a very considerable proportion of New York's foreign trade was on Massachusetts' account and was carried in Massachusetts-owned vessels. On such commerce New York collected the fees, but Boston salted away the profits. As a creator of commerce the Erie Canal was beneficial to Boston shipping interests, but not to Boston port.

Despite being dwarfed by New York, the port of Boston was highly active through the forties and the fifties. Boston's registered tonnage rose from 149,186 in 1840 to 270,510 in 1850.[43] A random inspection of issues of the *Boston Shipping List* reveals that on September 9, 1843, eight ships, four barks, and a brig were lying at Commercial Wharf; eight ships, four barks, four brigs, and a schooner were at Central Wharf; six ships, five barks, and a brig were at Lewis Wharf, and so on.[44] On April 18, 1843—reflecting, perhaps, a break in the weather—sixty-six schooners arrived at the port. All save one came from the eastward. Seventeen were from Nova Scotia; eleven were from Bath, Maine.[45]

On September 18, 1850, thirty-two ships, forty-nine barks, forty-seven brigs, and fifty-two schooners were reported at Boston. Twenty of the ships and thirty of the barks hailed from Boston.[46]

Foreign entries at Boston in 1849 included 215 ships, 305 barks, 908 brigs, 1732 schooners, and 23 steamers. Coastwise arrivals included 193 ships, 488 barks, 1087 brigs, 4287 schooners, 89 sloops, and 65 steamers.[47] The large number of ships and barks which arrived coastwise is especially interesting—no doubt many were cotton packets. Of the more than seven hundred Boston–New Orleans packets sailing from 1830 through the fifties, as listed by Carl Cutler, more than five hundred were ship-rigged and at least 160 were bark-rigged.[48]

One of the reasons for Boston's increased maritime prosperity was simply that Boston remained one of the great shipowning centers of the world in a time when there was a tremendous rise in tonnage demands. The decades from 1830 to 1860 saw the accelerated growth of the United States and the widespread migration of British capital and production. From 1830 to 1860 the total tonnage of all vessels entering and clearing United States ports rose nearly eightfold; the comparable British total increased by a factor of five.[49] The North Atlantic cotton and immigrant trades were particularly affected. Tonnage demands peaked in the late forties and the middle fifties, reflecting food shortages in England and Ireland and the repeal of the English corn laws, increased business activities, the Crimean War, and the phenomenal gold rush and settlement of California.

The California boom was especially important, as its peculiar nature caused a disproportionate expansion of American shipping and inspired rapid advances in the design of ships. When Dana visited the West Coast in 1835 only a handful of Boston hide-droughers and Yankee whalers called there in a year; in 1849, 755 vessels cleared East Coast ports for California.[50] One hundred and fifty of those left Boston; one hundred and sixty-six followed in 1850.[51] Since California was a United States territory, the voyage there from the East Coast was technically a coasting passage, restricted to American-flag shipping. Trade to California during the years of the great rush offered fantastic profits and inspired the construction of the California clippers, the fastest vessels and the largest merchantmen that the world had seen.

The clipper ship was a strikingly new type of vessel capable of revolutionary performance. Its conception, construction, and management entailed unusual skill and courage. Nevertheless, the basic theoretical concepts employed in its design had long been understood, and had been applied in the past when fast vessels were required.[52] Clipper ship designers were primarily concerned with the task of adapting lessons learned from generations of development of small clipper brigs and clipper schooners to vessels of vastly increased size and potential—thereby entailing the consideration of a multitude of complex new problems. Clipper ships therefore reflected more the radical application of accepted theories than the application of radical new theories. In addition to their command of aero- and hydrodynamics, clipper ship builders and designers (usually one and the same person) were necessarily masters of structural engineering. Given the same technological and material resources, it is unlikely that today's designers (or their computers) could produce superior results.

Compared with their packet ship predecessors, clipper ships featured flaring bows, finer ends, longer runs, increased deadrise, decreased relative carrying capacity, and generally greater size. Their rigs were usually at least the maximum that could effectively be carried. A crucial element responsible for record passages was the fact that clipper commanders were commonly sail carriers of rare skill and nerve who were permitted to drive the vessels to the limit by reason of the extravagantly large crews shipped for that purpose.

The first clipper ships, built at New York in the late forties, were intended for the Canton trade. Clippers built for the gold rush, however, represented the fullest development of the type, and Boston enjoyed a central position in both the building and financing of the California flashes. For a few grand years crack Boston-built clippers smoked along the great ocean highways, humbling every vessel that they met. Most, however, loaded even their first cargo at New York, and few ever returned to their native port.

The clipper era marked the peak of shipbuilding at Boston. During this, the greatest period of American maritime industry, Boston's yards were producing the largest and fastest merchantmen in the world. Although the demand for California clippers had largely ended by 1854, American shipbuilding was temporarily buoyed by the repeal of the British Navigation Laws which permitted British shipowners to purchase American-built tonnage.[53] Even in 1856 "Boston yards" (at East Boston, Medford, Chelsea, Quincy, Charlestown, and South Boston) launched forty-two ships, three barks, one brig, and one schooner.[54] The effect of the overall shipping boom on American shipbuilding was reflected in the rise of total American flag tonnage from 1,191,776 in 1830 to 5,353,868 in 1860.[55]

Technological and economic changes occurring throughout the world during this great boom profoundly altered the basic nature of American deepwater shipping. Shipowners decreasingly owned the cargoes as well, and vessels were less often sent out on speculative trading ventures offering possible fantastic profits. Increasingly ships became competitively hired vehicles engaged in the transport of vastly increased quantities of basic commodities. The shipowner's income became the difference between freight rates and expenses—even the remarkable California shipping boom was based on shipping rates, not merchant speculation of the old style. Working conditions aboard American ships steadily deteriorated as shipowners economized to meet foreign competition, and the native American sailor was forced to leave the sea.[56]

In a related development, American ports such as Baltimore and Philadelphia which had not been as heavily involved in shipowning (in 1855 Boston, Baltimore, and Philadelphia claimed 393,577, 77,107, and 47,739 tons of permanently registered shipping respectively)[57] became increasingly important as points of transshipment in interdependent networks of land and sea transport.

The shipping panic of 1857 marked the beginning of the spectacularly rapid decline of America's maritime industries. The causes of this decline, which followed so closely upon world leadership, were many. They included the rise of low-cost sailing ship production in Great Britain and Canada; the collapse of the California bubble; decreased advantages of design leadership; improved efficiency of foreign—primarily British—shipping; the early inroads of foreign steamships; and the commercial disruptions of the Civil War—particularly the destruction of the cotton trade.[58] Between 1862 and 1865, partially inspired by the threat of Confederate commerce raiders, over 801,000 gross tons of American shipping were sold or registered foreign, marking the first great migration of American shipping capital to foreign flags.[59] From 1855 to 1859, 67 percent of America's foreign trade was carried in American-flag vessels; by 1870 the total had fallen to 38 percent.[60] Boston's own fleet, which was overwhelmingly composed of registered shipping, declined dramatically. In 1855, Boston's total registered (permanent and temporary) tonnage was 482,438; in 1870 it was 275,436.[61] (The difference between these totals is somewhat inflated by the adoption of a new system of admeasure in the sixties which decreased vessels' tonnages by varying degrees).[62]

The great age of American deep-water shipping had passed. No longer would major American ports be judged by the fleets of far-wandering ships that called them home; never again would people in remote and distant lands believe that "Boston," written in gold upon the sterns of so many fine vessels, was a nation in itself. After the Civil War the ocean commerce of the world was increasingly carried in hulls of iron and steel, which America was unable to construct at competitive cost. The profits of deep-water shipping, driven down by international competition, were not sufficient to lure away the American capital employed developing the West. In the future the major American ports would be large metropolitan areas and railroad centers capable of employing the rapidly growing protected coastwise marine—the child of industrial and demographic expansion—and of attracting the steam deep-water shipping of England and Europe with the agricultural produce of the great West. In the sixties Boston was forced to watch the steady decline of her deep-water fleet, and from every indication the Boston of the future might well be a third-rate seaport, attracting little shipping beyond that required by her immediate consumption and production. At this decidedly dismal phase of Boston's maritime fortunes it would be appropriate to shift our focus from the sea to the land, and to observe the growth of the railroads that were to become the absolutely essential factor explaining the eventual revival of the port of Boston—although of vastly changed character—in the vastly altered world of the second half of the nineteenth century.

After the end of the War of 1812, New England—Massachusetts and Boston in particular—grew increasingly paranoid and pessimistic—with good reason. Politically, New England lay in disgrace, felled by the excesses of radical reactionism. As a mature and largely interdependent economic unit, New England was left behind as the nation moved westward. From 1790 to 1820 the population of the United States grew 150 percent, while the population of Massachusetts increased by only 30 percent.[63] The population of eroded Berkshire County actually declined. In the light of the blazing success of New York, Boston felt especially threatened, and, if possible, the effects of the Erie Canal were overestimated by local prophets of doom and depression. The evidence lay at every hand—even at Boston's very back door the Blackstone Canal, completed in 1828, began to drain off the commerce of agricultural Worcester County to Providence.[64] Providence, of course, was already in New York's camp.

Not surprisingly, the first panacea proposed was a trans-sectional canal which would cleverly tap the western trade of the Erie as it flowed out into the Hudson. Had not the Middlesex Canal captured the commerce of the Merrimac Valley, leaving poor Newburyport to wither on the vine? [65] Despite the force of the arguments, the indisputable existence of the Berkshires could not easily be dismissed (although a tunnel through Hoosac Mountain was proposed). After surveys, the Commonwealth officially dropped the canal plans in 1828, thereby turning the stage over to a band of active railroad agitators. In the meantime, transportation projects designed to force trades through the Alleghenies for Philadelphia and Baltimore were under construction. Pennsylvania, acting too quickly for her own good, was building a system which combined many of the worst qualities of both railroads and canals; Maryland was wisely at work on the great Baltimore & Ohio Railroad.

The Boston & Lowell Railroad was incorporated in June 1830, with the Boston & Providence and the Boston & Worcester following suit shortly thereafter. Owing to the intransigence of interior farmers, who were not eager to see the golden grain of the West rolling past their fields of stone, no state aid was forthcoming. The quick and largely unexpected financial and operational successes of the three roads greatly influenced the future of railroading.[66]

The rail route intended to connect Boston and industrial Massachusetts with the West was built in sections. It must be remembered that the railroads were soberingly large financial, physical, and managerial undertakings, and were hardly considered certain investments. The Boston & Worcester was built over relatively easy terrain and was completed in 1835. From this success grew the logical extension of the Western Railroad, chartered in 1835 and incorporated by the directors of the Boston & Worcester. The route from Worcester to the Hudson entailed physical difficulties and provided little local traffic. It was then not even known for certain whether trains could surmount the steepest grades planned.[67] Raising money for the road became a test of Bostonian loyalty rather than of sound financial judgment—some prominent Bostonians, including David Sears and Harrison Gray Otis, were so hesitant that they chose simply to contribute funds, refusing stock for fear of future liabilities. Bostonians eventually purchased over three-fourths of the road's stock.[68]

The first trains traversed the entire route at the end of 1841. Despite the oratory of the occasion— and the fears of New York and Philadelphia—the connection did not contribute measurably to the prosperity of the port of Boston for many years. The stubborness of Troy, at the Western's Hudson terminus, prevented the construction of a bridge to Albany and the canal. The filling in of part of South Cove in Boston Harbor for a rail terminal disrupted tidal flows and caused silting which prevented ocean-going vessels from loading grain directly.[69] Financial and legal difficulties prevented the use of rail connections to the deep-water East Boston piers. Relations between the short-haul Boston & Worcester and the long-haul Western deteriorated over rate-setting, and union into a single road, the Boston & Albany, was not effected until 1867.[70] Despite the respective hopes and fears of railroad owners and sloop captains, it is indicative that water rates from Albany to Boston remained highly competitive for many years.

The Boston & Albany was a profitable enterprise, and it laid the foundations for the revival of Boston's foreign commerce. Created under the excellent management of the Western, it became the most technologically advanced road in New England. A bridge spanned the Hudson, and a million-bushel grain elevator was constructed at East Boston (reached via the road's Grand Junction Railroad). In 1868 Boston had been humiliated by the Cunard Line's decision to suspend its separate steamship service to the port. Although there were extenuating circumstances, the decision was based primarily on Boston's inability to provide sufficient export cargoes for the line's newer and larger steamers. With its new facilities, the Boston & Albany was able to guarantee Cunard weekly cargoes of grain in exchange for the line's business. Cunard accepted the offer and resumed its Boston service in 1871.[71] Similar arrangements made with other British steamship lines gave the Boston & Albany a temporary monopoly on inland imports from the port.

By necessity, the road was forced to develop a friendly working relationship with the New York Central, which had become a great trunk line to the West. Virtually all of the Boston & Albany's eastbound freight came via the Central. Although the Central earned more on a car going to the port of New York, it desired the tremendous tonnage of freight coming out of New England—by 1851 the Central Vermont "Great Northern Route" was eager for the same business. The long and happy relationship was finally consummated in 1900 when the desirable Boston & Albany, a money-maker to the end, became a part of Vanderbilt's great Central.[72]

In 1900 the port of Boston was served by three major rail systems—the New York Central–Boston & Albany, the Boston & Maine, and the Consolidated, or "New Haven." For our purposes, perhaps the wisest course would be to review the latter two systems from the perspective of 1900, observing the major roots, rather than working from the fibril level of the forties and the fifties.

The Boston & Maine Railroad of 1900 was composed of almost 140 once-separate railroads and overspread northern New England like a great cast seine.[73] It contained the systems of the Maine Central, the Boston & Lowell, and the Fitchburg. The Fitchburg had gained sole ownership of the four-mile "Great Bore" through Hoosac Mountain in 1887. Financed by the Commonwealth, fifteen years under construction, the Hoosac Tunnel gave the Fitchburg trunk line connections at Troy. By 1895 the Fitchburg had become the primary bulk freight carrier to Boston from the West, providing 60 percent of the freight—mostly grain and livestock— exported from Boston.[74] In 1900 the Fitchburg was joined to the Boston & Maine. Union of the roads allowed Hoosac traffic the use of the spacious Mystic Docks (acquired by the Boston & Maine through its lease of the Boston & Lowell in 1887) in addition to the Fitchburg's cramped Charles River terminal. The arrangement provided the Boston & Maine with a western route of its own for its extensive northern New England traffic.[75]

The Consolidated "New Haven" system of 1900 was composed of more than eighty once separate roads,[76] and resulted from the expansionist policies of the New York & New Haven Railroad, which in 1872 joined with the Hartford & New Haven to form the domineering New York, New Haven, & Hartford Corporation. After buying up the Connecticut House of Representatives, the combine began the systematic and cold-blooded monopolization of transportation in southern New England.[77] In 1893 it leased the profitable Old Colony Railroad, thereby gaining the territory between Boston and New Bedford, Fall River, and Providence. In 1895 it finally cornered and conquered the ailing New York & New England, which it had reduced through ceaseless torment to a state of living death. This key addition gave the Consolidated both an entrance to Boston and routes to trunk line territory which were fully competitive with those of the Boston & Albany and the Boston & Maine—as well as a virtual monopoly south of the Boston & Albany. A road which possessed only 519 miles of track in 1886 had grown by 1900 into a 2,073-mile monster.[78] The completion of magnificent South Station at Boston in 1898 (which the New Haven shared with the Boston & Albany), adjacent to its spacious waterfront terminal on the South Boston Flats, celebrated the railroad's blazing rise.

East of Chicago and west of New York lay the land of the great trunk lines, roads built to carry the produce of the West to the cities and ports of the East. Of the leading Atlantic ports, only Boston was without a trunk line of her own—New York had two, the Central and the notorious Erie; and even Portland was served by the unstable Grand Trunk, a Canadian road. By means of rail links or water service, all of the trunks had connections to Boston. Although some Bostonians bewailed the fact that Boston capital had not seized ownership of the New York Central when the road was young, their fears of manipulation by outside interests were not realized. The history of the great trunks clearly indicates that they could not afford to operate in the interests of their "home" cities unless they benefited as well. Railroad managers sought traffic for long hauls, not civic accolades. For example, two-fifths of the eastbound tonnage carried to Baltimore was delivered by the Pennsylvania Railroad. A "Boston trunk" would have acted no differently. Instead, Boston's construction of connections with several competing trunks was a wiser course of action.[79]

Boston's problem, therefore, was not trunk lines, but rather her relative proximity to the West and her eager rivals. This position was reflected in shipping rates, and therein lies a complex, not entirely logical, and vitally important story. The great agricultural tonnage bound for the East Coast ports would naturally tend to seek the cheapest route. The distance from Chicago to New York was considered the basic trunk line measure. The Baltimore & Ohio and the Pennsylvania railroads maintained, therefore, that Philadelphia and Baltimore deserved lower rail rates than did the ports to their east. The New York Central, understandably, did not agree, citing its superior route and equipment as a more accurate basis for rate setting. The fragile Grand Trunk, on the other hand, claimed that it deserved the lowest rates because it was the longest, the weakest, and the poorest.[80] Unbridled rate competition eventually hurt all the participants. The years from the late fifties to 1877 saw the eruption of fierce rate wars, interspersed with periods of exhaustion. Combat established important patterns and agreements which acquired lives of their own, to be perpetuated in future federal regulation.

Setting westbound rates was relatively easy, as the freight was of small bulk, and transportation of imports was initially confined to a small number of roads. In the fifties the trunk lines agreed that Boston and New York rates should be the same, thereby advancing the relationship between the Central and the Boston & Albany. The sulking Grand Trunk, however, refused to play. In 1875 the other roads attempted to discipline the stubborn Canadian road, and soon Boston's rates were one hundred percent lower than New York's, inspiring the Erie and the Pennsylvania to ship westbound goods eastward to Boston by water.[81] A shaky truce was eventually established.

By the late sixties the all-important eastbound rates gave New York a five-cent (per hundred pounds) differential over Boston; Philadelphia a five-cent differential over New York, and Baltimore five cents over Philadelphia.[82] However, the agreement worked out between the Boston & Albany, the New York Central, and the Cunard Line—which began the resurrection of foreign commerce at Boston—included a five-cent drawback on agricultural exports, thereby giving Boston an export rate equal to New York's.[83] In 1877, during the aftermath of a particularly destructive rate war, the trunk lines signed a treaty setting new differentials supposedly based on through-charges from interior cities to European ports. This agreement gave Philadelphia and Baltimore two and three cents respectively over New York. Boston was told that its rates could not be less than New York's, and its split differentials for domestic and export freight remained.[84]

The weariness of 1877 led to the creation of a trunk line association, or pool, ruled by Albert Fink, who had been the driving force behind a successful pool of southern railroads and coastal shipping lines. Fink's plan was to divide freight at its source between competitors. Roads carrying more than their share would pay into a common fund.[85] Problems of omission and commission immediately developed. Differentials caused the greatest unhappiness, as it was impossible to maintain the underlying concept of equalized through-rates. Ocean rates at a single port changed by the hour, reflecting sailings, vessel types, and other more mysterious considerations.[86]

In 1881, because of port improvements, the general ocean rates from Baltimore and Philadelphia to Europe fell to New York's level, and New York interests pressed the Central into challenging the differentials. Damaging conflict followed, and the differentials situation was put before an ad hoc arbitration commission. In general, the commission upheld the 1877 rates and agreements. Although Baltimore and Philadelphia were rewarded on the grounds of distance and port costs,[87] these factors were not cited in Boston's case. Rather, Boston was allowed to maintain her export rate equal with New York's on the grounds of historical precedent. Later decisions by the Interstate Commerce Commission generally reaffirmed the differentials structure.[88]

Despite persistent local visions of persecution, the effects of the differentials on Boston's commerce were far from disastrous. Beginning in the early seventies Boston experienced a dramatic revival of foreign trade as European (primarily British) steamship companies were attracted by the free wharfage and active cooperation of the port's railroads.[89] In 1869 not one steamship departed Boston for Europe; in 1877 there were one hundred such departures.[90] In 1896 there were 361 steamship sailings from Boston to Europe.[91] Comparing 1870 with 1885, the number of barks and ships arriving at Boston from foreign ports declined from 451 to 266; however, the number of steamships arriving from foreign ports (including arrivals from the Maritime Provinces) increased from 132 to 621.[92]

In 1875 Boston's share of the total grain exports from the four principal Atlantic ports was about 5 percent; by 1899 Boston's share of a much larger total was about 14 percent.[93] In the seventies Boston gained a strong position in the new and growing North America–Europe livestock and provision trade; in the late nineties Boston was clearly the nation's major cattle exporter,[94] and the provisions trade had made the Boston area a major meatpacking center. Although some cattle were driven or shipped to the stockyards of Brighton and Watertown from New England and northeastern points, the vast majority were western animals delivered by the Fitchburg and the Boston & Albany. Steamship lines calling at Boston were also active in the transatlantic passenger and immigrant business.

Throughout these decades of expansion Boston maintained a considerable and growing lead over Baltimore and Philadelphia in terms of the total value of imports and exports.[95] In most years Boston also enjoyed an advantage in terms of the tonnage of shipping entered and cleared.[96] Reflecting the great increase of British steam shipping and the conspicuous lack of American-flag deep-water steam tonnage, the overwhelming body of Boston's foreign trade was carried by British ships operating to British ports. Unlike Baltimore and New York, Boston lacked the necessary grain supplies to attract tramp shipping, and the great majority of steamers calling at Boston were liners. Boston's transatlantic trade was of sufficient importance to warrant the construction of a respectable number of steamers specifically intended for the run.

For the first time in the history of the port no major foreign shipping activity (excepting the quasi-domestic trades to the Maritimes and the

Caribbean) was associated with the waterfront of Boston proper. Ocean-going steamers called at the rail terminals of Charlestown, East Boston, and South Boston. The city's old waterfront served the active coastal steamer lines, the fishing fleet, Caribbean fruit vessels, and steadily declining numbers of deep-water sailing vessels that could afford to discharge and receive cargoes in the casual manner of the past. Coasting schooners discharged at numerous coal pockets and lumber wharves located all about the port (many were owned by the railroads).

Because of the scarcity of data, there is a dangerous tendency to underemphasize the importance of coastal shipping at Boston. Nothing could be more mistaken. By any measure the coastal trades were of greater importance to Boston and New England than were the foreign trades. Many of the factors that contributed to the revival of Boston's foreign commerce—specifically, the rail connections with the West and the rail systems of New England—were also crucial to the health of the industrial activity of New England that supported the coastal traffic. Of the approximately 8,000,000 tons of waterborne freight received at Boston in 1895, only 1,500,000 tons were delivered by foreign line steamships; 2,000,000 tons of generally high-grade freight were delivered by coastal line steamers. Over 3,500,000 tons of coal arrived, carried by a vast fleet of schooners and barges.[97]

The coastal shipping industry experienced a great expansion after the Civil War, largely in response to the demands of rapidly growing manufacturing and population. At no port was this process more evident than at Boston. Between 1850 and 1890 the population of Massachusetts increased from 994,000 to 2,239,000;[98] the average number of employees engaged in manufacturing advanced from 177,000 in 1850 to 485,000 in 1890.[99] Despite the fact that the dollar of 1890 was worth more than double the inflated dollar of 1870, the gross value of Massachusetts' products rose from $553,913,000 to $888,160,000.[100] The recorded domestic arrivals at the port of Boston in 1870 were 6060; in 1885 they totaled 8485; in 1900 they exceeded 10,000.[101] Throughout this period the average size of coasting vessels increased. (Also, to be practical, the two thousand or so annual arrivals from the Maritime

Provinces could be added to the totals.) In 1891 Boston's own enrolled tonnage was more than twice her registered deep-sea tonnage; of her total 236,281 tons of shipping, 186,702 tons represented sailing vessels.[102] Between 1900 and 1910, close to half of the new members admitted to the ancient and prestigious Boston Marine Society were coastwise masters.[103]

Having been forced out of the packet business by steamers and railroads, coastal sail was generally employed in the carriage of bulk, low-grade commodities—particularly New England ice, Middle Atlantic coal, and Southern pine. No ice was landed at Boston, but Boston was probably the foremost coal-receiving port in the nation. The great expansion of the coal trades to New England—particularly the bituminous trade, in which sail and steam competed—was directly responsible for the development of a breed of giant wooden schooners capable of delivering huge cargoes with remarkable economy. Steam captured the anthracite trade by means of coastal towing of barges. Regular steam colliers were not employed to any great extent until after World War I (the fourteen steam colliers built by the Reading Railroad between 1869 and 1874 and operated to New Bedford, Salem, and Newburyport, were the one major exception). In 1864 Boston reportedly received 103,000 tons of coal;[104] by 1900 coal receipts at the port exceeded 4,660,000 tons.[105]

A heavy traffic of fast coastal steamers connected Boston with the Maritimes, Maine, New York, Baltimore, Philadelphia, and southern ports. Most of the steamers operated to the eastward were big wooden sidewheelers, largely engaged in the passenger business. The southbound steamers that rounded Cape Cod were ocean-going steel and iron screw vessels principally employed carrying freight. At Boston steamers on southern runs loaded New England manufactures; they returned with raw materials and foodstuffs.

With the development of relatively swift steamer and rail transportation to Middle Atlantic and interior points the fresh fish industry expanded rapidly, and Boston became one of the world's major fishing ports.

The story of the roles played by Bostonians and their capital in relation to the port is of great interest and relevance. Boston's transformation in a few decades from a deep-water shipowning port to a major center of integrated transportation systems indicates that it was a community of economic flexibility. Since the basis of Boston's early wealth was shipping, it is apparent that to an important degree shipping financed the railroads, thereby confirming the observation that Bay Staters were proficient maritime opportunists, and not a true seagoing race.

The first large-scale wandering of shipping capital occurred after the War of 1812. F. C. Lowell, the founder of Massachusetts' first textile mill, was a wealthy merchant. The Appletons, of the Canton trade, invested early in Merrimac mills. John Bryant and William Sturgis, pioneers of the Canton trade (who later employed Richard Henry Dana aboard their brig *Pilgrim*) invested heavily in Lowell textiles. Harrison Gray Otis, a great champion of shipping interests, controlled a mill at Taunton.[106]

Shipping men proved to be the ideal pioneers of railroad development. As a class, they became wealthy when relatively young, were accustomed to taking risks and engaging in distant speculation, and formed a compatible community of investors with widespread credit. The men of the China trade, in particular, made a contribution to railroad development that belies their small number. No doubt this was partly because they were getting out of the China trade at the very beginning of the railroad boom, but they also clearly possessed the above-mentioned qualities to a great degree.[107]

Elias Hasket Derby, of Salem, the grand old man of the China trade, was a leading proponent of the Western Railroad, served as president of the Old Colony, and doubtless held many directorships. The Perkins brothers, leading China traders, were heavily involved with railroads, as were Bryant & Sturgis and the Cushings. Perhaps the most dramatic switch from Canton to railroads was made by John Murray Forbes. Forbes returned from Canton in the mid-forties, a wealthy young man looking for new fields to conquer. Soon he headed an extremely active and influential group of railroad investors, and qualified as an important railroad promoter. Among other positions he became the first president of the Michigan Central.[108] Railroad men of Forbes's caliber were not armchair investors or desk-bound executives. They traveled in the West for months

on end, and were continually immersed in all the difficulties that the financing, organization, construction, and operation of the roads entailed.

In 1848 the heavily New England-owned Philadelphia & Reading Railroad experienced some very rough sailing, and Boston interests in the road prevailed upon David Neal, president of Massachusetts' Eastern Railroad, to take the Reading's helm.[109] Neal skillfully piloted the Reading to safety, and went on to an extensive career in western railroads and real estate. Previous to becoming a railroad expert, Neal had been a Salem shipmaster in the China trade. An equally fascinating example of the curious interaction between the China trade and the railroads was provided when the great merchant Houqua, the patron saint of Boston's China traders, entrusted a large sum to John Murray Forbes to be invested in western American railroads.[110]

On the eve of the railroad boom of the forties Bostonians had already invested an estimated $30,000,000 in railroads.[111] In 1845 an analyst wrote, "The Boston people are certainly the only Community who understand Rail Roads," [112] and the *American Railroad Journal* noted that:

. . . the opinions of half a dozen eminent Boston merchants—if decidedly unfavorable—will be quite sufficient to deter foreign capitalists from investing in the securities of the Western States, be the advantages offered ever so great.[113]

Railroads created a multitude of economic prospects, and interest in railroads led directly to interests in real estate and timber and mineral rights. Bostonians invested eagerly in all. To cite one example, the *Transcript* reported in 1897 that in the Kansas boom of the eighties New Englanders purchased $85,000,000 worth of Kansas mortgages. The sheriff of Garden City recalled those times:

We used to wonder where all the money came from. There seemed to be no end to it. Seven loan agencies in Dodge City handled Boston and Providence capital only, and each must have put out over $300,000 in one year.[114]

A great bust followed the great boom, and prosperity did not return to Kansas until 1897. Kansas mortgages were not the only poor investments. W. T. Glidden and J. M. S. Williams, Boston's foremost California clipper ship operators; Elisha Atkins, a West Indies trader; the Nickersons, prominent shipowners; and Ezra Baker, a shipowner, were involved in the notorious Credit-Mobilier-Union Pacific scandal.[115] Many Bostonians got badly trimmed on the Santa Fe.

Referring to the decline of the deep-water merchant marine, Samuel Eliot Morison has written,

> The Civil War merely hastened a process that had already begun, the substitution of steam for sail. It was the ostrichlike attitude of maritime Massachusetts towards this process, more than the war, by which she lost her ancient preëminence.[116]

There is no question that steamship development at Boston was greatly retarded—in 1860 Boston's total steam tonnage was not much greater than Charleston's.[117] It would appear considerably more doubtful, however, that the benefits of steam power at sea were not realized by the sea-minded merchants who pioneered in the development of steam mills and railroads. How else can we explain the great encouragement (including the construction of a rent-free wharf) that the merchants of Boston gave the Cunard Line? On three separate occasions (1847, 1855, 1864) Boston merchants tried to organize their own transatlantic steamship line, although all attempts failed. Two of the incorporators of the 1855 attempt were Donald McKay and Enoch Train—two men who, above others, might be suspected of harboring a blind adherence to sail. It is recorded that in 1855 Elias Hasket Derby publicly predicted that, before long, steamships would dominate the commerce of the world [118]—if anything, he might be accused of being overenthusiastic.

The failure of the 1864 attempt was the most discouraging and the most educational. Prominent Boston businessmen and merchants (including Osborn Howes and William Perkins) financed the construction of two splendid big wooden screw steamers, and learned, to their great financial loss, that the line could not succeed without government subsidies (such as buoyed Cunard). By the mid-sixties it was also increasingly apparent that the future of steam at sea lay with hulls of iron, and not of wood.

Large-scale iron shipbuilding was a heavy industry having almost nothing in common with the New England shipbuilding establishment. Nor could any American yards expect to be competitive with the iron shipbuilders of Great Britain. Nevertheless, wooden deep-water sailing vessels remained competitive for several decades after the Civil War, and it is reasonable to assume that the Bostonians who chose to operate such vessels did so because sail offered them more profits than did steam—and not because of blind conservatism.

The steady transformation of deep-water shipping from small speculative enterprises into a large utilitarian industry profiting from margins of efficiency has already been noted. A Philadelphia shipper described the change:

> . . . in place of the merchant masters of the old days we now only need capable navigators and engine drivers. It is . . . a most prosaic and practical business.[119]

In 1903 a witness testifying at a congressional hearing investigating the sad state of the American merchant marine stated:

> When I urge enlisting railroad men in our cause, I want to say that if you do you will enlist nearly 1,000,000 of the brainiest, ablest men who control affairs in the whole world . . . Every man who has come in contact with the railroad men of this land knows that they are the supreme men, whether they are running a train in the wilderness West or in the most congested section of the East.[120]

A century previous this was precisely the class of men who put to sea in the ships of New England.

All this is not to say, of course, that Boston and New England capital turned entirely from the sea. Many individuals were simultaneously involved in both shipping and railroads, and no doubt considerable funds were invested under foreign flags. Previous to his retirement in 1861, William F. Weld was a director of three New England railroads, including the Boston & Maine. He was also one of the nation's largest shipowners: William F. Weld & Company, of Boston, operated deep-water square-riggers until 1875. Arthur Sewall, the great Bath shipbuilder and operator, was one of the great railroad men of New England. Many Bostonians invested and profited in the protected coastwise trades. Henry A. Whitney, of the Merchants' & Miners' steamship line, was a director of the Boston & Providence; Henry M. Whitney of Boston's Metropolitan Steamship Company was a director of both the Boston & Maine and the Maine Central Railroads. (The Whitneys also invested extensively in urban electric transportation, and created Boston's trolley system.) [121] Although there were profits for some in shipping, the prospects were limited, and the industry probably could not have successfully supported much additional investment. The evidence appears to indicate that both Bostonians and their port benefited more from investments in railroads, industry—and even Kansas mortgages—than they would have had that same capital been drained directly into shipping.

In 1900 the port of Boston was evidently the second ranking port of the nation; yet in only a few years its decline was well under way. World War I provides the most convenient turning point in the story of the port's fortunes—even though the war itself created a spectacular temporary shipping boom. The word "decline" is used subjectively and selectively. In terms of value and tonnage, the coastal, intercoastal, and import trades continued to grow—although at reduced rates—since they reflected Boston and New England's immediate consumption and production. Nevertheless, exports declined absolutely, and, on an overall basis, the port lost considerable ground to her rivals.

Nor are columns of data listing tons and dollars all that matter. World War I perhaps more definitely marked the final and precipitous decline of the port's unique and traditional characteristics of commerce and community, its irreplaceable intangible assets. In terms of simple interest and human participation the many arrivals in the 1920s of large oil tankers from Los Angeles and great steam colliers from Norfolk could scarcely match the ancient flocks of small Down East coasters or the legions of many-masted coal schooners that had crowded the port only decades before. The draggers and short-rigged auxiliary schooners of the fishing fleet lacked something of the spirit of the all-sail fleet. Steamships trading to the Far East and the River Plate did not impart the atmosphere of the lofty deep-water square-riggers of even the recent past. Nor could the hurried visits (only a few hours' long) of British passenger steamers preoccupied with New York ever hope to provide Boston with

the pride and security of its "own" fleet of liners. As vessels grew larger and more efficient, fewer crew members, pilots, tug men, stevedores, chandlers, agents, boardinghouse masters and barkeepers were required per ton of shipping.

The most serious area of decline was foreign trade. In terms of value, Boston's exports declined from $88,126,444 in 1903 to $50,558,550 in 1922.[122] From 1891 to 1900 Boston handled 9 percent of the nation's imports, and 9.7 percent of its exports. From 1901 to 1910 these proportions fell to 8.3 percent and 5.8 percent, respectively. From 1911 to 1915 exports fell to 3.2 percent; in 1922 imports were 6.25 percent, and exports were only 1.3 percent.[123] The situation worsened despite the efforts of an active port authority (1911), and considerable port improvements.

Several factors were responsible for Boston's problems. For one, the creation of J. P. Morgan's colossal shipping conglomeration, the International Mercantile Marine Company, in 1901–1902, put most of the important transatlantic steamship lines associated with the port under New York management. The consolidated management exerted no special effort to load ships at Boston.

The basic patterns of American and North Atlantic trade were changing. Growing industry and population increased the demands for imports while decreasing agricultural exports. The growing competition of Montreal and New Orleans had considerable effect on all North American ports—although Boston, a traditional "Canadian" port, probably suffered the greatest loss (The Canadian Pacific Fleet, established in 1903, quickly became one of the world's largest). Nor was Boston helped by the Interstate Commerce Commission's decision to raise Boston's import rail rates. Between 1903 and 1913 Montreal's import trade nearly doubled in value, and surpassed Boston's by a wide margin.[124]

Boston's once great export trade of livestock and provisions fell victim to increased American appetites and the refrigerated beef trade from the Argentine to Europe. Whereas in 1904 exports of cattle and provisions were valued at $48,000,000, by 1913 they were worth only $18,000,000.[125]

The general decline of the North American grain trade once again left Boston without sufficient bulk exports. The only bulk freights emanating from

New England itself were apples in the fall and cotton wastes. Boston and New York overlooked a real opportunity to capture the growing western Canadian grain trade with the lower differentials that the rail distances would have justified—it went by the board, and the regular American differentials were applied by default.[126] In 1913 Boston's excess of entered tonnage over cleared tonnage had grown to 1,135,421 tons,[127] as steamers departed Boston empty to load export cargoes at other ports.

World War I was also a factor. Losses of "Boston" ships were very high. In the unsettled and depressed years that followed, several weakened "Boston" lines disappeared in mergers or liquidation. Central to Boston's difficulties was the continued growth of the port of New York and the advance of motor trucking. Restrictive post-war legislation largely ended the immigrant trade.

The situation today is not improved. In 1967, in terms of cargo tonnage, Boston was surpassed even by Portland (though Boston had more dry cargo), to say nothing of her old principal rivals.[128] It seems certain that in proportion to its surrounding population the port of Boston handles a smaller tonnage of goods than does the port of any other major East Coast metropolitan area. The greatest activity at the port today is found not on the docks, and not in the railroad yards, but at the airport. Indeed, much of the freight now produced in the Boston area—small-volume, high-value electronics—is shipped by air. The metropolitan area and its hinterland are now chiefly supplied by trucks, and much of the freight entering and leaving the region passes through the port of New York. (Even in 1928, 65 percent of all New England's exports were routed through New York.) [129]

The revival of the port in the foreseeable future seems most unlikely. The harbor is too shoal for the construction of a supertanker terminal, and the port's location appears unsuited for any real development of containership operations. With costs of vessel operation and port services continually rising, ships are less inclined to call at Boston to discharge freight which may be trucked from New York. The inherent disadvantages of the port's geographical location have now taken a firm grip on its future.

With the future of the port apparently foreordained by economics, only the future of the once magnificent old harbor remains in doubt. One wonders how sensitive Bostonians of the past would react to its present state of degradation. Some planners advocate a giant jet port that will cover the Brewsters, crowding out old Boston Light, destroying the last spiritual remnants of the harbor's pre-European state, and ending any prospects of the area's aesthetic rehabilitation. On the other hand, if people care enough, the water could be cleaned of pollution, the islands cleared of rubble, the marshlands and shorelines restored, the waterfronts redeveloped, and the watery territory south of the city could become a wonderful regional park, an invaluable resource to enjoy and protect in our crowded future.

Maps

Boston Harbor, 1877. This is a detail from the United States Coast Survey chart of the Atlantic Coast, Cape Sable to Cape Hatteras. Lamont Library, Harvard University.

The New England Coast, from Portland to Nantucket, 1877. This is a detail from the chart listed above.

J. H. Colton's Map of Boston and Adjacent Cities, 1855. W. H. Bunting.

A detail from Sampson, Murdock's map of the Boston area, 1886. Lamont Library, Harvard University.

Atlantic Avenue and a part of the old waterfront. The docks west of the avenue were reclaimed with fill. This is a detail from a map of Boston in A. Williams' *Boston in the Future*, published at Boston in 1871. Widener Library, Harvard University.

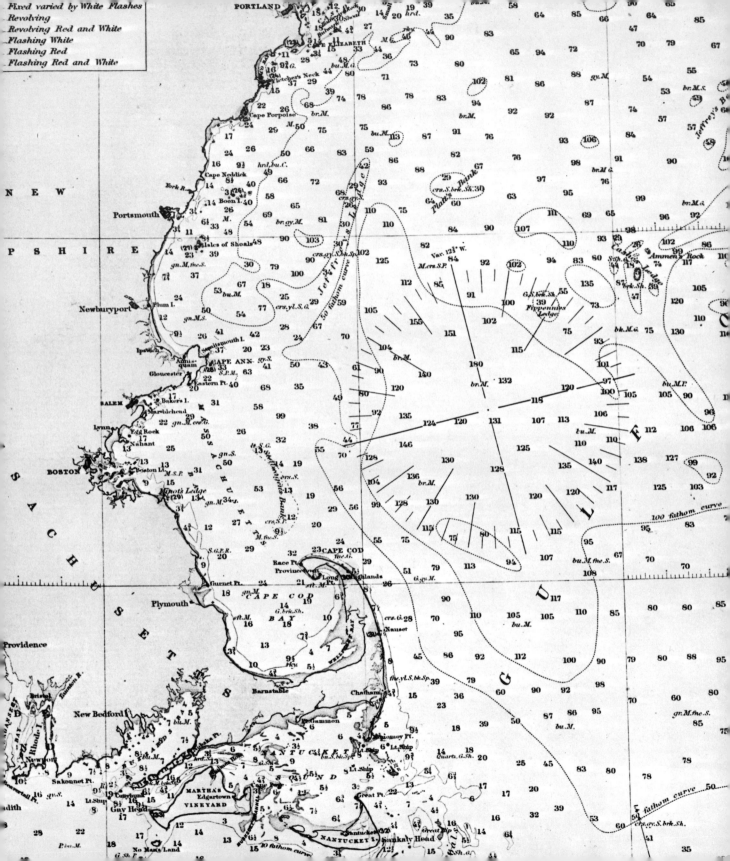

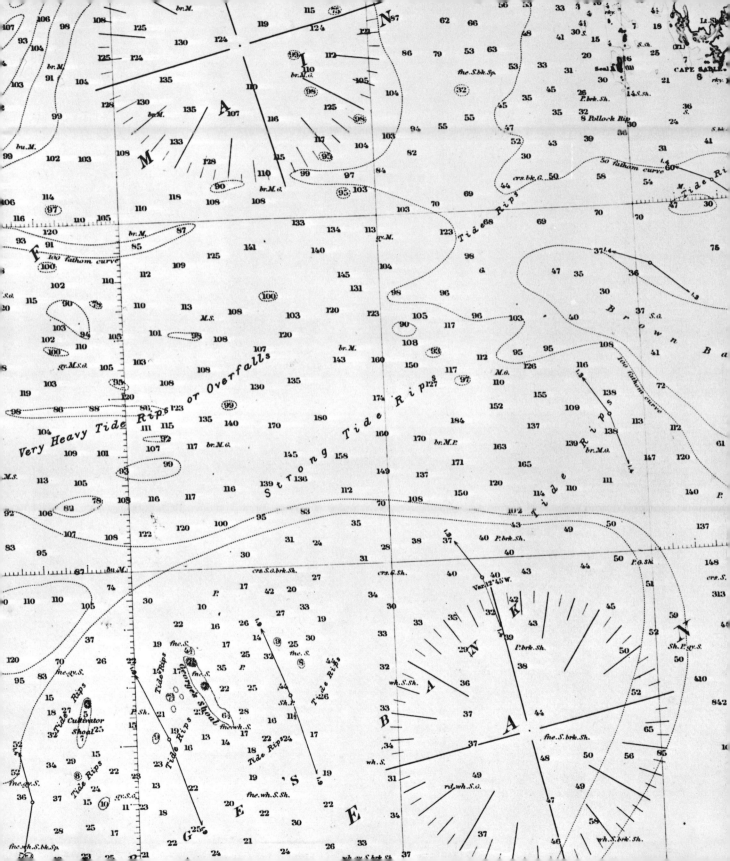

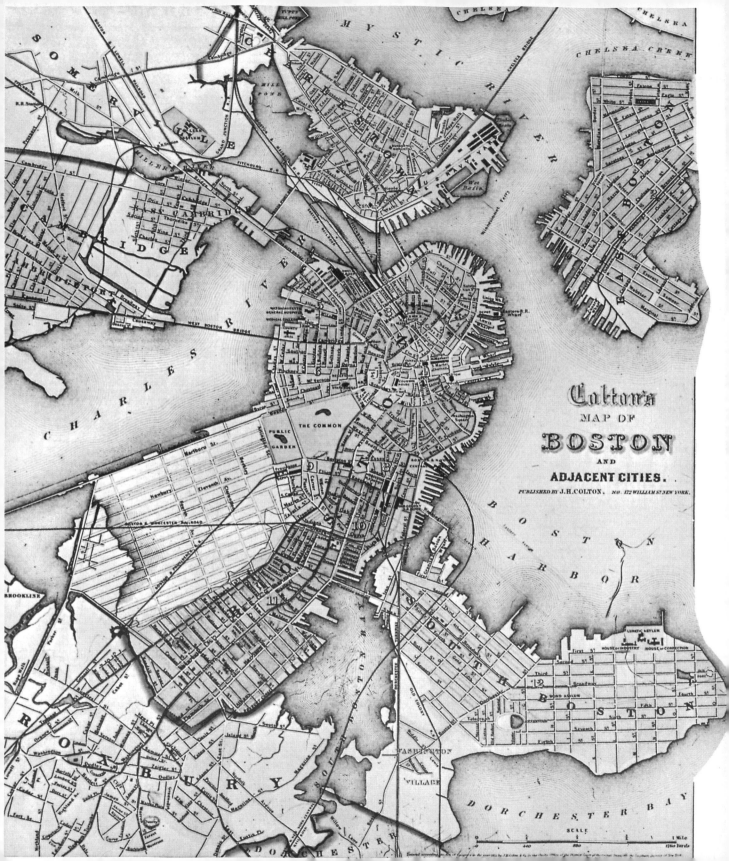

Colton's
MAP OF
BOSTON
AND
ADJACENT CITIES.
PUBLISHED BY J.H. COLTON, NO. 172 WILLIAM ST. NEW YORK.

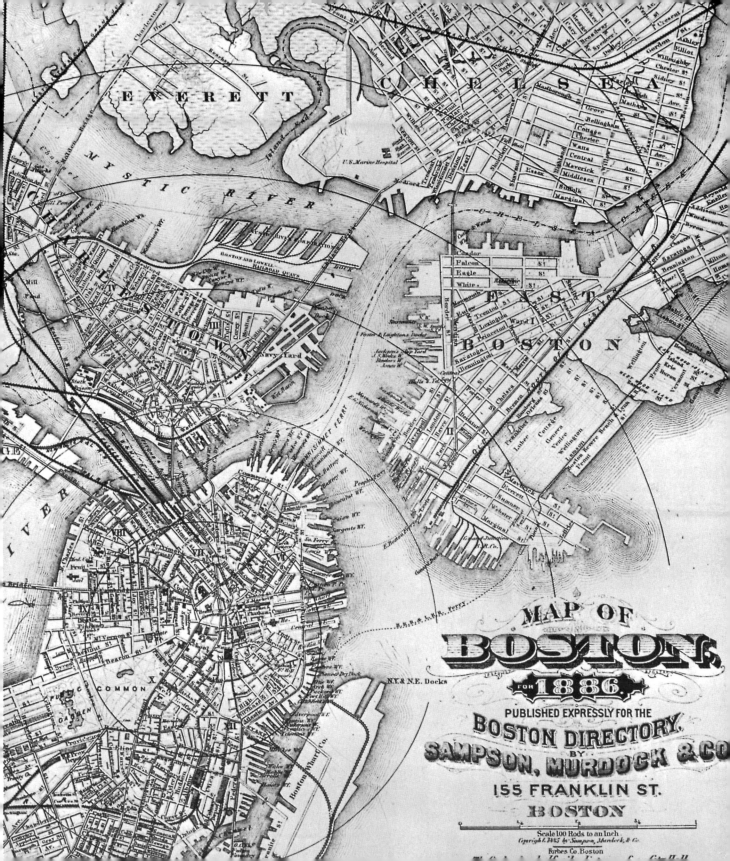

MAP OF
BOSTON
FOR 1886
PUBLISHED EXPRESSLY FOR THE
BOSTON DIRECTORY,
BY
SAMPSON, MURDOCK & CO.
155 FRANKLIN ST.
BOSTON

Scale 100 Rods to an Inch
Copyright 1885 by Sampson, Murdock & Co.
Forbes Co. Boston

[2] Some Waterfront Views

[2.1] Mid-eighties. A small coasting schooner and a sloop lie nearly becalmed off Minot's Light. Point Allerton and the southern entrance to Boston Harbor lie beyond, about six miles to the northwest. Located on Outer Minot Rock, standing at the outskirts of the extensive Stellwagen Ledges off Cohasset, Minot's Light remains one of the great sea-rock lighthouses of the world. The 114-foot granite tower was constructed by the United States Engineers under extraordinarily difficult conditions from 1855 until 1860. The working season at the site was less than six months long, and the first three seasons were required to prepare the ledge. Stonecutters did much of the preliminary chiseling under several feet of water. Progress was set back during the third season when a cotton-laden bark brought up against the staging.

The completed tower replaced a lightship station which had been maintained since the original year-old iron light tower was destroyed by a gale in 1851. Prior to the establishment of a warning light at Minot's the ledges of Cohasset annually killed many Boston-bound ships and sailors. Many mariners stood boldly into danger, mistaking old Scituate Light to the south for Boston Light to the north.[1]

[2.2] A view of the outer harbor, looking north from Hull, during winter in the eighties. A big bark, probably British, tows for the Narrows, the channel between Lovell's Island and Gallup's and George's Islands. The Narrows Channel was the principal entrance to the inner harbor previous to the dredging of the channels to Broad Sound from 1892 to 1916. The Narrows Channel, first dredged in 1867, was 27 feet deep and 1000 feet wide.

The bark's tug is obscured behind the bow of a salvage schooner busy picking over a wreck, possibly the remains of a coasting schooner. Bug Light, marking the southern end of the Narrows, is faintly discernible just to the left of the salvage schooner. George's Island lies just beyond, made nearly invisible, like the other island, by haze and snow cover.

[2.3] Quincy in the eighties, with the harbor and islands beyond. The charm and serenity of the scene belie the great social and economic changes and problems which faced the nation in the late nineteenth century; yet it is typical of the profound natural beauty of the harbor environs in an age of relatively small population, when the countryside still lay only a short distance from cities. In the eighties South Shore commuters traveled to Boston by rail or steamboat (Charles Francis Adams II occasionally sailed from Quincy to his Boston office); and the Southeast Expressway would have been an unimaginable horror. The contrast between this view and the reality of the overcrowded, over-polluted, overdeveloped, and ugly shores of Boston Harbor today is shocking, frightening, and revealing.

[2.4] Boston—a city by the sea, a city of the sea. The view is east from the State House in the late fifties—probably 1858—when Boston's shipping interests had entered their dismal decline, initiated by the Panic of 1857. Symbolically, the light-domed Customs House (seen above the "Boston Museum" sign, slightly left of center) had just been insensibly deprived of its noble position at the head of Long Wharf south dock by the erection of the grey mountain of State Street Block directly to the east. Jeffries' Point, East Boston, juts into the view at left; Governor's Island lies at the right.

It is difficult to view any photographs of American scenes in the late fifties without reflecting that these were the haunted years that culminated in the Civil War. Although Boston was the hotbed of abolitionism, it was also a community with unusually strong social and economic ties with the South, emanating from the shipping and textile industries. It is worthy of note that in 1865 citizens of New York and Boston—the two great northern port cities—contributed money for the relief of the inhabitants of stricken Savannah, a major prewar cotton port. Nearly $35,000 was raised at Boston, and the list of contributors includes nearly the entire mercantile community.

The Boston committee sent the mayor of Savannah a letter which read in part:

Sister cities on the Atlantic, long connected by friendly offices and commercial ties, it gives us great pleasure to witness the re-opening of an intercourse which has been temporarily suspended and which we believe will never again be closed.[2]

[2.5] 1877. The view southwesterly across the old South End (east of the present South End) toward Roxbury. Fort Hill, leveled to provide fill for the Atlantic Avenue project, was located behind the high brick buildings to the right. Much of the city in the center of the view was burned out by the great fire of 1872, which covered sixty-five acres, and destroyed the wholesale district. The initial blaze gained headway because of the lingering effects of that summer's epidemic of distemper, which drastically reduced the ranks of able fire horses. At its height, the fire could be seen from Nashua, New Hampshire, and men and equipment responded from as far away as New Haven, Connecticut.[3] The photograph testifies to the speed with which the area was rebuilt.

This is a rather dense photograph, and some of the details mentioned in the following description may be very difficult to see; nevertheless, they are included as part of the record.

Looking along the waterfront, at the far left we see the white steamer *Emeline,* ex-*Nantasket,* probably employed on the Strawberry Hill run. The northern end of the new Congress Street Bridge is astern of the *Emeline,* at the very edge of the photograph. The lofty rig of a big two-masted schooner, rising above Piper's coal pocket on Litchfield's Wharf, appears to the right of the *Emeline*'s stack.

At about the center of the picture three sailing vessels are lying alongside the salt fish dealers at Snow's, Arch, and Otis Wharves. A small, white half-brig and a smaller schooner lie facing the *Emeline;* a larger, dark half-brig faces outward. The dark brig's crew is apparently employed refinishing the yards, as the furled square sails are suspended free of the jackstays. The three vessels are almost certainly from the Maritime Provinces. (Barely discernible beyond the white brig is the rigging of another half-brig occupying the Fort Hill Dry Dock).

The large, white side-wheel steamer at right, lying at Foster's Wharf, is the Sanford Independent Line's beloved *Katahdin,* which ran between Boston and Bangor from 1863 until 1893. In thirty years on the run she missed only one winter season, which was spent on the Fall River Line.

In the palmy days of Boston shipping before the Civil War this waterfront was as crowded with vessels as were the better known docks to the north. Russia Wharf, sacrificed for the Congress Street Bridge, was patronized by foreign traders. Fort Hill Wharf was the center of the heavy trade to the Maritimes. Arch Wharf served both the Provincial and the West Indies trades. Foster's Wharf (two wharves, actually) was long occupied by John H. Pearson & Company, a firm extensively involved in trade to Europe, and the operator of packet lines to Philadelphia and New Orleans.[4]

[2.6] 1877. A view of the north side of Commercial Wharf, with the Mercantile Block, left background, and the end of Lewis Wharf, to the right. Commercial Wharf Block, like Central and India Wharf blocks, was cut into two separate buildings by the construction of Atlantic Avenue. The new façade of the western, landlocked segment shows clearly above the left-hand corner of the shed on Lewis Wharf.

The three-masted schooner *Jacob M. Haskell,* of Boston, lies at the extreme left of the picture. The white side-wheel steamer *New York,* running on the International Line to St. John, New Brunswick, dries her riding sail at center. Several fishing schooners occupy the dock beyond her. To the right, the *Panay,* of Salem, a full-rigged ship or "ship" as vessels square-rigged on all three masts were commonly called, loads at Lewis Wharf for her maiden voyage, to Melbourne, under charter to Henry W. Peabody & Company. The vessel across the dock, also rigged as a ship, is Thayer & Lincoln's East Indies trader *Majestic,* of Boston, loading for California, where she will be sold.[5] Both vessels are probably receiving cargoes of general merchandise.

The Pilot's Office at the end of Lewis Wharf was occupied by pilots awaiting assignments to take vessels out. It was a very salty place, decorated with vessel portraits, brass telescopes, charts, a compass, and retired pilots.[6]

[2.7] Long Wharf in the early sixties. The passage between the brick and wooden buildings led to T Wharf, which was an appendage of Long Wharf. T Wharf was for many years patronized by coastal sailing packets, and the masts of schooners lying in the dock appear over the low wooden buildings.

Built early in the eighteenth century, Long Wharf originally extended some one thousand feet into the harbor from the shore of Town Cove. Subsequent encroachments from the land reduced its length to less than half the original. In the thirties part of the dock between Long Wharf and Central Wharf was taken for the new Custom House. In the fifties more of the dock was lost by the construction of the State Street Block. In 1869 Atlantic Avenue cut across the wharf from No. 43—the store to the right of the large "Salt" sign—over to, and including part of No. 47—the first low wooden building.[7] The wharf in the foreground, thus, became an addition to State Street. The portion of the south dock west of the avenue, where the little bark is shown lying, was filled with the remains of Fort Hill, and became dry land.

The middle low wooden building was Acorn's Salt House, a favorite meeting place for Boston's artists and writers. "Acorn" was the pen name of James Oakes, the proprietor, and a prominent prewar drama and music critic.

It is interesting to read on the packet depot that there was water service to Albany and Troy. Although Boston had enjoyed rail connections to those towns since 1842, rates by water remained competitive for many years after. Signs along the wharf advertise Cadiz, Liverpool, and Trapani salt. Until our own times salt was a vital preservative—for thousands of years it was one of the foundations of civilization. Boston was a center of several salt trades. The little bark lying at right is rigged with old-fashioned single topsails.

[2.8] Long and Central wharves, probably in 1866, when a photographer atop the State Street Block was at eye-level with the royal yards of square-riggers in the dock. A steamer for Philadelphia lies at the end of Long Wharf, drying her square foresail. She is operated by Sprague, Soule & Company (later called the Boston & Philadelphia Steamship Company). Across the dock, facing outward, is a beamy steamer of the Neptune Steamship Company, an early Boston-New York freight line. A fleet of square-riggers lies at anchor in the harbor.

The handsome granite building at the end of Long Wharf is the Custom House Block (in the previous photograph it was obscured by the sails and rigging of the bark). The block was built in 1846 and was rented to the Government for the use of customs appraisers. For many years it housed the port's immigration detention station; the station was later located in a wharf shed. Beneath the block were deep cellars kept tight and dry by sheet piling and clay. After being flooded by an extreme tide the cellars automatically drained through hollow logs fitted with clapper valves.

Central Wharf was one of the results of the dynamic development of Town Cove by the Broad Street Corporation, which was led by Uriah Cotting, a great city benefactor.

In the course of the last year, Central Wharf, and the extensive range of stores which it supports was begun and compleated. The completion of this undertaking, unparalleled in commercial History, is a proof of the enterprize, the wealth, and the perservering Industry of Bostonians . . . From an octagon cupola over the pediments you have a charming view of the Harbour and neighboring towns, and the liberality of the proprietors has furnished it with a telescope and other apparatus for the accommodation of the public—*Shubael Bell, 1817* [8]

The handsome cupola may be glimpsed at the left hand side of the opening photograph of Chapter 8.

Central Wharf possessed the longest continuous block of warehouses in the country and housed many prominent merchants from various trades. Perkins & Company, Bryant & Sturgis, and William F. Weld & Company were all once located there. The Wharf's south dock was for many years the center of the large Mediterranean trade, and was a lively, colorful location during the "fruit season."

[2.9] The view from State Street Block north toward Commercial Wharf, about 1870. Most of the vessels in the dock are fishing schooners. "Snow's" marks the head of T Wharf. Previous to the construction of Atlantic Avenue—the diagonal roadway—the brick buildings in the foreground were at dockside. The avenue also landlocked several wharves and piers to the west which once constituted the busiest section of the waterfront. Colonel Frank Forbes reminisced about the old days, before the Civil War:

The packet lines to New York, Philadelphia, Baltimore, and Washington, represented fully a hundred sail of vessels, barques, brigs, and schooners, and a large portion of this fleet centered in this locality. The sailing days were Wednesdays and Saturdays, and on these days, especially during what was known as the packet season, Commercial Street was almost impassable. Commercial Street was practically the centre of the grain trade, and fifteen or twenty vessels would be discharging their cargoes all the time.

The entrance from the harbor to the upper North side of Long Wharf to City Wharf, Mercantile Wharf, and the piers, was between Commercial and T Wharves through a series of channels, having very much the appearance of the canals of Venice. The entering and departing of this great fleet was one of the most exciting and interesting sights one ever beheld. This was before the day of steam tugs, when vessels of any description from a ship to a sloop, used to beat in and out the harbor, and . . . a whole fleet would pass in between Commercial Wharf and T Wharf, under full sail, and not let go a halyard till the berth at pier or wharf was reached.[9]

Even into the late sixties most of Boston's corn and wheat arrived from New York, Baltimore, and Philadelphia in schooners, although by 1870 the railroads had suddenly taken the bulk of the business.[10] Railroads and steamboats together replaced most of the sailing packets.

Commercial, or Granite, Wharf (built from 1832 to 1834) was the first of the great North End wharf structures, and originally housed East Indian, South American, Mediterranean, West Indian, and North of Europe merchants. According to Colonel Forbes: "It was a high-toned wharf in those days, and if a fishing smack, or a lobster boat, stuck its nose into the dock, it would have been fired out instanter." By 1870 Commercial Wharf housed many fish dealers, and fishing vessels crowded the dock.

[2.10] The view from the end of T Wharf across the north dock toward Atlantic Avenue. Mercantile Block appears in the center distance; Commerical Wharf is at right. An unidentified bark and the coastal steamer *Commerce* lie in the foreground. The date is probably the early seventies, when shipping activity at the port remained much reduced from pre-Civil War decades. Nevertheless—perhaps because it is dimmed by age—this photograph seems to impart something of the feeling of the old days, when:

Our wharves . . . were in every truth water parks for the people, and contained no end of object lessons. On pleasant Sundays whole families resorted thither. On holidays and special gala occasions, they were immensely attractive; each vied with the other. Every description of craft, from sloop to a full rigged ship, was rich in the display of canvas and bunting. It was a picture that . . . can be more easily imagined than described.—*Colonel Frank Forbes* [11]

[2.11] Gentlemen, presumably from the firm of Loring & Company, commission merchants at 54 India Wharf, pose at the southeastern corner of the great brick wharf block. The stubby gentleman in the center would be well advised to seek a new tailor. The dray (possibly called a "sloven") at the far right is of interest, as its bed is lower than its rear wheel hubs. The photograph was probably taken in the early sixties, before Atlantic Avenue bisected the building through the archway.

India Wharf was incorporated in 1808 as part of the development of Town Cove by the Uriah Cotting group. The wharf was designed by Charles Bulfinch, who was apparently the planner for the project. Wharf construction was a difficult business, and the foundation stones had to be placed by men working in wooden diving bells. Pile drivers were manually operated. The completed block was initially occupied by merchants engaged in the West Indian and East Indian trades and the New Orleans cotton trade.

In their day, the big wharf buildings of Boston formed one of the great waterfront complexes of the world, but they were not suited to post-Civil War conditions. The docks were too narrow for large vessels, and facilities were inadequate for handling or storing bulk cargoes. Rail facilities were hopelessly deficient—prewar shipping had not involved railroads to any significant extent, while postwar shipping was very largely dependent on them. Increasingly, the old waterfront buildings were occupied by shoreside concerns, and the major shipping activities moved to the railroad freight terminals at East Boston, South Boston, and Charlestown. Although many coastwise steamer lines continued to use the Atlantic Avenue waterfront, this was primarily due to considerations of passenger convenience, the lack of alternate facilities, and to the fact that most of their freight was shipped in bales, barrels, or boxes, and could be carried in wagons ashore.

The great swath of Atlantic Avenue through the old wharves was symbolically fitting, however painful it was to witness. Practically speaking, it was unavoidable. No doubt the traditionalist maritime alarmists who opposed practically all harbor-filling or river-bridging felt it was a perfect horror. Writing many years after, Colonel Forbes probably reflected the sentimental tone of opponents of the project: "In the sixties, when Atlantic Avenue was constructed, then and forever departed the traditional glory of the old wharves of Boston." [12]

The avenue clearly demonstrated the changing character of the port. It was primarily intended to connect the railroad terminals of the North End and Charlestown with those of the South End. The terminals, in turn, linked Boston to the growing commerce of the Continent. Additionally, it created valuable new commercial real estate. A rail connection between the northern and southern terminals was provided by the Union Freight Railroad, which ran along the avenue. This facility never fully met expectations, as it was impossible to operate adequate rail service on a public thoroughfare choked with teams.

In 1873 Josiah Quincy addressed the Street Commissioners on the matter of widening Atlantic Avenue from one hundred to two hundred feet:

The keenest regret is often expressed that the city government, some fifty years ago, did not carry out the plans that were suggested by the second mayor for laying out, widening and improving our streets . . . And yet it is not very wonderful that the opportunity was not accepted by your predecessors. Remember that at that time *there was not a steamship on the ocean or a railway upon the land*. The croakers of that day said, and said with considerable plausibility: "Why should you prepare for a large population or an increase of business? Our back country extends about forty miles into the interior, and a little further when snow is on the ground, but commerce is passing off to New York, and Boston may become a mere fishing village on the Atlantic." There are no such croakers today. [13]

[2.12] A glimpse of Lewis Wharf Block in 1884, before its disfigurement by the addition of outsized dormers. Lewis was perhaps the finest of all the great wharf buildings, having been constructed of Quincy granite in the most extravagantly substantial manner during the booming thirties. In the forties it was home to Enoch Train's Liverpool packet line; in the fifties it could boast of Glidden & Williams' famous California clipper line.

The opening of the Quincy quarries in 1825 to supply the thousands of tons of stone for the Bunker Hill Monument began Boston's age of granite. The vogue for granite construction may have cooled after the Great Fire of 1872, when it was observed that the intense heat had caused the stone to blister and crumble.[14]

In the early twentieth century certain no-nonsense shipping experts were advocating the drastic redevelopment of the Atlantic Avenue waterfront to better serve the needs of coastal steamer lines. This would have necessitated the complete destruction of the old wharf buildings.[15] Fortunately, their ideas came to nothing, perhaps partly because of the great difficulties of demolition. Several of the old wharf blocks, including Lewis, remain standing today, and despite crass alterations they are still handsome and impressive.

The odd-looking vessel in the foreground is the auxiliary barkentine *Morning Star* of Boston. She was financed by public subscription, owned by the American Board of Foreign Missions, and operated as a missionary vessel in the South Pacific. Her furnaces exhausted through her iron mainmast. The barkentine ahead of her is the *Albert Schultz,* also of Boston.

[2.13] The view southeasterly from Bunker Hill Monument in the seventies. In the foreground we look down upon houses of Charlestown, which was annexed to the City of Boston in 1874. Beyond, along the near shore, are the grounds of the Navy Yard. At the far right, a rigged-down sailing warship occupies Dry Dock Number One. At center, steam issues from a tall-stacked engine house; the big joiner shop lies beyond. The watery areas to the left are timber docks, where ship timber was stored and seasoned. The square white building on the dike, far left, is the heavy shell magazine. The big warship moored off the dike, at center, is the old "74" (gun) *Ohio,* serving out her days as a receiving ship. Her short and spindly rig is for decoration— and for hanging out the laundry suspended between her fore and main masts.

Bustling East Boston, across the channel, was comprised of two islands and some filled land. Breed's Island, still fields and marshes, is out of the picture, to the left; Noddle's Island, thickly settled and heavily masted, stretches across the top of the view. Governor's Island lies beyond. The high structure to the right is the Boston & Albany Railroad's first Grand Junction grain elevator. In 1830 Noddle's Island was empty and treeless, inhabited by a single family. In 1850 the population was over 5,000; by 1875 it had grown to 27,420; by 1905 it totaled over 50,000.[16] The initial growth resulted from the owners' planned development. Their project was greatly advanced by the shipbuilding boom of the forties and early fifties which temporarily transformed East Boston into one of the great shipbuilding centers of the world, and permanently established the area as the principal home of the port's marine tradesmen. The dramatic population growth after the Civil War resulted from the inflow of immigrants.

[2.14] East Boston, probably in the late eighties, viewed from the Navy Yard. The gathering of half-brigs and coasting schooners, at left, marks a distinctive region of the East Boston waterfront, extending into Chelsea Creek, which was chiefly occupied by lumber yards, shipyards, and marine repair concerns.

The naval vessel doing her laundry and interfering with our view is the sloop-of-war *Galena,* one of five similar wooden vessels built during the seventies. Their hopelessly obsolete design well reflected United States naval policy of the period. With characteristic lack of urgency, the *Galena* was under construction (at Norfolk, Virginia) from 1871 through 1878. These vessels were said to be quite capable of fulfilling the duties of a naval cruiser "in time of peace," and were, at least, very saving of coal.

The record should show that the photograph which occupied this berth in previous printings of this book has been revealed as an impostor. In fact, it was taken at New York, along the East River. The Compiler confesses to deep humiliation over this affair, but feels that the Annotator is also not without blame.

[2.15] Boys of the eighties capture an East Boston dock—a sapper scales a roof on Carlton's Wharf while his companions inspect the prizes—three caulkers' floats. (Caulkers have fitted the dock with blocking for taking-on vessels for inspection.) Lying beyond, a big half-brig and a barkentine are also fast in the mud and will not escape. A second brig lies at the wharf end, almost entirely obscured by the rigging in the foreground. In the distance, a big mainskysail yard full-rigger tows up the ship channel.

If not a problem of major importance, the shoaling of docks and channels was a continual nuisance in the port. The blame was often laid to the filling-in of the tidal reservoirs, the outward growth of wharf structures, and the construction of the many bridges across harbor channels. All these "improvements" were thought to reduce the velocity, and thus the scouring power, of the ebb tide. During the mid-century decades considerable concern also arose over the obvious deterioration of the harbor islands, which in many instances could be laid to ballast digging. Certain groups— especially the Boston Marine Society—were actively concerned about the condition of the harbor early in the century. In the late forties and fifties this concern became more widespread, and various scientific-sounding theories, observations and solutions to the problems were proposed. Although the City established a Harbor Committee in 1852, the Great and General Court (the state legislature) retained its ancient and generally ineffective jurisdiction. Over the years a very considerable area of the harbor has been lost to fill. Even Faneuil Hall, first built in 1742, is constructed on filled land.

In 1881 Captain R. G. F. Candage commented upon a petition for leave to extend the Grand Junction wharves beyond the established harbor lines, toward Bird Island Flats. Captain Candage, the pilots, and others feared that lengthening the wharves would shoal the channel and hinder the outward passage of ice floes.

We have land enough and to spare—a continent even, stretching from the Atlantic three thousand miles away to the Pacific—and yet . . . strange as it may appear, men are found who advocate a further contraction of the limited navigable area of the harbor. The harbor of Boston is a highway greater than any ever laid out and constructed by Street or County Commissioners; it is an avenue for the travel and convenience of the ships of all nations seeking commercial intercourse with our city, State, and country, which was laid out and constructed by none other than the Great Creator Himself, and woe be to him who obstructs or encroaches upon the King's highway.[17]

[2.16] 1883. A line of Charlestown and Chelsea horse-cars are stalled as a three-masted schooner tows through the Charlestown Bridge. Warren Bridge is to the far left; Charlestown is across the river. The schooner has probably delivered a cargo of coal or hard pine to Cambridgeport or the West End. The large coal pile in the right foreground is on the premises of the Boston Gas Light Company, and was delivered by schooner.

In 1888 there were thirty-nine drawbridges in the port.[18] Towing through the bridges was a tricky business, and towing charges increased with every bridge passed. Since a tow could not be quickly stopped, bridges had to be opened while the tow was still relatively distant. Traffic delays were frequent and long, giving rise to public complaint. Charlestown politicians occasionally courted local favor with cries for fixed bridges over the Charles. In 1902, 8,789 vessels passed through the Charlestown Bridge, while 13,454 vessels entered and departed the Fort Point Channel through the Congress Street Bridge.[19]

[2.17] Probably 1875. The bark *Albert Russell,* of Boston, newly built at Newburyport, lies at Damon's Wharf, Charlestown. Protective fenders hang against the bark's metal sheathing. Two half-brigs (one is obscured) and a three-masted schooner lie in the dock to the left—the unequal athwartship placement of the schooner's mainmast indicates that she has a centerboard. A small Boston bark, with her lower yards cockbilled, and a half-brig, lie to the right. The Bunker Hill Monument rises in the center background.

The Charlestown waterfront from Charlestown Bridge east to the Navy Yard, including Tudor's, Hittinger's, Damon's, and Gage's wharves, was for many years the center of the Boston export ice trade. From 1830 to 1870 Charlestown was home to a dozen firms engaged in shipping cargoes of area ice to—among other places—South America, Europe, Australia, and the Orient.

Damon's Wharf, formerly Harris Wharf, was owned and improved by John W. Damon. Although Damon made his fortune from ice, I have seen no indication of the extent of ice shipments from the wharf. Damon was originally a mechanic who became involved in the business when hired to construct ice houses for the great Charlestown ice pioneer, Frederick Tudor. After completing an ice house at Havana he was promoted to manager of the facility. Later, he became Tudor's partner. Tudor and Damon subsequently had a falling-out over business matters, and the two maintained an active feud for over twenty-five years.[20]

[2.18] Charlestown, 1911. The Boston & Maine Railroad's Hoosac Tunnel Docks occupied the former sites of Tudor's, Hittenger's, Damon's, and Gage's wharves. The large steamer to the right is the White Star Liner *Canopic*, which first came to Boston as the Dominion Line's *Commonwealth*. A Warren Line cargo steamer lies in the shadows across the dock, her decks cluttered with ventilators required by her employment in the cattle trade. A small Nova Scotia schooner lies at left. The large, ugly building in the center background is a grain elevator. The Bunker Hill Monument stands behind the *Canopic*'s stack.

The long-delayed opening of the Commonwealth's remarkable Hoosac Tunnel in 1875 connected the Fitchburg Railroad with the great western trunks. Previously just a local road, the Fitchburg was transformed into the port's major freight carrier. Originally the waterfront treminal of the tunnel route had been intended to be located on the South Boston Flats—when this plan was blocked by actions of the New York & New England Railroad, the Hoosac Tunnel Dock & Elevator Company developed the old ice wharves instead.[21] The principal exports of the Charles River waterfront became livestock, provisions, grains, and apples. In 1900 the Fitchburg was joined to the Boston & Maine. Charlestown's Mystic River waterfront, originally developed by the Boston & Lowell Railroad, was transferred to the Boston & Maine in 1887. It became the center of Boston's export lumber trade and was the receiving point for great quantities of domestic and Cape Breton coal used and distributed by the railroad.

Previous to the construction of Commonwealth Pier 5 at South Boston in 1913, all of the large steamship facilities in the port were railroad-owned. The railroads granted free wharfage to steamship lines in exchange for agreements of preferential treatment, and tended to view steamship connections as industries located in their exclusive territory. Although the railroads were chiefly responsible for the rebirth of the port in the eighties and the nineties, their maintenance of policies which favored their particular steamer connections hurt the port as a whole.[22]

The published "Boston rate" was the cost of shipping freight from an inland point of origin to the pier of the inland carrier. If the freight was sent to the pier of another railroad, extra switching charges were added. Since the Boston & Maine had the largest local territory of any road serving Boston and was practically the sole carrier of the important New England apple crop, Charlestown was long the most fortunate terminus for a steamship line. In order to compete for any of the freight produced in the Boston & Maine's territory, the steamship lines using the Boston & Albany's East Boston facilities had to settle for smaller profits due to the Boston & Albany's extra charges for switching the cars from East Somerville to the piers.[23]

[2.19] 1906. The view southwest from East Boston toward the New York, New Haven & Hartford Railroad's South Boston harbor terminal, constructed on reclaimed acreage of the South Boston Flats (also called Dorchester or Commonwealth Flats). The heights of South Boston proper rise in the left background, beyond the five masts of a coal schooner discharging at New Haven Pier 4. The peak-roofed building to the right of the schooner is a grain elevator. An ocean freighter lies at Pier 2, beneath the tall chimney. Fort Point Channel, separating the reclaimed flats land from Boston proper, is at the right. The white steamer headed down the main ship channel is the *Calvin Austin*, running on Eastern Steamship's International Division to St. John, New Brunswick. She has just left Union Wharf in the North End.

The reclamation of the South Boston Flats apparently began in the 1830s, at about the time that filling operations commenced at South Cove, on the Boston side of Fort Point Channel.[24] Although the area in the picture was sold by the Commonwealth to the Boston, Hartford & Erie Railroad in 1868, the largest area of the flats was reclaimed in the early 1900s. After the great Boston fire of 1872 large quantities of rubble were used for fill. For many years Boston oyster dealers used undeveloped areas of the flats for the storage of live oysters, delivered by schooner from Buzzard's Bay and Chesapeake Bay.[25]

Boosters long predicted that the flats terminal area would become the port's major commercial center, although this did not really happen until after World War I. Plans to make this the terminus

of the Hoosac Tunnel route did not succeed. Of the various railroads which at some time owned or leased the property—the Boston, Hartford & Erie, the Boston & Albany, the New York & New England, and the New York, New Haven & Hartford—only the Boston & Albany carried heavy western traffic or maintained important steamship connections. Yet even the Boston & Albany's interest in the location was fleeting, perhaps because it was so poorly situated with respect to the other roads serving Boston, especially the Boston & Maine. The only direct local rail connection with the Boston & Maine was provided by the very inadequate Union Freight Railroad, which ran up Atlantic Avenue and Commercial Street. As a result, the New Haven generally switched cars bound for the Charlestown piers at Concord Junction; cars bound for Boston & Albany piers were either switched across the South Boston passenger yard at night, or were switched to Boston & Albany tracks at South Framingham. By any route extra shipping charges were incurred. No doubt most of the vessels using the terminal were coastal colliers. In 1914 the Merchants' & Miners' Line and the Boston and Philadelphia Line, which had been docking at Battery and Constitution Wharves, and at Fiske Wharf, respectively, shifted operations to Pier 2, South Boston.

Fort Point Channel, a backwater both in spirit and in fact, long attracted coastal and deep-water sailing vessels carrying coal, lumber, West Indies molasses, and (I suspect) wool from South America and elsewhere.

O15517 BOSTON HARBOR FROM EAST BOSTON, MASS.

[2.20] A panorama of the lower inner harbor, facing page 68, as viewed easterly and southeasterly from the lower Atlantic Avenue waterfront in 1906. Many of the differences between this scene and conditions in the port today are obvious and profound. The most important component of the contemporary port is Logan International Airport, which occupies a site that was under water when this photograph was taken. The remarkable changes which occurred in the other direction—say, between 1856 and 1906 —are perhaps less apparent, although equally dramatic.

The harbor of 1856 was almost wholly dominated by sail—even steam tugs were scarce—and the port was still largely a port in the sense that it was the home of ship-owning merchant speculators. In 1906, by contrast, the port was a major center for the transshipment of commodities—as inspired by the great developments of industrial New England, connecting rail systems, and the metropolitan Boston area—and was operating within the context of vastly increased world commerce. The harbor of 1906 was frequented by sophisticated steel steamships bearing striking testimony to the astonishing advancements in industrial technology of the previous half-century—as well as suggesting something of the magnitude of the corresponding social and economic alterations.

For two months in the summer of 1905 the four-masted schooner *Alice Holbrook* swung at anchor off East Boston. Loaded with coal, she was held hostage by a longshoremen's dispute. Captain Sydney Ellis, of Harwich Port, Cape Cod, had his family aboard, and more than sixty years later his son Lester recalled that summer with great fondness. (The *True Life Story of a Master Mariner*, Philadelphia, 1969.) Between watching the endless traffic of vessels, memorizing tug whistles, riding the South Ferry for free and in the pilothouse (thanks to a Cape Cod captain), salvaging floating United Fruit bananas, and listening to the band concerts on illuminated naval vessels on warm evenings, Lester did not think life could get much better. The panoramic photos of the harbor taken the following year support his memory.

Captain Ellis was lost ten years later when in command of the Boston schooner *R.W. Hopkins.*

Our tour of the harbor will progress panel by panel, from left to right. In the immediate foreground of the left-hand panel the Boston & Philadelphia liner *Indian*, of Boston, is seen lying at Central Wharf. The fact that the better portion of Central Wharf Block is occupied by a manufacturer of baby food is a reflection of the declining maritime activity along the old waterfront of Boston proper.

The tall stack with the white diamond at the far

left belongs to a steamer of the Boston-based United Fruit Company, discharging Caribbean bananas at Long Wharf. The many masts of fishing schooners lying at T Wharf appear above Long Wharf Block. A South ferry crosses the stream beyond.

Looking to the right—at about the center of the panel—we see the two short, raked stacks of the wonderfully dependable Dominion Atlantic Railroad steamer *Boston,* operated between Boston and Digby, Nova Scotia, now lying at the end of Long Wharf. Just off her stern, steaming down the channel, is the superb Dominion Atlantic liner *Prince George,* bound for Yarmouth, Nova Scotia. Peering through her smoke one can hazily see a tall-stacked Cunarder—either the *Ivernia* or the *Saxonia*—lying at the Cunard Pier, East Boston.

The end of India Wharf dominates the foreground of the middle panel. The Metropolitan liner *H. M. Whitney,* running to New York, lies on the north side. Rail-car floats reflect both the lack of adequate dockside rail service along the Atlantic Avenue "coastal" waterfront and an attempt to supplement the poor rail connections between the Charlestown and South Boston railroad terminals. Wagons crowd the end of the wharf—Boston-based Metropolitan Line carried much produce, and the wagons are likely trucking for the city's grocers.

Out in the stream, the trim *Prince George* is still squarely in view. Further toward the East Boston shore, a tug is towing a wooden American bark (the tug is fast to the bark's quarter). By this date an American-flag square-rigger is something of a rarity. Just ahead, three white five-masted schooners of the Boston-based Palmer Fleet lie at anchor, deep with coal and heading into the flood tide. The nearest schooner has hoisted her dark coil of towing hawser on a fore halyard to dry; the farthest schooner is the *Prescott Palmer.*

On the East Boston shore, left distance, stands the Boston & Albany Railroad's obsolete Grand Junction grain elevator. The stern and the stack of two Leyland steamers appear just to the right of it. Leyland, like Cunard, was a Liverpool line. To the right of Jeffries' Point—the end of East Boston —we look across what is now Logan International Airport toward the lovely town of Winthrop, as yet unmolested by the roar and fumes of jet aircraft.

In the foreground of the right-hand panel the big wooden Portland-Boston steamer *Bay State* lies to the south side of India Wharf. The Boston–Portland steamer *Portland,* lost in 1898 with 176 lives, was of very similar design. Note the huge decorated paddle-boxes, covering out-sized and obsolete fixed-bucket "radial" paddle-wheels. Her twin stacks and massive walking beam rise between two rows of staterooms on the hurricane deck. The English-built screw steamer *Prince George*—now making smoke down the ship channel—offers a striking comparison in coastal steamer design.

To the right of the *Bay State,* over the shed roof on Rowe's Wharf, one can see the upperworks of a Nantasket excursion steamer. The Nantasket Beach Steamboat Company operated one of the most popular and best-run small steamboat lines in the country.

To this side of the smoking *Prince George* several yachts lie moored in the yacht anchorage. Beyond the *Prince George* two dark five-masted schooners are anchored in the lower reach of the Bird Island Flats anchorage. They are probably members of the Boston-based Crowley Fleet. Like the white Palmer schooners, they have likely recently arrived from a Hampton Roads bituminous port. Because of delays caused by wind, weather, and tide, northbound coal schooners often arrived "bunched up."

Beyond the schooners (also, two anchored coastal coal barges, a white-plumed harbor tug, and the tall-stacked coastal steamer *City of Gloucester*) rises Governor's Island, not yet leveled to form a section of the airport.

The dark square-rigger seemingly touching the top of the *Bay State*'s foremast is the Massachusetts Nautical Training School's auxiliary bark *Enterprise.* Close inspection of the original print of the photograph reveals cadets drilling at stowing headsails. Beyond the *Enterprise* lie three empty coastal coal barges (two are alongside each other). Two white-sailed schooners—probably fishermen—pass in the distance beyond. Further to the right lies a collection of small Down East two-masted schooners; a big, empty four-masted coal schooner, and several smoking dredges. The central lower harbor islands appear in the distance. The view of the New York, New Haven & Hartford Railroad's South Boston Flats piers jutting into the photograph at the far right, across the Fort Point Channel, completes our tour.

I

I

II

II

III

[3] Shipbuilding and Repairing

Probably no major Boston industry emerged more profoundly changed into the turbulent post-Civil War period than did shipbuilding. Between 1850 and 1875 Boston shipbuilding moved from world leadership to general bankruptcy and obsolescence.

In the early years of the nineteenth century the most important shipbuilding areas in Massachusetts were on the Merrimac and North rivers. The Middlesex Canal, opened in 1804, provided the Boston area with new timber resources, and Medford developed into a major shipbuilding center prominent in the construction of fast vessels for the China trade. Between 1830 and 1859 Medford's yards launched at least 269 ships and approximately 120 barks, brigs, and schooners into the Mystic.[1] But the Mystic was too shoal for the larger vessels required by mid-century, and after 1850 Medford was decisively overshadowed by East Boston.

In 1839 Samuel Hall, a shipwright from the North River, established a yard at East Boston. Other outstanding builders followed, and in a decade or so East Boston could claim one of the most productive and progressive shipbuilding complexes in the nation. The East Boston boom was directly related to the dramatic but short-lived clipper ship phenomenon, and the port of Boston was the center of clipper construction. Local yards excelled in both vessel design and means of production, and produced a great quantity of superior vessels within a very short period. For example, between 1845 and 1856 Donald McKay built forty-six square-riggers at East Boston.[2] Samuel Hall built fifty-three vessels in twenty years.[3] In 1855

there were ten yards at East Boston engaged in the construction of full-rigged ships, while nine other yards were similarly employed at Medford, Chelsea, South Boston, Charlestown, and Quincy.[4] At one time in the fifties, over 30,000 tons of shipping was under construction in the port of Boston.[5] The authoritative Henry Hall described these times in his classic report included in the 1880 Census:

Few of the Boston builders took shares in their vessels, but built on contract or speculation. Studying closely the requirements of trade, they devoted themselves to the production of vessels especially suited for the various employments of the day, leaving to others the operation and management of the ships. They often made voyages to Europe and to the West Indies, and even to the Mediterranean, in order to study the behavior of vessels at sea . . . it is probable that the superior excellence of Boston vessels sprang from the particular fact that builders gave their whole attention to the art . . . The Boston yards launched the best, largest, and finest specimens of marine architecture in New England.[6]

Except in 1856 and 1859, the New York customs district produced more tonnage than the Boston district throughout the pre-Civil War era.[7] Simple tonnage figures, however, do not tell the entire story. In 1857, for example, Boston launched thirty-eight ships and barks, ten more than New York. Yet New York's total tonnage exceeded Boston's by 3,000. The difference consisted largely of small steamers, schooners, and seventy-three "sloops and canal boats." [8] Steamers, due to their rapid technical obsolescence, were of notoriously flimsy construction;[9] canal boats were slightly pointed boxes—their construction can hardly be compared with the building of deep-water sailing vessels.

The shipping depression of 1857, followed by the general decline of American shipping after the Civil War, caught the vulnerable high-cost Boston yards especially hard. Just as New York shipbuilders had once been underpriced by those of Boston, Boston builders now felt the competition of Maine yards. By 1870–71 the sailing vessel output of Boston and Bath were nearly identical.[10] In 1880 the principal ship work at Boston consisted of repairs to the growing, chiefly Maine-built, coastwise fleet. New construction was largely confined to an occasional schooner, tug, ferry, or local steamer. Hall reported: "Repairing can be as advantageously performed in Boston . . . as in any part of the country; like the other branch of the business, however, it is in a general state of decay."[11]

The one striking exception to this general deterioration was the growth of the Fore River Ship & Engine Building Company and its corporate successors. The original firm was founded at East Braintree in 1883 as a marine engine builder. In 1893 it received a major naval contract, the first of the many which have turned the operation into one of the nation's largest shipbuilders. Expansion was rapid, and by 1901 the yard was moved to a deep-water site at Quincy to provide room for the construction of two 15,000-ton battleships.[12]

The story of Boston shipbuilding is instructive of the profound economic and technological changes of the nineteenth century. At mid-century, the largest and fastest merchant vessels in the world were being built at Boston on a speculative basis by "wooden" shipyards that required a minimum of capital investment. By 1900, shipbuilding was a capital-intensive heavy industry, dependent in large measure on the industrial structure of the entire nation. In 1850 shipyards had depended on the supplies of white oak, hard pine, and hackmatack.

[3.1] This rare and wonderful daguerreotype of the *Champion of the Seas* is perhaps the sole existing photographic image of a virgin American clipper ship, as fresh and new as she would ever be. It is perhaps the same picture mentioned in the following article excerpted from *The Boston Daily Atlas* of May 20, 1854. (The daguerreotype of the *Great Republic* mentioned in the article must have been of a painting).

THE NEW CLIPPER SHIP "CHAMPION OF THE SEAS"

This splendid vessel registers 2,447 tons, and is the largest sailing merchant ship in the world. She was built at East Boston, by Mr. Donald McKay, and is intended for Messrs. James Baines & Co.'s Liverpool and Australian line of clippers . . . Mr. McKay has already built for them the celebrated clipper *Lightning* . . . The *Champion of the Seas,* in beauty of model, strength of construction, and all other elements of perfection is a decided improvement upon the *Lightning.* Her ends are as long, though not so sharp or concave, and are even more beautiful in their form. She is 238 feet long on the keel, and 259 feet on deck, between perpendiculars . . . The run is long and clean, and blends in perfect harmony with the general outline of the model. Broadside on she has all the imposing majesty of a ship of war, combined with the airy grace of a clipper. Outside she is painted black, and inside white, relieved with blue water-ways . . . Over the transom sofa [in the after cabin] are three panels, which contain daguerreotype pictures. The first is a representation of the ship *Great Republic,* under all sail by the wind; the second is the outline of the *Champion of the Seas,* as she now lies broad-side on . . . These pictures were taken by Messrs. Southworth & Hawes, and are about the best of the kind we have seen . . . Nothing that ingenuity could devise has been omitted to render her accommodations the most perfect in every particular . . . She is a full rigged ship and has a noble set of spars . . . the harmony of her masts and yards is complete . . . The *Champion of the Seas* is now lying at Grand Junction Wharf, East Boston, and in a few days will be towed to New York, and there load for Liverpool.

The *Champion* was the second of a famous quartet of big ships, including the *Lightning,* the *James Baines,* and the *Donald McKay,* built by McKay for Baines' Black Ball Line. Launched in '54 and '55, the first three, at least, were among the last genuine clippers built in America.[13] All were intended to operate between Liverpool and Australia, and they account for many sailing records. Carl Cutler, a clipper authority, held that the *Champion of the Seas* very likely made the best day's run of any sailing vessel, covering 465 nautical miles in twenty-three hours, twenty minutes.[14] As with other such records, this should be accepted with reservation. Although Captain Newlands, the *Champion*'s commander, was a seaman of high reputation and furnished supporting navigational data, celestial navigation left a certain latitude for personal variation, despite the purest of intentions. There can be no doubt, however, that the *Champion* was smoking along at a wonderful rate.

It is indicative that the *Champion* and her three sisters were built for a foreign owner. By 1854 the big, extreme, heavily sparred clippers that McKay favored were being priced out of the settling California trade. The Australian boom was also short-lived, and big clippers were too expensive in operation to be competitive in anything like a normal trade. But as the newspaper article demonstrates, they gave Boston its last moments of clipper euphoria. Pride goeth before a fall.

Many details of the photograph are of interest. The big single topsails must have been of great power. The ship's healthy freeboard reflects something of the conditions she will meet when running before the powerful westerlies of the Great Southern Ocean. The American ensign indicates that she is under temporary American register until delivered to Baines at Liverpool; she was built on McKay's own account.[15] It is interesting that her topsails are bent, although royal yards have not yet been crossed. Perhaps she is soon to tow to New York for loading, and Captain Newlands wants at least to be able to set his topsails in an emergency. There will be ample opportunity to complete rigging at New York. (The Boston Marine Society owns a painting that shows McKay's enormous clipper bark *Great Republic* sailing under topsails en route from Boston to New York to load for her maiden voyage. No upper yards are crossed. The ocean-going screw tug *R. B. Forbes* of Boston is shown in company with the giant vessel.)

The sloop in the foreground occupies a position at the opposite end of the social register from the *Champion,* but she is fascinating nevertheless.

[3.2] Donald McKay's shipyard at East Boston, probably in 1855, when he produced only two vessels. In 1854 he had built eight; in 1856 he built seven. McKay utilized many labor-saving devices in his operation and was very prolific. The identity of the vessel in frame is not known. It was common practice in big vessel building to begin framing amidships, then work toward the ends. The keel was pieced together as it was required.

Despite the significance of the scene, it is not very dramatic to look at. A wooden shipyard was an unassuming place, marked principally by a carpet of wood chips strewn with raw timber. The growing vessel dominated the area, and after a launching the yard seemed unnaturally empty. The Mystic River bridge stretches across the background.

McKay launched his last true clipper-type vessel, the bark *Henry Hill*, in 1856. Many of the fuller and more moderately rigged vessels that he produced from 1854 onward were called "medium clippers"—a rather tenuous term often loosely applied. The true clippers have received a disproportionate amount of attention relative to their overall economic importance. Although they were a stirring breed of vessel and influenced the development of the design of other vessel types, true clippers accounted for only a small proportion of America's ocean freighters.

[3.3] A famous photograph taken on the launching day of the ship *Glory of the Seas,* East Boston, October, 1869. Her builder, Donald McKay, stands center under a high hat. The coppering has not been completed, but she will float high. Apparently the paint will not yet stick to her bow planking. The figurehead is the goddess Athene—McKay had a romantic streak to his soul that wouldn't quit. Notice the large size of her dolphin striker.

The *Glory* was built on speculation, and, except for two sloops-of-war, was McKay's last creation. He had not been notably successful designing the fuller cargo carriers and steamers of the sixties, and, although intended for the California grain trade, the *Glory* was in certain respects a throwback to the good old days. Her construction was exceedingly rugged. She was sold to Boston owners and proved to be fast, lucky, and long-lived; in short, a most worthy final effort.

Donald McKay is considered by many to have been the outstanding designer and builder of American clipper ships. In terms of his total output of superior vessels of varied types, he was not the equal of the New Yorker William Webb, who was probably the greatest designer and builder of the era. At Boston, Samuel Hall was likely as respected a builder, and Samuel Hartt Pook was certainly a more scientific designer. McKay was a practical genius with a background of minimal formal education, and he was not notably well-versed in the theoretical aspects of naval architecture. Nevertheless, the records of his ships speak for themselves, and in this light his less sophisticated approach only adds to his stature. Though he may have devised no complicated formulas, he had some magnificent "hunches." [16] He was a handsome man, and was always the thorough gentleman.

[3.4] Shipbuilding at Medford. The vessel-in-frame is probably the ship *Don Quixote,* built by J. B. Foster in 1868. The inside and outside surfaces of all her frames have been smoothed and beveled by a gang of skilled "dubbers," armed with sharp adzes and good eyes. The interior planking, called "ceiling," is nearly completed, and the first strakes of her exterior planking are in place. The ceiling was vital to the hull's strength, was often thicker than the planking, and was usually of southern hard pine. Planking is either hard pine or oak. Although many British writers have called American pine-planked vessels "soft wood ships," hard pine is, in fact, exceedingly hard, durable, and compact. The frames are compounded of separate timbers, called "futtocks," and are of oak—preferably a white variety. The cheerful shipwright is sitting on a "top timber," an extension of the frame which will support the bulwarks. In this instance, the frames have been assembled with breathing spaces between the futtock surfaces in an attempt to retard rot.

It is not surprising that the "flitch timbers," the naturally curved sections of the frames shaping the turn of the bilge, look a bit rough. Good shipbuilding timber had become scarce. Compared to today, nineteenth-century New England was relatively treeless. Although much of the oak used at Boston-area yards came from around Nashua, New Hampshire, it was not uncommon for timber to be shipped by schooner from Virginia, or by rail and canal boat from as far as Ohio. Often a gang of carpenters from a yard would take a set of patterns, called "moulds," directly to the woods (even to Virginia), where they would select and cut timber for frames, stern, stem, keel, and other such parts.[17] Some yards acquired timber from numerous subcontractors in different areas, supplying each with certain moulds.

[3.5] Shipbuilding at Chelsea. The ship *Comet,* shown nearly ready to launch, was typical of the ocean carriers built at Boston for a decade or so after the Civil War. Generally classified as "Down Easters," they were fuller and more efficient than the clippers.

In 1868 and 1869 Peirce & McMichael built a pair of small and fast full-riggers, the *Ringleader* and the *Comet,* for the Boston firm of Howes & Crowell. Both vessels were named for earlier clippers, and both traded to California and the Far East. The *Ringleader* was cut down for a barge in 1894; in 1896 the *Comet* was still under sail, employed in the transatlantic trade under the German flag.[18]

Partners Osborn Howes and Nathan Crowell both belonged to outstanding Cape Cod seafaring families and represented the migration of Cape Cod mariners to Boston in mid-century. In the fifties, the firm owned six clippers, five of them Medford-built. The Howes-patented double-topsail rig, which quickly became standard around the world, was first fitted to the Howes & Crowell clipper *Climax* by Captain William Howes, her master and the inventor.[19]

No shipyard portrait is complete without a horse or a yoke of oxen, employed to haul timber about. One of the many circumstances contributing to the difficulties of shipbuilding is that the vessel must be constructed on an incline.

SHIP COMET,

Built by PEIRCE & McMICHAEL, Chelsea, Mass.

LAUNCHED AUG. 12, 1869.

Length of Keel, 178 ft.   Depth of Hold, 23 ft. 6 in.   Breadth extreme, 37 ft. 2 in.   Length on Deck, 189 ft.   Length over all, 205 ft. 6 in.   Tonnage, 1157 71-100.

[3.6] 1884. The celebrated pilot schooner *Hesper* on her launching day, at Montgomery & Howard's, Chelsea. Everything looks ready to go; the rudder has been immobilized with a clamp; the hawser led around her stem is probably bent to a drag, to check her run; the launching party is aboard; and the launching gang stands ready, topmauls in hand. Vessels were commonly christened aboard, thereby eliminating the expenses of a platform at the bow. Usually the bottle was broken forward, on a knighthead or chock, but in this instance it appears that the ceremony will occur aft.

The photograph affords another opportunity to observe the nineteenth-century fondness for hats. If hats were items of less than considerable importance you would expect to find at least two hatless heads in the hundred-odd assembled here. But only one is visible, and that belongs to a babe-in-arms.

[3.7] 1890. Joiners at work on the three-masted schooner *Alma Cummings,* building at William McKie's East Boston yard for service in the southern hard pine trade. George B. McQuesten & Company, of Boston, was her managing owner.

A cofferdam, used when working on the ends of large vessels, afloat, is tied to the pier astern. The white steamer beyond is the ancient *New York,* of Eastport, Maine, built at Clayton, New York, in 1852. For many years she was a stalwart on the International Line to St. John, New Brunswick. To the right, a four-masted schooner lies in the cradle of a marine railway at the East Boston Dry Dock Company either before or after being hauled-out for bottom work. Across the harbor may be seen three shiphouses at the Navy Yard which protected building ways. After the Civil War they saw almost no use.

[3.8] 1890. A group, including the joiner gang, poses on the *Alma Cummings'* poop. Wooden shipbuilding was generally a clean occupation, and a joiner, at least, could work in tie and waistcoat. Most of these men are probably Down Easters. According to Captain W. L. Josselyn, the majority of the shipwrights who built the bark *John D. Brewer* at Smith & Townsend's in 1882 were from Nova Scotia.[20]

A natural knee, probably hackmatack, lies in the foreground. A jack lies in the shavings by the hatch coaming. The inward bevel of the rail stanchions is in conformity with her tumblehome aft.

By 1890 Boston shipbuilding had been seriously depressed for several decades. High wages and frequent labor difficulties had long hurt the competitive position of Boston shipyards. A particularly bitter strike in 1871 ruined several builders and seriously embarrassed the survivors. When the strike was called, Robert Jackson had begun construction of a big full-rigger for William F. Weld & Company. In order to complete the vessel, as well as to weaken the strike, Jackson rented a building site at St. John, New Brunswick, and Weld & Company shipped the framing material there from East Boston. The resultant vessel, the *Lightning,* could not, of course, qualify for American registry.[21]

[3.9] Shipbuilder John Brooks poses in the doorway of his classic East Boston office at 334 Border Street. His yard, in the background, occupied a portion of the grounds of the old Donald McKay yard. In later years it became the property of lumber-shipper George McQuesten. Brooks served as McKay's foreman for six years, and in the seventies was a partner in the firm of Campbell & Brooks. About 1877 he went into business for himself; in the late nineties he shifted operations to the old Crosbie yard.[22] Brooks was the last of the old-time Boston shipbuilders. He launched an impressive fleet of vessels in his long career, including many fine Down Easter ships and barks. In 1893 he built one of the very last square-riggers launched in the port, the bark *Holliswood*. Brooks built many fine schooners, possibly including the three-master alongside his mill. Note the pile of knee-timber.

[3.10] The Atlantic Works, East Boston, probably in 1889. The firm was incorporated in 1853 by a half-dozen mechanics. It flourished, and in 1869 moved to the spacious site partly shown here. The Works principally built and repaired steam vessels and engines, and supplied the port with many of its tugs, ferries, and lighters. Several notable iron and steel vessels were built here, including the Merchants' and Miners' coastal liner *William Lawrence,* and the iron brig *Novelty,* used as a molasses tanker.[23]

From left, we see the Work's one hundred-ton shears; a boiler; the tug *Wesley A. Gove;* a tug under construction (the white propeller has been drawn in); and a new barkentine, almost certainly the *Bruce Hawkins,* built by William McKie. She has probably just recently been alongside the shears having her spars stepped—close inspection reveals that her mast hoops are still tied to her mast heads.

The ferry at the city-owned pier to the right is likely a reserve boat, used only during rush hours. She is lying just beyond a public bath house, one of eleven operated by the city, and a sign of the times in a city with a large immigrant population living in tenements and rooming houses without plumbing.

[3.11] 1878. Engine-building in the main machine shop of the Atlantic Works, East Boston. The mechanic is apparently securing two separate frames to a base preparatory to leveling their upper surfaces with a planer. Bottom surfaces must also be machined to insure proper engine alignment. The cross-head guides are clearly visible on the inside surfaces of the legs, or "columns."

To the left, a crankshaft is being turned on a lathe. Overhead is a fifteen-ton traveling crane. Power for the works was supplied by four stationary steam engines. In a sense, the machine shop— especially an engine-building shop—was the essence of the spirit and the changes of the second half of the nineteenth century in America.

[3.12] 1902. "What have I done?" We can only wonder what designer B. B. Crowninshield is thinking as he surveys his colossal creation, the seven-masted steel schooner *Thomas W. Lawson* of Boston, soon to be launched at the Fore River Ship & Engine Building Company, Quincy. Her size can best be realized in comparison with the white-shirted worker appearing above Crowninshield's hat. Thomas Lawson, a celebrated wheeler-and-dealer from Brookline, was an influential owner in the schooner. (One suspects that Lawson was attracted as much by the novelty of the project as by its financial prospects—in 1905 he spent $30,000 to have a newly developed carnation named after his wife).[24] There is some evidence that the *Lawson*'s owners may have intended her to sail coal to Manila for the Navy.[25] Instead, she was employed in the New England coal trade for nearly four years, then was converted to a tanker.

While the schooner was building, there was a great amount of speculation by the press to the effect that she was the first of a new class of vessel that would revolutionize shipping. She was wonderfully economical and could carry 11,000 tons of coal with a crew of about twenty. When so loaded, however, she drew thirty feet, and was confined to operation between Norfolk and Boston. No doubt she made money, but she was not an unqualified success as a sailing vessel. Only two other big steel schooners were built in New England; one of them, the six-masted *William L. Douglas,* was built by Fore River in 1903.

[3.13] Under the stern of the schooner *Thomas W. Lawson* during launching preparations, at Quincy, 1902. A ship out of water is very heavy and surprisingly fragile. Moving a big vessel from her building site into the water is a difficult and dangerous undertaking. While building, the vessel rests on keel blocks and bilge blocks and is supported by various shores. When launching, she is held by a cradle, or "sliding ways," which slides down greased "standing ways." At the bow and the stern the cradle must be built up with "poppets"—here we see the starboard half of the stern poppet. The heavy chains connect the sides of the poppet, utilizing the vessel's weight to prevent the cradle from spreading. The weight of the vessel is transferred from the blocks to the ways by lifting the cradle—and the vessel—with hundreds of wedges, as shown. The process of wedging-up a big vessel may begin the day before launching and is a delicate operation. In hot weather the vessel must not be allowed to rest too long on the ways, as the weight may squeeze out the grease, and she may not "start." After the vessel is raised, the blocks and shores are knocked or cut out, and, at the proper time—when the tide suits—the sliding ways are released. The most critical moment occurs just as the vessel enters the water, a position of inherent instability. Occasionally vessels have fallen over at this point; others have been damaged when their sterns failed to lift, thereby creating great strains on a short section of hull.[26]

[3.14] The cruiser *U.S.S. Marblehead* departs Harrison Loring's City Point Iron Works, South Boston. In 1892 patriotism was simple, overt, and colorful.

As the stern lifts upon entering the water, the entire vessel pivots for an instant on the bow poppet, which must accordingly be very strong. The design of most sterns precludes the construction of heavy poppets. Moreover, the stern is the more fragile end of the vessel, and therefore, ships are usually launched stern first, or, more precisely, bow last.

Harrison Loring was primarily a manufacturer of stationary engines, especially sugar mills. The most notable vessels from his yard were the superb steamers *Massachusetts, South Carolina, Mississippi,* and *Merrimac,* built for Boston's pre-Civil War trade to the South.[27]

[3.15] 1907. The submarine *Tarantula* is launched at the Fore River Shipbuilding Company, Quincy. The old tug *Confidence* warily stands by to retrieve the sinister little underwater device. The *Tarantula* was one of ten submarines launched by Fore River between 1907 and 1909. Early submarines were intended as weapons of coastal defense.

[3.16] About 1890. A big half-brig has her planking refastened at East Boston. The brig is fastened in the traditional manner with locust or white oak treenails. When properly installed, treenails were at least the equal of metal fastenings. Wherever possible both the planking and the ceiling were fastened through the frames with the same treenails. After being carefully driven, the ends of the treenails were wedged tight and cut flush. Butts were fastened with metal.

[3.17] A cofferdam is used for repairing the Cunarder *Pavonia,* in the eighties. The port lacked large vessel graving facilities previous to the opening of a major dry dock at the Navy Yard in 1905. The *Pavonia* has probably had difficulties with her tailshaft—the aftermost section of her propeller shaft—and it is probably being replaced with the spare carried either in the shaft alley or the after hold. Screw steamers had frequent tailshaft troubles, since the shaft was exposed to salt water and was subjected to severe strains. On single screw vessels the shaft had to be removed and replaced from inside the vessel—an exceedingly laborious job. The cofferdam was required for removing and replacing the propeller. A steam pump is mounted on the opposite side.

[3.18] In the seventies. The bark *Anna Walsh*, of New York, and the Boston–Bangor steamer *Cambridge* in dry docks at Simpson's Dry Dock Company, East Boston. In 1854, J. E. Simpson built the first timber dry dock in the country.[28] A handsome row of trees lines Marginal Street. The cluttered area to the left is a portion of the Boston & Albany Grand Junction property. The furnace in the right foreground may have been used for heating pitch.

Appreciate the *Cambridge*'s handsome sheer, sweeping gracefully aft from her pilot house. Notice also the elaborate paddle-box. The steamer was fast and comfortable, and was the pride of the Sanford Independent Line. In February 1886 she ran into Old Man's Ledge, off Port Clyde, and became the only Boston–Bangor steamer lost in over a hundred years service.

[3.19] 1889. The lean and lanky pilot schooner *Hesper* is readied for a match race with the fisherman *Fredonia* (which may be the schooner sharing the dock). One of her two rugged "canoes," used for transporting the pilots to and from ships, lies under her bows. The pilots took great pride in their vessels, were dependent on their abilities, and maintained them in the finest manner. Since her launching day portrait, the *Hesper* has received a new bowsprit, some outside ballast (not visible), and has been coppered.

Notice the construction of the dock, probably of hard pine timbers. Simpson's docks were drained by two large steam centrifugal pumps.

[3.20] About 1885. The schooner *Emma M. Vickerson,* of Grand River, Prince Edward Island, is caulked in the Fort Hill Dry Dock, 454 Atlantic Avenue. Since she was engaged in the ancient West Indies salt fish trade, her bottom is probably being prepared for sheathing with copper or yellow-metal to protect her planking from the secret tunneling of the southern shipworm.[29] Canadian vessels came under British registry, and were commonly termed "British."

[3.21] South Boston, probably in the seventies. A beamy little schooner—possibly a pilot-type or fisherman-style yacht—undergoes some bottom work at low tide. Halyards led to the pier heel her against the pilings. Is the dark shape in the rowboat an umbrella carried by a second person? The man standing may be scrubbing the schooner's bottom—a wet job. Beyond, yachts lie moored in Dorchester Bay.

Boston Harbor's average range of tide is 9.5 feet. In early times, before marine railways and dry docks were available, a respectable range of tide was of great assistance in the maintenance of modestly sized vessels, although it made the task of heaving-down a large vessel at dockside all the more difficult. At dockside, tides have always been a great nuisance; coastal steamers, which worked their cargoes through side ports, were especially sensitive. But rare was the mariner who at some time in his career had not been saved the immense labor of lightening and kedging-off a grounded ship by a rising tide.

[3.22] The America's Cup defender *Volunteer* fitting out at George Lawley & Son's City Point yacht yard, 1887. The long reefing bowsprit has just been installed; her centerboard stands waiting on the pier. Uniformed crew members aid the yard riggers, under the eyes of the curious. A smaller sloop, also being rigged, lies outboard of the *Volunteer*. The defender's plating is rather rough, as she was designed and built in a matter of only several months' time.[30] Lawley built wonderful rowing tenders—several are in the picture.

Looking across partially reclaimed South Boston, or Commonwealth Flats, very close inspection reveals the State House dome on Beacon Hill, and the sails of a schooner in Fort Point Channel. The main ship channel is to the far right.

Although Lawley built the wooden defenders *Puritan* and *Mayflower* in 1885 and 1886, the steel *Volunteer* was built by Pusey & Jones at Wilmington, Delaware. All three sloops were designed by Edward Burgess, under the close supervision of General Charles Paine. Paine organized the *Puritan* syndicate and was the sole sponsor of the *Mayflower* and the *Volunteer*.

Previous to the *Puritan*'s success, Burgess was unknown outside of the Boston area. He was one of the first designers to cross the traditional American beamy-centerboard concept with the deep-keel model favored in Great Britain. The resulting keel-centerboarders were over-all superior to vessels of either extreme. In recent years this concept has returned with great vigor.

04923 RIGGING THE VOLUNTEER AT LAWLEY'S.

DETROIT PHOTOGRAPHIC CO.

[3.23] March 1905. A Lawley displacement speed-ster in the Back Bay, being delivered to the boat and automobile show held in Mechanic's Building. The very fastest speed boats in 1905, powered by European automobile engines, were reaching about thirty miles per hour.

[3.24] 1901. Ship-building, *ergo*, ship-breaking. The 1867-built Fall River Liner *Providence* is broken up at Nut Island, Quincy. Massive "hogging frames," looking and acting like bridge trusses, gave her immense shoal wooden hull longitudinal strength.

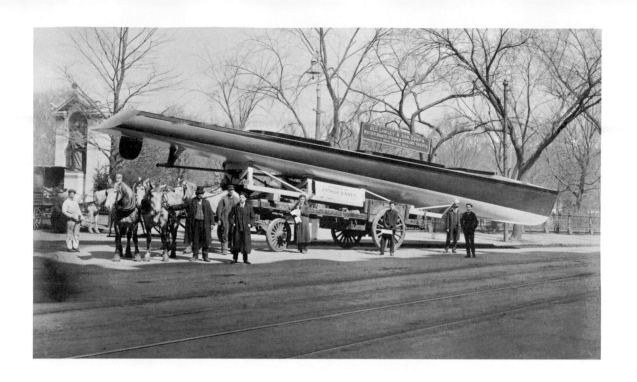

[4] Some Useful Vessels and Institutions of the Port

This chapter is something of a catch-all, yet it remains incomplete. It is intended to present some of the men, vessels, businesses, and agencies contributing to the daily activity of the harbor, or concerned with the operation of the port. There are many omissions. There are no photographs of longshoremen, immigration officials, wharfingers, switchmen, marine surveyors, coastal surveyors, insurance agents, baggers, bakers, shipping agents, or doctors at the Marine Hospital. There is no mention of the vital, though unspectacular, army of clerks who made the whole show work. There are no intriguing interiors of nautical instrument shops; no agonizing scenes taken in navigation and engineering cram schools; no photographs of the Customs House, of shipping offices, of the old sailors' home at Quincy; or of the activities of the several religious organizations dedicated to the aid and salvation of destitute or intemperate seamen. There are no fireboats, floating coal or grain elevators, water boats, water taxis, dredges, salvage vessels, barges, lighters, or pile drivers.

This dismal listing is not to be considered an apology. If photographs of all these subjects existed, and were of good quality, there would not be room here for a quarter of them. Nor would many necessarily be of much interest. As it is, the selections for the chapter have been made from a relatively limited group of photographs, for these were apparently the classes of vessels and professions generally taken for granted. The imbalance is all the more obvious when viewed in the light of the exceptions—for example, there exist many more fine photographs of piloting than are here reproduced, which may reflect the fact that the pilots were a notoriously introverted group, proud of their profession and their schooners.

[4.1] Boston Lightship station, six miles east of Boston Light, was established in 1894, and was primarily intended to reduce the danger incurred by vessels running in to Boston Light in fog. (Not surprisingly, the greatest danger faced by lightships was collision with vessels homing-in on their fog signals). This particular lightship, pictured in 1915, was probably the second regular vessel on the Boston station. In 1900 the station was shifted one mile to the north after the Cunarder *Ultonia* struck the rock now bearing her name while running out to the lightship. The move increased the controlling depth from 26′ to 32′.[1] Lightships were maintained by the Lighthouse Establishment, a Treasury Department agency that was transferred to the Commerce Department in 1903.

[4.2] 1893. Captain Joshua James, Keeper of the United States Life-Saving Service Station at Point Allerton, poses with his crew, two boats, and three beach apparatus carts. In the background, a three-masted schooner tows into Nantasket Roads, past Boston Light on Little Brewster Island.

Boston was a dangerous port to enter in bad weather, and the stretch of coastline from Point Allerton to Scituate had a high incidence of shipwreck. Most difficulties occurred during winter northeasters when vessels which failed to fetch Boston Light were forced to anchor off the lee shore. Between 1889 and 1902 eighty-six vessel casualties occurred within the field of operations of the Point Allerton station.[2]

The area's first lifeboat stations were established early in the nineteenth century by the Massachusetts Humane Society. Before the extension of federal service to Massachusetts in 1874, the Humane Society maintained seventy-eight lifeboat and thirteen mortar stations.[3] The U.S.L.S.S. station at Point Allerton was established in 1889. Other government stations were located at Nahant and North Scituate; there were Humane Society stations at Strawberry Hill, Gun Rock Cove, and Crescent Beach. The Humane Society boats were manned by volunteer crews; the government stations had professional crews, usually locally recruited. All crews were composed of superior surf and broken-water boatmen who drilled frequently. The government life-savers maintained beach patrols in the night and during thick weather. In addition to rescuing people, the life-savers—especially those stationed in areas remote from tugs—would always help the crews of endangered or stranded vessels set out anchors, secure gear, or kedge off.

The smaller boat, in the background, is apparently a Beebe surfboat, strongly but lightly constructed of cedar and oak, and weighing about 700 pounds. The bigger surfboat to the right has built-in flotation tanks, and was probably intended for use closer to the station. The boats used by the Life-Saving Service were developed from the surfboats used by the beach fishermen of Long Island and New Jersey.[4] The boats used by the Humane Society were generally heavier, and often of carvel construction.[5]

The three carts contain apparatus for the breeches-buoy. If conditions were so bad as to make the use of the surfboat very dangerous, and if the wreck were within range, a light line was fired to the stranded vessel from the Lyle gun (the gun muzzle may be seen between the wheels of the middle cart). The light line was bent to a stouter line, which, when set up with tension, served as a bridge for the operation of the breeches-buoy (or metal life-car), which was laboriously hauled between the shore and the wreck. The white, round buoy may be seen on the left-hand cart. The wooden "crotch," folded and slung beneath the cart, was erected on the beach, stayed with sand anchors, and served to elevate the shore-side end of the line. In bitter winter cold, whether out in the boat or heaving on the wet and sandy buoy line, the life-saving crews frequently suffered nearly as much as the wreck survivors. The stations were not manned during summer.

[4.3] Captain Joshua James, Keeper of the United States Life-Saving Service Station at Point Allerton, poses grandly with his crew and some apparatus of the business. The captain holds a brass speaking trumpet in his weathered hand. The men in the back row hold Coston lights—red flares—used to signal wrecks and to warn wayward vessels that they were standing into danger. A bronze Lyle line-throwing gun is in the foreground; its solid cylindrical projectile is well displayed. With a light line attached, the Lyle gun had a range of about 700 yards, although the effective distance of breeches-buoy operation was considerably less.[6] The white, round breeches-buoy, with traveling block attached, is to the right. A metal life-car—an elaboration of the breeches-buoy idea—is suspended in the background, behind the flag. The big lantern to the left was probably used to illuminate beach operations; the middle lantern, with reflector, may be a beach lantern, carried on patrol. The man sitting to the right holds a cork life-vest. Not shown is the clever device that was hauled out to the wreck at the very last and which cut the lifeline at the knot when tripped.

Captain James was a native of Hull who joined the volunteer crew of the Humane Society in 1842, at age fifteen. In 1876 he was appointed keeper of the Society's four lifeboats at Stony Beach, Point Allerton, and Nantasket Beach. The exploits of Captain James and his crews were many. On November 25 and 26, 1888, they rescued twenty-nine persons from five vessels wrecked along eight miles of beach in a terrific gale. In 1889 Captain James became the first keeper of the government station at Point Allerton, despite the fact that at age sixty-two he was seventeen years over the prescribed age limit.[7]

The exertions of life-savers all along the coast during the long and destructive "Portland Gale" of November 1898 were extraordinary. At Hull the force of the wind was so great that Captain James's men frequently had to turn their backs and crouch to the ground. The seas were so heavy that it was necessary to launch the boats at Pemberton Landing, on the inside of Hull Gut. Twenty lives were saved from six wrecked vessels.[8]

On March 17, 1902, the entire crew, save one, of the Monomoy Point station was lost while attempting to rescue the crew of a coastal coal barge. Captain James was deeply affected. Two days later, in a northeast gale, he called out his crew for an unusually early boat drill. For an hour he manned the steering oar in the surf. When the drill was completed and the boat landed, the old life-saver jumped to the sand and said to his men, "The tide is ebbing." Within a few steps he fell dead, several months shy of seventy-six.[9]

[4.4] 1898. The United States Revenue Cutter *Manning*, newly built by the Atlantic Works, East Boston. The Revenue-Marine (later called the Revenue Service) was founded by Alexander Hamilton in 1790 to enforce customs regulations. In 1832 cutters began to cruise the coast during winter months to aid distressed mariners.[10] The service had a varied history, often suffering from lack of centralized control—at times cutters became political annexes of particular customs houses. The nineties were a period of reform, and saw the service's responsibilities increased to include patrolling of regattas, and the regulation of anchorages. The steel *Manning* was representative of the first-class vessels built by the service during this period. In 1915 the Revenue Service was merged with the Life-Saving Service to form the Coast Guard. The Steamboat Inspection Service, the Bureau of Navigation, and the Lighthouse Establishment were eventually also included in the Coast Guard.

[4.5] The Lighthouse Establishment (or Lighthouse Service) tender *Gardenia,* 1891. The Lighthouse Establishment maintained all federal aids to navigation, including the two spar buoys resting diagonally aboard the *Gardenia.* Spar buoys measured up to sixty feet long, and were of pine, spruce, and—preferably—cedar. Additionally, there were iron can, nun, whistle, gas, and ice buoys. An ice buoy was compartmentalized and, being shaped like a spar buoy, was not easily carried away by ice. Iron buoys were preferred over wooden spars at important locations because they would not be cut by propeller blades. Whistle buoys, introduced in the late seventies, were constructed with a long tube extending downward, open at the bottom. Air was drawn into the tube as the buoy rose on a sea, and was compressed as the buoy fell in a trough, producing a mournful tone. Gas-lighted buoys were introduced in the eighties. The modern buoyage system in United States waters dates from 1850.[11]

Tenders were also used for servicing lightships and lighthouses. The Lighthouse Bureau (as the service was then termed) was merged with the Coast Guard in 1938, and it is a pleasure to report that the Coast Guard has continued the tradition of naming tenders after plants, in refreshing contrast to the generally characterless bureaucratic vessel-naming practices of governmental services and agencies.

[4.6] A federal license which was required to pilot enrolled and licensed steamers on the waters of Boston Harbor and Massachusetts Bay, issued by the Steamboat Inspection Service to Captain Thomas Cooper of the Boston Pilots. Such a federal license was not required for the vast majority of a pilot's duties, as the regulation of pilotage of "registered" or foreign-going American and all foreign-flag vessels was under the authority of the individual states. Federal steamboat inspection was begun in 1838, and the Steamboat Inspection Service was created in 1852. Although the Service was primarily concerned with the inspection and certification of boilers, machinery, and engineers, its jurisdiction extended to steamer hulls and deck officers.

To become a working pilot at the port, an experienced mariner had to be recommended by the Boston Pilots' Association and approved by the Trustees of the Boston Marine Society—not surprisingly, many pilots were related. A pilot candidate working up through the ranks had to serve a long apprenticeship as a boatkeeper on the pilot schooners. The Boston Marine Society Trustees were empowered by the legislature with the general supervision of pilotage, although such matters as rates were determined by the Commonwealth.[12]

In addition to the Harbor pilots, there were special pilots for Hull, the Charles River, the Neponset River, East Braintree, Weymouth, and Quincy.

Issue   Nº 3.

United States

Inspectors' License to PILOTS.

This is to Certify that **Thomas Cooper**
has given satisfactory evidence to the undersigned Local Inspectors of Steam
Vessels for the District of *Boston* that he is a skillful **PILOT** of
Steam Vessels, and can be entrusted to perform such duties upon the Waters of
Boston Harbor and
between Massachusetts Bay

and he is hereby Licensed to act as **FIRST CLASS PILOT** on Steam Vessels of
gross tons for the term of *five* years from this date on the above named route.
Given under our hands this *19th* day of *November* 1897

Albert C. Crandall
Inspector of Hulls.

1182

Andrew Savage
Inspector of Boilers.

[4.7] 1891. The wonderful pilot schooner *Hesper* romps along off Pemberton under her summer rig. Previous to 1901, piloting was internally competitive, and except for the two schooners required to be on station off Boston and (after 1873) Highland Light, the remaining schooners (usually numbering six) were free to go hunting for "good," or, eligible vessels. With certain exceptions, under state law, all foreign vessels and all United States vessels returning from a foreign voyage were required to take pilotage.[13]

Racing, with the schooners, and even with the "canoes," which were rowed, was very much a part of the business. The pilots, therefore, required fast vessels with the ability to safely and comfortably maintain station throughout the winter. Their demands were admirably met by several talented and progressive local designers who probably produced the finest pilot schooners in the world. The *Hesper* was perhaps the finest of all. Designed by Dennison J. Lawlor, of Chelsea, for Captain George Lawler, she was for many years the standard measure of performance by which new fishermen and yachts were rated. Her sharp, deep hull had considerable influence on subsequent fisherman design.[14]

[4.8] Winter 1884. The pilot schooner *Sylph* (II) drives crisply home to Lewis Wharf against a cold norther. Her crew appears to consist of one pilot and four boatkeepers, some of whom may be apprentices. When the schooner is "manned out," with all her pilots gone, the first boatkeeper brings her home—often a distance of several hundred miles. The two "canoes"—one for launching on either tack—lie overturned amidships. Sails are neatly reefed. Halyards are clear and on deck, ready to run, for the *Sylph* is going to sail to her berth. She is the picture of trim good health.

[4.9] 1891. The pilot schooner *Varuna* is beating out of Nantasket Roads and has just tacked. The forestaysail, or "jumbo"—which has been backed to windward to help her bow fall off the wind—is being slacked to leeward. (In typical pilot fashion, the jumbo has a "bonnet"). The forward-most hand slacks the windward jib sheets to allow the sails to set better. The prominent building in the left distance is the Hotel Pemberton on Windmill Point, one of several giant Hull resorts. The pilot vessel keeping the Boston Light station often put into Hull to land pilots retrieved from outbound ships.

The *Varuna,* a centerboarder, survived the terrible "*Portland* Gale" which wrecked her sister the *Columbia.* When the storm struck, the *Varuna* was headed offshore for a cruise. During the fearful night of wind and ice she just managed to clear the Cape. In the morning there was a great deal of sand on deck, apparently scooped up by the seas as she slid by Peaked Hill Bars.[15]

[4.10] To be at sea aboard a small sailing vessel in a 70-mph gale, full of snow, with the temperature near zero, is to be in a considerable situation.

Pilot boat *Lilly,* No. 1, Capt. George Lawler, was out in the bay all Saturday night, being unable to get inside the harbor, owing to the storm. The mainsail was frozen stiff and the light was completely encased in a covering of ice . . . The cold was so intense that the sailors could not remain on deck for more than five minutes at a time, and only by keeping their hands well soaked with kerosine oil were they able to keep them from freezing.—*Boston Evening Transcript,* Jan. 25, 1879

The able *Lilly* was designed by D. J. Lawlor. She is pictured at Lewis Wharf the morning after the night before.

[4.10] Detail

[4.11] Captain Thomas Cooper puts the helm a-lee and tacks the pilot schooner *Columbia* to pass close astern of a coaster from the Maritimes. The man aft hauls in slack in the main sheet. Foreign vessels of under two hundred tons' burden or of less than seven feet draft were not required to take a pilot, but if they were hailed by a pilot they were nevertheless liable for half of the regular fee.[16] This was collected in port by the Pilots' clerk. Obviously, this was a very cosy arrangement for the schooner keeping the Boston Light station, and in a good morning she could pay all the expenses of the cruise without losing a pilot. According to Mr. Thomas Lampee, Captain Cooper's grandson:

Grandfather would spend the mornings on the Boston station chasing the Johnny-boats. He'd sail close under their sterns to get their names, and holler, "Do you want a pilot?" Of course, they'd always holler back, "Nooooo!" I think that if one of them ever answered "Yes," Grandfather would have shot him![17]

In addition to the large number on the mainsail, pilot schooners identified themselves by flying a large blue and white pilot flag, and by showing rockets and blue lights at night. A brass signal gun was carried, for use in fog, and no doubt to attract the attentions of near-sighted Provincial skippers.

[4.12] Piloting was not all gales and ice. In the summer, especially, it could be a very pleasant way of life. Here, pilots on the *Columbia* play cards aft of the white deck icebox. Each schooner had four to six pilots regularly working from it. At sea, correct discipline was maintained, and the crew kept forward unless called. When a schooner was manned-out, with the first boatkeeper in command for the run home, it was customary for the crew to eat at the cabin table, although discipline was not otherwise relaxed. It was not unknown for the homeward-bound schooner to be met within the harbor limits by a tug carrying her pilots, who— to the disgust of the crew—were ready to put about for another cruise.[18]

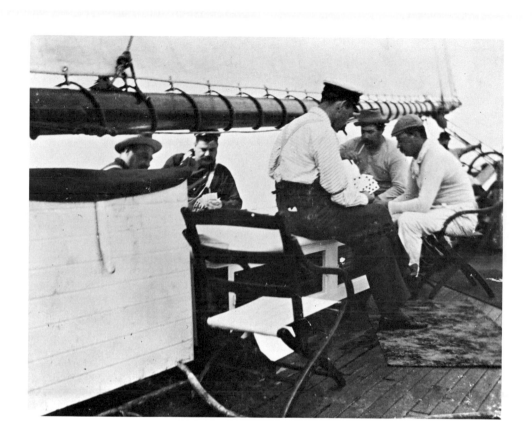

[4.13] When the *"Portland* Gale" struck during the evening of November 26, 1898, the pilot schooner *Columbia* was returning to Boston manned-out, in the charge of her first boatkeeper. Her last pilot had boarded the Allan Line steamer *Hibernian* off Race Point at noon. She was seen from the lightship at dusk, nearly becalmed. The hurricane struck suddenly, with thick snow, and the *Columbia* was apparently put about to find sea-room. When she would not fetch clear of the land there was no choice but to anchor. Shackle pins on both chains let go, and she grounded on a Scituate ledge, staving-in her port side. Big seas picked her up and drove her ashore on the Sand Hills, throwing her into a cottage. It is a tribute to her builder that so much of her hull remained intact.

On Wednesday, the first day that the railroad line was open we went to Scituate accompanied by a marine junk dealer. When we saw the wreck her starboard side seemed OK outside of the loss of her rudder, the lower end of her stern post shredded, some sheets of copper missing and her masts broken off close to the deck with the sails securely furled to the booms. But her port side resting on the sands was mostly open and the Skipper [Captain Thomas Cooper], realizing that she could not be salvaged sold her as she lay for $300. She had cost over $12,000 to build . . . All five of her crew were drowned, two of the bodies never recovered. The Skipper naturally was distressed over her loss, but more by the loss of the men, some of whom had served with him for years. He was never the same after this catastrophe. The Skipper found no fault with the way the *Columbia* was handled in this storm.—*Mr. Charles I. Lampee, one of Captain Cooper's grandsons.*[19]

[4.14] The police steamer *Patrol* in July 1890. The waterfront police force was established in 1853. The Harbor Master, an officer of the Boston Police Department, was responsible for enforcing harbor regulations, including the anchorage of vessels. For many years members of the force performed some of their harbor duties in a Whitehall rowing boat—very likely it is the boat shown in the right background, with a mast for a sprit rig stepped in the bows.

[4.15] The *J. Putnam Bradlee* was owned by the City of Boston for many years and was primarily used for servicing the penal and charitable institutions on the islands. For gala harbor events she doubled as the official city yacht. Here, she heads down the harbor through the ice with a load of hay on her foredeck.

Notice her large paddle-boxes. Large paddle-wheels reflected the desirability of having the static, radial paddles enter and leave the water as near to the vertical as possible to reduce vibration and inefficiency. This problem was solved in the eighties with the adoption of "feathering" paddles which were geared to an eccentric and changed angle as the wheel turned.

[4.16] Late nineteenth-century Boston was a city of immigrants and contained some of the most crowded and unhealthy neighborhoods in the country. Hot summer weather was the special curse of the slums, and during July and August the mortality rate for Boston's children under age five was commonly three times the rate for the rest of the year. The Boston Floating Hospital, supported by private charity, was opened in 1894 for the purpose of providing sick children under age six with medical care, good food, cool breezes, and a change of scenery. Mothers accompanied by their other (healthy) children were welcome to join the daily cruises. The hospital was chiefly inspired by the spectacle of crowds of parents with infants and children in arm walking the South Boston Bridge through sweltering nights.

The first hospital vessel was the ex-steamer *Clifford,* which had to be towed about the harbor. The hospital steamer pictured here was new in 1906 and was fully air-conditioned. It accommodated 100 permanent patients and 150 daily patients in six wards, and contained an operating room and a laboratory specializing in milk research. The steamer operated during July, August, and September from North End Park.[20]

[4.17] Although the date of the first instance of steam towage at Boston is unknown, the business apparently did not develop to any appreciable degree previous to the 1840s—and even then a series of warping buoys were maintained along the waterfront, and vessels were regularly warped from wharf to wharf.[21] Much of the towing that did occur was accomplished by passenger steamers working between runs. By contrast, New York's first regular towboat was built in the early 1820s.[22] No doubt the slow growth of towing at Boston was largely due to the compactness of the waterfront and its near proximity to the sea.

Early tugs were side-wheelers, although the screw propeller was quickly adopted. Boston's most famous pre-Civil War tug was the iron twin-screw *R. B. Forbes*, built at Boston by Otis Tufts in 1846. The *Forbes* was an able seagoing vessel and towed many new Boston-built square-riggers to New York for loading. She was lost in the Civil War.

The vessel pictured is the tug *Leader*, built at Philadelphia in 1881, and operated from Lewis Wharf by N. P. Doane. Although lacking a pilothouse eagle and a canvas window "visor," the *Leader* otherwise admirably displays the handsome proportions of the eastern harbor tug of the later nineteenth century. There is a certain affinity of spirit between a tug and a locomotive, and, in fact, the *Leader*'s pilothouse windows are stylistically similar to those found in locomotive cabs of the day. American tug design was distinctive—Europeans built side-wheel tugs and usually towed ahead, the better for turning in confined basins. Consequently, for maneuverability, the towing bitts were placed nearly amidships. Americans, however, preferred screw tugs, and often towed lashed alongside. In most harbor situations this method increased efficiency, safety, and control. It also permitted the large, ventilated deckhouse demanded by local climate.

Wooden tugs were substantially constructed, with a mammoth main beam intended to withstand the compression inherent with certain situations— as when a tug is jammed by the tide between her tow and a bridge pier. Cramped boiler rooms grew dry-rot like a hot-house, and older tugs often became extremely ripe.

[4.18] A receipt kept by the master of the Boston schooner *Rebecca J. Moulton* upon payment for towage by the tug *Leader* from sea to McQuesten's East Boston lumber wharf. The schooner probably carried a cargo of Georgia or Florida hard pine. The derivation of the engraved illustration will not have to be impressed upon the observant reader. The Doanes were Cape Codders, as were so many of the people who made the port work. Schooner captains who were fellow Cape Codders favored Doane tugs.

N. P. DOANE, - Agent,
Office, 109 Commercial St.

LEADER.—Capt. W. S. Doane.

Boston, *Sept 8. 9* 1899.

The *Sch. R. J. Moulton*

AND OWNERS,

To The Steam Tug Boat **LEADER** and Owners, **Dr.**

To Towing said Vessel from *Sea*

to *Mc Martens* $ *25.*

APPROVED   Received Payment for Agent,

S. W. Rogers

☞ TOW BOATS AT LEWIS WHARF, NORTH PIER ☜

[4.19] 1884. Tugs of the Boston Tow Boat Company lie at the end of T Wharf. The near dark-hulled tug is the *Confidence,* a large tug fitted with pumps for salvage operations; inboard of her is the big *Storm King,* which towed coal barges coastwise. Two harbor tugs lie to the right. Close inspection reveals a tug model atop the flagpole erected from the wharf building. Boston Tow Boat Company was incorporated in 1872 as an outgrowth of the T Wharf Tow Boat Company, established in 1857. Other tug fleets were operated by Rogers & Sears, Central Wharf Tow Boat, Commercial Wharf Tow Boat, N. P. Doane, Ross Tow Boat, and Suffolk Tow Boat Companies.

The two tugs with white houses lying left, at Long Wharf, are Quarantine Department steamers. The Quarantine Department, which was under the control of the city health department, enforced federal health regulations pertaining to foreign entries. Vessels arriving from foreign ports with cases of contagious disease aboard were required to anchor in the outer harbor at Quarantine. Infected persons were treated at the hospital on Gallop's Island.

[4.20] Boston Tow Boat Company tugs hang off the end of Lewis Wharf in 1906. From left, they are *Ariel, Vesta, D. Roughan, Dione, Vim, Zetes,* and *Juno.* White hulls indicate that oil pollution was not yet a harbor problem. The hogsheads on the lighter may contain rosin or naval stores brought by coastal steamer from Savannah or Charleston. In 1900 nearly sixty tugs were owned in the port.[23]

By waterfront standards, a tug skipper was enviably employed. His work was often challenging and of great variety. He played to a critical waterfront audience, and skilled performance was certain to be noted. He spent his days on the water and was home in bed most nights. In the summer he was cooled by sea breezes; in the winter he enjoyed steam heat. Food on tugs was outstandingly good and was served in outrageous quantity. You could often identify a tow boat man by his great girth.

[4.21] About 1890. The East Boston ferry *Gen. Hancock,* running on the North, or People's Line, heads for the Boston terminal at Lincoln Wharf. Despite her awkward appearance and mundane employment, she possesses a certain appeal, as does nearly every manner of floating craft. She was not intended for a looker, and her only concessions to vanity are the wonderful round pilot-houses topped with white range lights, and the carved nameboards over the team gangway. Her frothing paddle-wheel and broad white wake are the essence of marine steam power.

The port's first ferry, the Winnisimmet ferry between the North End and Chelsea, was established in 1631. In 1831 steam ferries were introduced on the run. The East Boston Ferry Company was established in 1852, and came under City management in 1870. The People's Ferry was established in 1853 and became a city line in 1864.

Like most forms of public transportation, the ferry service was frequently criticized, especially by citizens of East Boston, who felt that the one cent passenger fare was discriminatory and oppressive. In 1890 the two City-run East Boston lines (a third East Boston line was privately owned) carried over 10,200,000 foot passengers and over 900,000 horse-drawn vehicles.[24] Vehicle rates varied with the horsepower—for example, a one-horse carriage containing three passengers paid four cents.

In a sense the ferry lines were major cargo carriers, especially before the Grand Junction Railroad was completed to the East Boston waterfront in 1869. In 1871 East Boston shipbuilder D. D. Kelly reminisced: "Formerly, all the [ship] timber that came in on the Worcester, Providence and other roads came across on the ferry on drag wheels or very heavy caravans. The sticks were heavy, sometimes weighing three or four tons."[25]

Every shipping trade had its own particular problems. On the ferries teamsters overloaded wagons to save fares, and then were unable to negotiate the off-ramp at low tide without aid from willing passengers.[26] (By the 1890s, at least, steam winches were installed at the head of the ramps). In winter, ice in the slips was an occasional problem for the pilots, while the deckhands struggled to maintain a solid base of snow on the team gangway for the sleighs and pungs.[27]

One might conclude that commuting to work on the water, in the open air, daily seeing the city from its most advantageous and natural perspective, was a far happier arrangement than the present fume-choked tubes dug through the bottom mud; in fact, the ferries became badly congested, and since the average commuter probably valued the harbor scenery only slightly more than his modern counterpart does the view in the tunnels, there were cries for an underwater route at least by the seventies.

Milford T. Cunningham of Ashburnham grew up in East Boston. He remembers the ferries:

My father did most of the ice-breaking for the ferry lines with his tug the *Bessie B.,* and he was friendly with most of the engineers on the boats. When I wanted to take the ferry I would walk aboard and say that I wanted to visit "Medcalf, the engineer", and even if Medcalf wasn't aboard they would let me stay in the fire-room for the crossing, so that I did not have to pay the penny fare. Boston harbor was a paradise for a boy in those days.

[4.22] The Boston, Revere Beach & Lynn Railroad was a narrow gauge line which ran from East Boston to downtown Lynn. It began operations in 1875 and shut down in 1940. As a feeder it operated a ferry line from 350 Atlantic Avenue (the slip was between Rowe's Wharf and Foster's Wharf) to the railroad's western terminus at Marginal Street, East Boston. The boats were painted dark red, ran on railroad time, and possessed great character. They carried passengers only, at three cents a head.

The *Newtown* is pictured fresh from her builders in 1908. Her tall stack improved the furnace draft and reduced the number of cinders which spotted commuters' white collars. Paddle-wheels provided strong backing power, and ferries entered their slips at a great rate of speed. The employee standing foremost on the "Boston end" was very likely the man who shifted rudder pins between trips, locking the forward, unused rudder.

In the left distance two city-run North ferries are passing each other. The busy East Boston waterfront is at right.

[4.23] From 1869 to 1877 the fast *John Romer* was one of the several steamers operated on the popular Boston–Nantasket run by the venerable Boston & Hingham Steamboat Company. Appreciate the calculated architecture of her pilothouse, the graceful visor above the windows, the finely carved eagle, and the sartorial excellence of her master and mate. The Pilot Rules are framed on the after pilothouse bulkhead. The diagonal brace appearing beneath the pilothouse is part of the starboard hogging frame which contributed longitudinal strength to the *Romer*'s shoal wooden hull.

Appearing aft of the stack is the skeletal, peculiarly American "walking beam." The forward end of the beam is attached to the single piston rod; the after connecting rod turned the crankshaft. Steam entered first one, and then the other end of a single vertical cylinder. At half stroke, steam was cut off, and the stroke was completed by the steam's expansion. Steam was exhausted into a condenser, which created a vacuum on the opposite side of the piston from the expanding steam. Engines of this seemingly antediluvian design were still being built in the early 1900s, as they were quiet, economical, and could tolerate great latitudes of wooden hull flexibility without getting out of line. The cheapness of wood construction was an important factor explaining the slow adoption of the screw propeller in protected coastal waters.

[4.24]

The perfection of physical comfort is enjoyed, when on a warm day of summer, one leaves the hot and crowded streets and many cares of the city, and passes down Boston Harbor on one of its luxurious excursion-steamboats . . . And on a day of unusual heat and sunshine, all roads lead to the harbor; and the horse-cars for Atlantic Avenue are crowded with people eager to inhale the bracing air of the ocean. The fares on the steamboats are so small that even the poorest can go; the accommodations are so luxurious that the veriest Sybarite of the Back Bay need suffer no discomfort.—M. F. Sweetser, 1882 [28]

The handsome *Gov. Andrew* presents a most satisfying picture as she backs away from Foster's Wharf on a Friday afternoon in August 1908. Unless this is a special excursion, her run is to the old summer resort of Nahant, which had been served by almost continuous steamer connections since 1817, and, according to Samuel Eliot Morison, "exhibited every known atrocity in cottage architecture." [29] The sun glints off the eagle perched on the foremast, and off the instruments playing in the band on the foredeck. The polished brass rail used by the oiler when attending to the walking beam, and the stern spring line hooked to the paddle-box, with heaving line bent, bespeak a well run vessel.

Beyond, at left, the *City of Bangor* prepares to receive the weekend crowd for Penobscot Bay, while the two raked stacks of either the *Yale* or the *Harvard,* for New York, appear over the shed on Rowe's Wharf. The rather outlandish stack just forward of the *Bangor* belongs to a "narrow gauge" ferry.

[4.24] Detail

[4.25] This little cat-rigged vessel of unknown employment will have to serve as a stand-in for the vast and motley fleet of lighters, dredges, water taxis, and other such craft, which were employed at the more menial chores of the port, and are not pictured in the collection. This photograph is unusual in that the photographer exposed it despite the fact that the lowly cat boat was blocking the middle of the view.

Governor's Island is in the left background. The vessels at anchor are all coasting schooners. A diminutive dark fishing dory and a white cat-rigged yacht tack up the harbor astern of our anonymous friend.

Occasionally . . . [Little Brewster Island] is visited by a swarm of boarding-house runners, in longboats, who dash out thence upon foreign vessels entering The Roads, to lure the sailors to their dens in the North End. These are the stuff that pirates are made of,—bronzed and scarred fellows, with sinister faces, and language which the Puritans would have hung them for.—*M. F. Sweetser, 1882* [30]

Here we see The Sailors' Home, a plush North End den of the eighties. The sailor's district in the North End was rough country—in 1884 the Boston Port & Seaman's Aid Society reported that one precinct of Ward Six contained 140 "rum shops." [31]

The maltreatment of seamen in major American ports was a national disgrace, made possible by the wondrous gullibility of the sailor ashore. The institution of the seaman's boarding-house was central to the problem. Shipping masters, known as "crimps," controlled the hiring of seamen. Boarding-house masters either doubled as crimps or worked in league with them. Crimps negotiated the sailors' contracts with shipmasters and delivered the bodies for a fee, and, usually, a sizable advance upon the men's wages. In 1884 federal law made the payment of advances illegal, but this was soon circumvented by the legalization of payment-of-debt allotments, and by bonus systems. [32] Although seamen were required to sign articles at the office of the port's United States Shipping Commissioner (2900 men signed at the Boston office in 1886; 85 percent were foreign-born [33]), they often arrived with their crimps, who retained control of the manning business.

The situation at Boston was apparently quite rugged during the mid-century decades, although subsequently conditions seem to have improved. Toward the end of the century nothing on the East Coast could approach the conditions at labor-starved West Coast ports, where criminal and brutal methods of raising crews were practically an economic necessity. Boston usually seems to have had an adequate—or excessive—supply of seamen on hand.

This winter has been the hardest on Boston's colony of sailors that has ever been known here. It is almost impossible for a great many of them to get work, and when Jack cannot get work, it means that he is completely destitute . . . for not one sailor in twenty ever has any ready money after he has been ashore and paid off for a day or two. The Seamen's Friend Society has had all it could possibly do in taking care of these men . . . Almost the whole of Boston's [coastal] shipping now is carrying coal from the South, and in the summer time taking ice down as a cargo. This winter the competition of the barges which tow up with very large cargoes of coal have been felt to an unusual degree.—*Boston Evening Transcript,* March 2, 1895

Generally, Boston's crimps seem to have acted more the role of double agents, doing "favors" for both labor and management. The oversupply of seamen cramped their style and led to the formation of The Sailing and Boarding House Masters Association, which "absolutely controls all shipping offices," according to the *Boston Evening Transcript* of March 2, 1895.

If a man goes to a shipping office and asks for a berth, he is at once asked what boarding house he is staying at, and if it is not one of the association houses, he is put off and can never get a berth . . . the association houses will not take a man unless he has money, and the minute that his money is gone, he is kicked out into the street . . . It is probable that no class of men in the world are so thoroughly and systematically robbed as the sailors of this country.

[4.27] Ship chandlers were vital to the operation of the port. As indicated by the signs, they provided almost everything that a vessel required. Chandlers knew everyone and were valuable friends to shipmasters—often they acted as bankers and made substantial interest-free loans to embarrassed captains. As astute businessmen, they frequently owned shares in vessels of the port. At one time James Bliss & Company owned in all the vessels managed by Crowell & Thurlow, Rogers and Webb, and William F. Palmer.[34]

The Bliss firm was the oldest of the dozens of chandlers active at Boston during the late nineteenth century. Founded in 1832 by James Bliss, it was located for many years at 328 Atlantic Avenue, the address pictured. In 1876 old Mr. Bliss died, to be succeeded by the partnership of his adopted son James and long-time employee Israel Decrow, standing left and right respectively in the doorway.

[5] Fishing

Off the shores of Greenland, Newfoundland, the Maritimes, and New England lie extensive fishing grounds which have been of immense importance to much of the western world, to say nothing of coastal North America and Boston. These include the grounds of the Davis Strait; the Gulf of St. Lawrence; the Gulf of Maine; the Nova Scotia offshore banks; the Bay of Fundy; the New England shore; the dangerous shoals of George's Bank, east of Nantucket; and the great banks of Newfoundland, including Grand Bank, 37,000 square miles in area.

These rich old grounds have fed the Catholics of Europe, the slaves of the Caribbean, and fostered and sustained many of the early European settlements on the North American continent. For two centuries fishing was the most important industry of Massachusetts.

Our knowledge of the first European fishermen in these waters is slight. Likely they sailed from Bristol, inspired by the tales of fat cod told by sailors who were with Cabot off Newfoundland in 1497—despite the claim that the Newfoundland natives already knew the French name for cod.[1] The cod was an extremely valuable fish, not only because it was found in great numbers and was easy to catch but because it salts well.

There are indications that French fishermen were working the Newfoundland Banks in 1504,[2] and that in 1577 between three and four hundred European fishing vessels spent the summer in New World waters.[3] Nor did these resourceful and largely forgotten mariners confine themselves to the easternmost waters; at least, we know that in 1602 Gosnold discovered a Basque shallop commanded by Indians sailing off the Isle of Shoals, and Hudson made a similar discovery in Penobscot Bay in 1609.[4] When the unprepared and impractical Pilgrims were going hungry at Plymouth, forty or fifty fishing vessels were profitably employed seasonally on the coast of Maine.[5] Fortunately for *Mayflower* descendants, the Pilgrims' remarkable friend Squanto had once been employed as a Newfoundland fisherman.[6]

It is not my purpose to dwell unduly on these early incidents, but I believe that an awareness of the origins of the New England fisheries lends a valuable shading to one's vision when inspecting photographs from a far later era. Many of the elements and much of the spirit of the early fisheries remained.

From colonial days to the present, Boston's foremost role within the New England fisheries has been as the central market for distribution and export.[7] Although Boston's own fishing fleets have often been sizable, Boston's importance as a fishing center would have remained much the same had they never existed. Therefore any consideration of the Boston fish industry must take account of all the fisheries of New England.

Through much of the first half of the nineteenth century Boston's fishermen were prominent in the mackerel fishery, but were of no importance to the cod fishery.[8] At the beginning of the century Marblehead was the leading salt cod port, with strong competition provided by many Maine and Massachusetts towns, including Portland, Newburyport, Beverly, Chatham, and Provincetown. Marblehead saw its fishery largely destroyed by Jefferson's embargo, and was succeeded by Gloucester, which had a far superior harbor. In 1846 Gloucester and Boston were connected by rail, a link which became very important with the growth of the fresh fish industry.[9] The process of centralization continued, and by 1866 Gloucester was the leading fishing port of North America, a position it held at least into the early years of the twentieth century, when Boston was in serious contention.[10] The symbiotic relationship between the fish industries of Gloucester and Boston contributed to their mutual successes.

The major fisheries developments in the period covered by the photographs were the general decline of the New England fleet (as represented by the tonnage of vessels employed in the cod and mackerel fisheries); the tremendous growth of the iced-fresh fish business; and the steady development of improved vessels, gear, and techniques. The tonnage of the vessels in the cod and mackerel fisheries was at its zenith in 1862, and reached its nadir in 1899.[11] The growth of the fresh fish industry was largely responsible for the expansion of the Boston fish establishment, and was a factor in the deterioration of outport fisheries. The development of fast and able vessels was also partly a result of the growth of the fresh fish industry.

[5.1] An outstanding photograph of the north side of T Wharf, about 1885. The long wooden wharf building was built in 1882–83 and housed fish dealers, many of whom moved over from Commercial Wharf. The idle fish carts indicate that it is Sunday.

The cluttered vessel, extreme left foreground, is the *General Middleton*, a New Brunswicker. She has probably come from the north shore of New Brunswick with a cargo of herring. Topmasts and jibbooms indicate that it is not winter; therefore, her fish are probably smoked or salted, intended for human consumption, and imported under the terms of the 1871 Treaty of Washington. (From colonial times, an important aspect of the story of North Atlantic fishing has been the almost constant international litigation.) The winter fishery for frozen herring, which occurred primarily off the shores of Newfoundland, was a foundation of the New England deep-sea fisheries, since herring was the principal trawler bait. New England vessels predominated in the frozen herring fishery.[12]

The trailboards of the center schooner suggest that she is Essex-built; the Essex yards were known for their fine finish work. Her big forestaysail, or "jumbo," was typical of vessels rigged previous to the mid-eighties. The customary long, overhanging mainsails (see the outward-facing schooner, center background) must have been perfect joys to reef in a gale. In the immediate foreground, a man works at the masthead of a big sloop.

In terms of the tonnage of the New England cod and mackerel fleet, 1885 saw the acceleration of the post-Civil War decline.[13] The total recorded catch in 1885 was reduced from previous years, although receipts at Boston were larger, reflecting centralization and the growth of the fresh fish industry. At this time, the cured and fresh divisions of the fish business at Boston were of about equal capitalization.[14] Great quantities of fish cured elsewhere were packed by Boston and East Boston dealers. The catch of the vessels actually enrolled at Boston amounted to only about one-fifth of the port's total fish product receipts.[15]

In 1879 the fleet actually enrolled at Boston consisted of seventy-six vessels and 119 boats. Sixty of the vessels were engaged in the New England shore fresh fisheries; none went to George's or the Newfoundland banks. Six whalers and four menhaden steamers were also included.[16] By contrast, over four hundred vessels were enrolled at Gloucester.[17] Although the "outport" fleets were greatly reduced from former years, Marblehead still supported seventeen shore vessels and one Grand Banker;[18] Swampscott could still claim seventeen schooners winter fishing.[19]

In 1885 the recorded groundfish landings by vessels from Maine and Massachusetts totaled 528,000 quintals (1 quintal = 100 lbs.) from the New England shore and George's, as compared with 374,400 quintals from the Newfoundland banks.[20] In previous years the totals had generally been roughly equal; in future years the margin would greatly widen, reflecting the growth of the fresh fish market.

[5.1] Detail

[5.2] The south side of T Wharf, June 1907. Flags snap in the breeze; topsails are brailed-up, fisherman-style. The bell in the tower rang to announce fish auctions. The schooner in the right foreground has swung her long main boom to port to prevent locking horns with the big banker astern. The barrels in the white horse's wagon may contain some early mackerel. Landsmen stand along the caplog, just looking, feeling slightly out of place. Across the dock the Boston & Yarmouth (Dominion Atlantic Railroad) steamer *Prince George* lies on the north side of Long Wharf.

The year 1907 was a good one for the Boston fish industry. The tonnage of the New England vessel fishing fleet had made modest advances from its nadir in 1899. The Boston Fish Bureau reported that during the year a total of 476 separate craft landed their fares at Boston. The fleet included 307 vessels (schooners), 168 boats, and one steam trawler, and 4,912 men were reported fishing from the port.[21]

The data recorded by a 1908 Census report provide some interesting comparisons. The report listed a total of 2,305 active fishermen residing in Suffolk County; of these only 1,819 were vessel fishermen. Only 105 fishing vessels—but 384 boats—were listed under Suffolk County.[22] The differences between these data and those of the Boston Fish Bureau for 1907 provide a rough indication of the large number of "foreign" vessels and men (mostly from Essex County) who were regularly fishing for the Boston market. They also indicate that there were still active local boat fisheries serving other than the immediate Boston market.

Recorded fresh fish landings at Boston in 1907 totaled nearly 88,000,000 pounds.[23] Reflecting the size of the fresh fish industry, the over-all New England totals of the shore and George's fisheries amounted to more than twice the total catch of the Grand and Western Banks fishery.[24]

[5.2] Detail

[5.3] A fisherman making up a trawl in the early 1900s. The vast majority of the groundfish fares landed at Boston were caught on bottom trawls. By the last decades of the century only some Down East shore fishermen and some summer salt-bankers, principally from Gloucester, Provincetown, and Portland, regularly persisted in the use of simple handlines.[25] Bottom trawling is not yet extinct, but the practice is now so greatly reduced that the following description is best set in the past tense.

Halibut, haddock, and cod trawls all varied in detail, but a description of the standard cod trawl provides adequate illustration. Quite simply, a bottom trawl was a long line (called a ground line or a back line) with a great many short, hooked lines attached to it. It lay on the sea bottom, held at each end by anchors, which were marked by buoys. It was set and worked by fishermen in dories. Each completed trawl, as set, was composed of four to six separate lengths bent together; each such length was 300 fathoms long. When not in use each length was coiled in a barrel-half, and thus was called a "tub-o-trawl." A set trawl might have been two miles long. The three-foot hook lines, called "gangings" (visible in the photograph), were attached at six-foot intervals. A set trawl, therefore, was armed with as many as 1800 hooks.[26] The trawl was worked either by hauling it in, or by under-running. Hauling a halibut trawl up from 200 fathoms, with heavy fish on the hooks, was a very arduous task. Of course, every hook did not catch a fish, or an edible one. Worthless skates and dogfish plagued the fishermen, the dogfish destroying many marketable fish caught on the hooks.

[5.4] Baiting trawls in the eighties. Frozen and fresh herring, menhaden, mackerel, capelin, and salt clams, not to mention occasional seabirds, were common trawl baits. Not a few Boston trawler crews were all-Irish; the wicker trawl baskets shown here were peculiar to Boston's Irish fishermen. The wooden slide on the after side of the house protects one of the two compasses.

Fishing was a hard profession, appealing only to men inured more than most to danger and discomfort. When a banksman, rescued from his capsized dory, was asked how his ordeal had felt, he replied: "Well, I'd been fishin' all winter, I thought it was damn tough to go fishin' all winter and be lost in the spring." [27]

Although fishing was an exceptionally dangerous, rigorous, and ingrown profession, its characteristics bore some relation to working conditions ashore. In recent years young historians have been eagerly employed attempting to discredit the popular homilies of America's past. In many instances their work is long overdue. Nevertheless, I have yet to see evidence disputing the belief that America was built by hard physical labor (although the moral and practical results of the labor are debatable). For example, the stone walls of New England—now tumbled and covered with lichens, silently bounding and organizing the vast tracts of brushland and second growth—remain as monuments to a quality of human exertion that we of this century probably cannot adequately comprehend.

[5.5] Mid-eighties. From all appearances this vessel is being readied for a refit, and the "lumpers" may be discharging ballast before she goes on the railway. Fishing schooners were built low-waisted to ease the handling of dories and fish. It became common practice to include a break forward of the mainmast, which served to keep the afterdeck dry and braced the nested dories. This vessel is also fitted with davits, which, when connected by a plank across the top, served primarily as a platform for reefing. A comic cuts up at the helm.

[5.6] On March 17, 1909, sixty-one fishing vessels put into T Wharf, and it was described as possible to walk from Long to T to Commercial Wharf on the decks.[28] Conditions were not nearly so bad when this photograph was taken, but the picturesque inefficiency of the facility is quite evident. Apparent immediate problem: to get the ice from the wharf to the second vessel outboard, then to get under way. To shift one vessel meant shifting five. Protruding bowsprits and main booms were a continual nuisance. Fishermen have always been free spirits, not greatly concerned by bothersome details.

Recalling these times, an employee at Long Wharf wrote:

Not only did the teamsters from the Yarmouth boat mix it up with the banana teamsters, but the boat itself, being too long for the end berth was obliged to haul ahead whenever a fruit boat went in or out of the south dock. Often there was a delay in their doing so, and on these occasions I would get an irate telephone message from the manager of the Fruit Co. stating definitely just what kind of a blue nose steamer was in the way. Investigation usually showed that the Yarmouth boat was doing her best to haul ahead but that a dense mass of fishing schooners in the T Wharf dock prevented her from doing so. Then I had to get the hard working T Wharf wharfinger to come out and pull and haul till space was made. The fishermen were very independent and never would lift a hand themselves to help.[29]

[5.7] About 1890. Scale-spattered fishermen, probably aboard a North Shore trawler. The fancy coat draped over the fore gaff no doubt belongs to the photographer. It is likely that this gang is mostly Yankee, which would not often be the case aboard Boston-based vessels. In the mid-eighties, the majority of New England fishermen were native-born, although foreigners constituted a considerable and growing proportion, especially in the larger ports.[30] The biggest immigrant group came from the Maritimes—primarily from Nova Scotia. There were also many Irish, Scandinavians, and Portuguese. The Portuguese, for the most part, were from the Azores, and many came to New England signed aboard American whalers, which operated off the islands. Many Provincial fishermen arrived aboard American schooners which had completed their crews at Maritime ports. Newfoundlanders thus found employment in the summer Grand Bank cod fishery, and many young and ambitious Nova Scotians were attracted to the superior American mackerel schooners.[31] Many American Irish fished aboard Boston and Gloucester vessels trawling on George's and the New England shore. Yankees and Nova Scotians predominated in the mackerel, fresh halibut, and fresh haddock fisheries.[32]

The extensive deep-water fisheries of New England were unique in the nation. In 1907 nearly twice as many resident New England fishermen were "vessel" fishermen as were "boat" fishermen. This contrasted with the national average of three times as many "boat" fishermen as "vessel" fishermen.[33] At a time when the men of the merchant marine were largely foreign-born, the fisheries were the last stronghold of the native American mariner. By 1900, however, the Yankees in the New England vessel fisheries undoubtedly constituted but a small minority.

[5.8] The crew and mascot of a trawler in the early 1900s. On trawlers and seiners the wages and profits were paid through a share system which covered every detail of expense. For example, the vessel (owner) provided the compass and clock, while the skipper was responsible for his own charts. If a chronometer was needed to locate a small halibut "spot," the vessel and the crew split the rental and insurance fees. The fishermen supplied their own dory compasses, if desired.[34]

The discipline in the fishing fleet was lax in the extreme, being a holdover from the times when a vessel represented a community effort. The skipper was the only officer, and he was often paid less than the cook (who was the hardest-working man aboard, with duties exceeding food preparation. Fishermen were the best-fed of mariners). Although by law the fishermen were required to sign a form of articles, this, in fact, was almost never done, and the skipper had to command by tact and force of character. His only jurisdiction applied to fishing, navigation, and the owner's property.[35] In other words, if his crew decided to leave the vessel at a Provincial bait port, he could bring charges only if they left in the dories. Despite the system's disadvantages, it accorded fishermen the respect they demanded, and may partly explain why men—especially Yankees—remained in such a dangerous, uncomfortable, wearing, and low-paying profession.

[5.9] A cart-load of haddock, in the eighties. Two unfortunates are displayed impaled on a fish fork. The fish fork, like its cousin the longshoreman's hook, has been damaging property from the dim past to the present day. Notice the big wheels of the cart, and the noble blocks of granite in the wharf building.

The story of the haddock industry (according to Pierce, not fully supported by Goode) is instructive. Once upon a time, the haddock was considered to be a nuisance-fish, not worth the catching (it salts poorly). When fresh haddock was first offered on the market, the public showed little interest. Then, about 1870, some clever men began to push smoked haddock under the Scottish name of "finnan haddie." It sold well, and soon the public decided that even fresh haddock was edible, and a major fishery was begun.[36]

There are many such tales. Swordfish were once avoided by fishermen. Halibut were once considered "bait stealers" which interfered with cod fishing. Even in the eighties members of polite society spurned flounder, and the public has always been reluctant to eat pollock. The economics of Maine and the Maritimes have greatly benefited from the practice, originated in the seventies, of canning small herring under the name of "sardines." [37] Herring and true Mediterranean sardines are at least very similar—the unappetizing menhaden was optimistically packed in tins labeled "Shadines" and "Ocean Trout." Not surprisingly, this ruse did not succeed.[38]

[5.10] About 1890. In the low light of late afternoon the men of a shore fisherman dress the catch (cod, hake, cusk, and other groundfish), and put the deck in order. They have probably been fishing on Tillie's Bank, Stellwagen Bank (known to the fishermen as "Middle Bank"), or on one of the small rocky ledges located off the North Shore. The men are warmly dressed, and there is likely a clean chill in the air, as the last of the afternoon breeze sends the vessel happily on her way. Gulls wheel and squabble over the leavings. A nested dory is in the foreground. The shore fishermen worked in shoaler water than did the banksmen, and could fish one man to a dory. There were fewer dogfish inshore than there were offshore. It is not surprising that the shore fishermen often made more money than the offshore vessels, especially as their fish were fresher and fatter.

[5.11]
No class of vessels, not even the halibut schooners,
take more risks in running for market than do the
haddock schooners. It is of the utmost importance to
them to reach the market with their fish in good condition . . . In the stormiest of weather all sail that will
bear is crowded upon them, and harbors are made even
in heavy snow and thick fogs.—*G. Brown Goode, 1887* [39]

The schooner *Joseph Warren,* of Saco, Maine, at
T Wharf, 1885. Owner Joseph Smith poses forward of the coiled anchor cable. The *Warren* was
primarily employed as a fresh haddock trawler,
although, like many winter haddockers, she often
went mackerel seining during the summer.[40] A
mackerel seiner and another trawler lie astern.

The haddock fishery principally ran from October to April, with some vessels fishing the year
around. Most of the haddockers landed their fares
at Boston. Fish were caught on trawl lines worked
from dories. George's and Brown's Banks were perhaps the most popular, although by no means the
exclusive grounds. Today the George's Bank haddock fishery is in serious trouble.

In certain respects the haddock fishery was
unique. Each fisherman supplied his own dory and
gear. While on the grounds the schooners rarely
anchored, but dropped and recovered their dories
under sail. Shooting a schooner accurately and
safely alongside deeply loaded dories demanded
the highest skill. At night the haddockers jogged
along under reduced canvas. Navigation, especially
on tide- and gale-swept George's Bank, where the
currents run in a circle, was an art based on frequent bottom soundings.[41] Trips were short, usually
less than a week, and what with the time spent
fishing, dressing, and baiting the fishermen often
did not sleep while on the grounds.

Despite fatigue, they were notorious racers, and
schooners were often rigged with topmasts and
jibbooms throughout the winter. Since they were
frequently running for the land, they became exceptional pilots, and often entered Boston Harbor
running before snow-filled easterly gales, when
other shipping remained prudently offshore. The
harbor, with its outlying ledges and islands, is a
dangerous landfall, and the fact that few fishermen
were lost by going aground is an indication of their
superior abilities.

[5.12] In the eighties. The old tug *Fremont* assists the Gloucester seiner *Margie Smith* from Commercial Wharf, while the fishermen set the main. Mackerel seiners were always in a great heat to rejoin the fleet, as the season was short, the fishing unpredictable, and the competition fierce. With good weather, thick fish, and high prices, the next trip might make the summer. The purse seine, over 1200 feet long, is neatly flaked in the stern of the seine boat, ready to be paid out around a wily school of handsome mackerel.

Mackerel had long been caught by jigging with hooks, but the adoption of the purse seine after the Civil War revolutionized the fishery. The season's first schools usually appeared off the North Carolina coast in late March, and in the early eighties were met by as many as 150 New England vessels. Early season fares were landed at New York. Fish and fishermen would migrate slowly northward, and by mid-May would usually be off Block Island. At this point the fish would either head for George's, turn up the New England shore, or—occasionally—simply disappear. In the meantime, part of the fleet would have departed for the separate June "Cape Shore" fishery off Nova Scotia. In July they would return, working the original body of fish, landing much of the catch at Boston. If the season were a good one, many cod and haddock trawlers would refit and join the fishery, which generally lasted through October.[42]

In the eighties most mackerel were landed salted in barrels, although the flyers in the fleet often landed some iced fresh. Fishing often continued through the night, as the seine could be set around the phosphorescent glow of the schools. Once caught, the fish had to be promptly dressed and packed—mackerel fishing was either all work or no work.

The fishery reached its height in 1884, when 478,000 barrels of salt mackerel were landed in the United States.[43] In 1880 there were 468 vessels engaged in the fishery; 235 were so employed from March to November.[44] Many vessels spent the winter months in the exceedingly rugged frozen herring trade. Most of the schooners hailed from Gloucester and Maine.

Beginning in 1886 catches diminished rapidly, and many vessels sought other employment. The southern fishery was suspended from 1887 to 1893, on the supposition that overfishing was to blame. Results were inconclusive—most populations of surface schooling fish are subject to poorly understood fluctuations. In 1897 only 13,000 barrels of salt mackerel were landed[45] (unrecorded fresh landings may have doubled the total). In the early 1900s the fishery experienced a modest recovery, with the emphasis on fresh fish.

[5.13] A big halibut being landed at T Wharf in the eighties. Getting such a creature into a dory was difficult under the best of conditions, and conditions on the banks were often very bad. The regular halibut fishery was based at Gloucester, and most of the halibut coming to Boston rode the train or the steamer. This particular vessel, therefore, is probably a cod or haddock trawler. Such vessels commonly caught considerable fares of halibut on George's, Brown's, and on the shore grounds.

In the early nineteenth century there were so many halibut on Gulf of Maine banks that schooners often caught full fares in a single day. These stocks were rapidly reduced, until by the seventies halibut vessels were fishing on the banks of Newfoundland, Greenland, and even Iceland. These vessels usually fitted out in January and fished until October. Fares were landed both fresh and salted. Only big, first-class vessels were employed—vessels capable of being driven to and from the grounds in very bad weather. On the banks they often anchored in water over two hundred fathoms deep, and carried some four hundred fathoms of nine-inch circumference cable.[46] Fish were caught from dories on heavy trawls. Ice floes were one of many dangers. Fresh halibuters, homeward bound, were driven extremely hard. It was a prestigious fishery, employing only the most capable fishermen.

[5.14] . . . there is no vessel which requires so much skill and judgement in its management as the American [clipper fishing] schooner; none which is, perhaps, more capable of remarkable achievements when properly managed, and none which is more liable to disaster when in the hands of the unskillful.—*G. Brown Goode, 1887* [47]

The *Joseph Warren* is an example of the handsome clipper schooners which were popular in many fisheries from the sixties through the eighties. Moderately shoal, with a sharp entrance, heavy quarters, a long run, carrying their wide beam aft to the counter, and often very heavily canvassed, they were extremely fast under the right conditions. This design had inherent disadvantages, however, since such a vessel often could not recover from a bad "knock-down," and could be fatally "tripped" when running before big breaking seas. [48] Vessels engaged in the fresh fisheries were always hard driven, and this practice, especially in the winter, contributed greatly to vessel losses.

The rigging in the foreground is the topping-lift of a schooner's main boom, and is indicative of the manner with which fishing schooners were sailed. Fishermen preferred the single lift—as opposed to a coaster's double lifts with lazy-jacks—because the sail was less likely to foul when dropped on the run as the schooner was shot into her berth. Never mind that half of it landed in the water. Big crews allowed fishing vessels to carry more sail, longer.

[5.15] The *Carrie E. Phillips*, of Provincetown, built at Essex in 1887, was designed by the Boston yacht designer Edward Burgess. She was the object of much curiosity. Her deep, rockered keel outside of her keel-rabbet was a Burgess innovation. Her general form, however, with deep draft, narrow stern, eased quarters, hard bilges, and considerable deadrise, was inspired by Dennison Lawlor's pilot-type schooners. In 1885 Lawlor had built the pilot-type fisherman *Roulette*, which had proved very successful and had been followed by similar vessels.[49] These schooners were faster than the clippers under most conditions, and were far superior working to windward or heaving to. On one occasion, while mackerel seining, the *Phillips* tacked up the coast from Bodie Island, North Carolina, to New York, passing the rest of the New York-bound fleet along the way. Although she started in the rear, she had the market to herself when she arrived.[50]

This photograph was taken when she was on an early shakedown sail. She is newly rigged, and there is much to be set to rights. The double lifts on the main reflect someone's charitable intentions, but will be replaced by a single lift when the fishermen get her. Reefing tackle is missing. There are turns in one part of the main peak halyard, and in the jumbo halyard. The jibtopsail down-haul needs a stopper-knot. All of the sails look too small, but they will stretch out in time.

[5.16] Thomas McManus, the nephew of a famous Boston sailmaker, was a very successful and progressive designer of fishermen. In the late nineties he designed the first round-stem schooners, which, with a severely cut-away forefoot, were very quick in stays, and could heave to well.[51] With certain variations, this became the standard fisherman profile until the production of fully powered draggers. Edward Burgess had started the shallow forefoot trend with the introduction of the *Fredonia* model in 1889, which was itself a progression from the *Carrie E. Phillips* model, with a clipper bow.[52]

The first McManus round stemmers were named for Indians, and became known as "Indian headers." They were small, but their success led to larger versions, such as the *Ellen C. Burke*, of Boston, shown new in 1902. She is outfitted for trawling, and displays her complete suit of sails, including a big jibtopsail, and a fisherman staysail set between the masts. The jibtopsail did much to keep a schooner moving in light summer air. The characteristic big mainsails of American fishermen often made life interesting—sailing in confined waters with a quartering breeze on the end of the boom was a most unsettling business, since a sudden forced jibe could break the sixty- or seventy-foot boom. Pilots on steamers were wary of fishermen running and beating in Boston channels, as many fishing skippers were apparently incorrigibly guilty of frequent, arbitrary, and inconsiderate course changes.

Ellen C. Burke

[5.17] The schooner *Juniata,* of Boston, less than a year old, lies on Pleasant Beach, Cohasset, awaiting salvage. She was one of numerous vessels sunk or stranded by the fierce *"Portland* Gale" of November 1898. Fortunately, her people were able to leave in the dories, and all survived. To the far right, on the very horizon, Minot's Light rises out of the now-pacific Massachusetts Bay.

With her shallow forefoot, and narrow, tucked-up stern, the *Juniata* well displays the hull form of the round stemmers. She is unusual, however, in that she lacks a break in her deck forward of the mainmast.

[5.18] The knockabout schooner *Washakie* of Boston, goes through her paces under her short winter rig. Neckties and topcoats, as well as the absence of trawl gear, indicate that she is out for a trial romp.

Built at Chelsea in 1908, the *Washakie* represents the final evolution of the all-sail New England fishing schooner. She is a very different vessel from the clipper of the eighties. The knockabout bow first appeared in 1902 on the McManus-designed *Helen B. Thomas*. This new design eliminated the bowsprit and the long overhanging main boom, which were hazardous at sea and major nuisances in port. The *Thomas* was very successful, but since fishing schooners were priced by length on deck, not waterline length, later knockabouts—like the *Washakie*—generally had shorter overhangs.[53] Knockabouts proved fast and able, no doubt partly because of the increased waterline length they enjoyed when sailing heeled over in a blow.

Within a few years of this picture the all-sail fishing schooner was fast disappearing. Progressive New England fishermen rapidly adopted the internal combustion engine.

19062-Washakie

[5.19] The Fore River-built Boston "beam trawler" *Surf* approaches a berth at the new Fish Pier, South Boston. Built by the Commonwealth in 1914, the 1200-foot facility was one of the most advanced in the world and alleviated the congestion at T Wharf. The pier contained a huge ice and cold storage plant.

Launched in 1911, the *Surf* was a member of the fleet of beam trawlers operated by the Bay State Fishing Company, a combine of fish dealers. To be precise, the vessels were "otter trawlers" and not "beam trawlers." They dragged a heavy conical net over the bottom, the opening of the net being spread by two rugged wood and iron "otter boards" (commonly called "trawl doors"). Pioneer European draggers had used a large beam to spread the opening of the net; hence the origin of the persistent misnomer. To this day, large steel otter draggers are commonly called "beam trawlers."

The *Surf* and her sisters were basically copies of European vessels and were too expensive for the average American owners. Although the otter trawl was eventually widely adapted by New England fishermen, their vessels, for the most part, were versions of the standard wooden schooner model powered by internal combustion engines. Otter trawling was still extremely hard work, although in terms of manpower and casualties it was a great advancement over dory trawling. Possible deleterious effects upon the stocks of young fish and the seabottom environment are still subjects of debate.

[5.20] A Boston Irish fishing cutter about 1890. First built in the late fifties by Irish immigrants, the "Paddy boats" were themselves really immigrants, being modeled after the Galway "hookers" native to the west coast of Ireland. Like the children of immigrants, the Paddy boats became increasingly Americanized over the years. Although often roughly built and covered with pine tar, they were fast and able little vessels and ranged far along the Massachusetts coast. The fishermen often spoke Gaelic and wore beards, waistcoats, and bowlers.[54] They commonly fished along the ledges of the South Shore for lobsters and ground fish, and gill-netted for herring in Ipswich Bay. Whether running home past Boston Light, or noisily counting their catch at the Packet Pier, they added much character to the port. By 1900 most were gone.

[5.21] Toward the end of the century the Paddy boats faced strong competition from a large fleet of "Guinnie boats," manned by rugged Italian immigrants who commonly rowed fifteen or twenty miles in a day. Using boats related to the famed Swampscott dories, they usually fished for cod, haddock, and flounder around the lower islands, and off the Graves. The Irish market boats had driven out the Yankee Swampscott dory fishermen; and the Irish, in turn, gave way to the resourceful Italians. By 1910 the Guinnie fleet was largely motorized. Italians persisted in the fishing business, and at present own and man most of the medium and small draggers fishing from Boston.

[6] Coastal Sail

From colonial times through the shipping boom of the First World War, coastal sailing vessels were of importance to the social and economic development of New England. The American Navigation Act of 1817 reserved coastal trades to domestic vessels. In 1838 the "enrolled" (coastal) tonnage of the United States moved permanently ahead of the "registered" (foreign-going) tonnage.[1] Steam tonnage did not exceed sail tonnage in the coastal trades until 1894. In 1900, coasting tonnage was five times that of the withered deep-water fleet, and was 49.5 percent sail.[2] Sail tonnage peaked absolutely in 1907, when it represented 39 percent of the total coastwise tonnage.[3]

Small coasters provided the principal means of transportation for coastal New England at least into the middle decades of the nineteenth century. They carried passengers, livestock, lumber, fish, staves, hay, lime, manure, produce, manufactures, imported goods, and anything else desired. Ketches, sloops, and schooners were all active in the colonial period. The important West Indies trade was really an extension of coasting, and employed many small brigs and topsail schooners well into the nineteenth century. The unique pre-Civil War southern cotton trade employed ships and barks. In general, however, from the mid-1700s on, the simple fore-and-aft schooner was the overwhelming favorite. Local needs, limitations, and traditions combined with the peculiar demands of particular trades to produce many varieties. The reasons leading to the selection of the schooner as the "national rig" are obvious:

the schooner combined technical simplicity with efficiency and good performance. Schooners were generally more weatherly and cheaper to build, maintain, and man than comparable square-riggers.

The last half of the nineteenth century saw the Eastern (primarily New England) coasting schooner reach its maximum development, becoming, in its many varieties, a most appealing and interesting species of vessel. The expansion of the coastal sailing marine was a direct consequence of the growth of American industry, cities, railroads, and other economic activities. Ironically, these were the same forces that contributed to the decline of the American deep-water marine.

Accelerated schooner development began in the fifties. The loss of passenger traffic and high-grade freight to railroads and steamers, coinciding with an increasing demand for bulk cargoes, resulted in larger vessels. Prosperity, and the influence of the clippers, led to improved models. Whereas previously schooners were primarily two-masted and under seventy-five feet in length, in the fifties three-masters began to appear in number, and some monster two-masters of up to 130 feet on deck were built.[4]

These big two-masters very effectively demonstrated the limits of the type, and, as a result, through the seventies and the eighties the three-master population increased by the hundreds.[5] In 1883, for example, at least 138 three-masters were built on the Atlantic coast. At least eighty-seven were built in New England.[6] It may be argued that in handsomeness of proportion, fairness of model, and smartness of performance, these three-masters represented the highest development of the coasting schooner.[7] In the following several decades the pressure of competition from steam, and other economic considerations, led to the construction of far bigger schooner types of thoroughly impressive character, yet none possessed the delightful spirit of the crisp little three-masters.

The principal trades employing the coasting fleet were lumber, coal, and ice. Hard pine loaded in the narrow and muddy rivers of Georgia and Florida was sailed north to build the cities and suburbs of industry. Ice from the ponds and rivers of Maine was loaded from the banks of the grand Down East rivers and sailed to every southern and Caribbean port of consequence. The importance of this trade to the coastwise marine is apparent when one considers that in 1890 Maine's three million tons of exported ice was primarily shipped in schooners of an average 350 tons' capacity.[8] The coal trade, from the Middle Atlantic coal ports to industrial New England, was perhaps the most important of all. Coal was the vital lifeblood of New England, and the demand for tonnage, particularly in the bituminous trade, fostered the development of progressively larger schooners.[9]

The increased demand for coastwise tonnage, which by law had to be American-built, was a windfall for the depressed wooden shipbuilders of New England—Maine, in particular. In many eastern towns a dying industry was revived. Yearly outputs varied, reflecting fluctuating shipping rates. Several good years were often followed by several lean years. In 1890 and 1891 East Coast yards built at least 143 three-masters and seventy-two four-masters; in 1892 and 1893 production was reduced to thirty-four three-masters, and only six four-masters.[10] In terms of schooner tonnage (and not the number of vessels) the totals from the early 1900s are impressive, although after 1905 the demand for schooners steadily declined.[11] Many yards which had been in the schooner business ended their days building coastal coal barges of quite similar design.

Boston was an important coastal sail port for as long as sail survived. In the early years it was the principal port of interchange between the towns of coastal New England and the rest of the world. Later, as a major industrial, residential, and railroad center it attracted a tremendous traffic in coal and building materials. Cheap coal—cheap in part because of coastal transport—was the foundation of New England wealth after the Civil War, and Boston was the major coal-receiving port of the region. In 1864 Boston received 18,900 tons of coal from the Maritime Provinces; 10,500 tons from Great Britain, and 73,200 tons from domestic sources.[12] Ten years later, domestic coal receipts totaled 1,200,600 tons; foreign receipts were 32,400 tons. By 1880, coal received from domestic sources amounted to 1,718,000 tons.[13] Between 1889 and 1899, the installed horsepower of New England was increased by half;[14] in 1900 Boston's coal receipts, by sea, were 1,973,700 tons of anthracite, and 2,086,300 tons of bituminous.[15] A considerable proportion of the shipping tonnage engaged in this great business, especially in the bituminous trade, consisted of schooners.

The separation of coastal sail and coastal steam into two distinct chapters was prompted by the general mutual exclusiveness of their respective employments, and not because of differing means of propulsion. The one great exception to this pattern was the New England coal trade, in which steam and sail fought fiercely. The dramatic increases in schooner size reflect this situation. In 1900, nearly even numbers of schooners arrived from eastern and southern domestic ports, but the gross tonnage of the southern schooners was over five times that of the eastern. The gross tonnage of barges arriving from the south, however, was three times that of the southern schooners.[16]

In light of the above, it may reasonably be asked why, in terms of the number of photographs, this is the longest chapter. I might have attempted to defend the situation by citing the traditional lack of consideration tendered by historians toward coastal sail. I might even have openly admitted my partiality for East Coast schooners. Fortunately, confession was unnecessary, since an adequate argument may be presented based on the underlying ideas of the book as a whole—the coasting schooner was simply the most visible species of vessel inhabiting the port of Boston during the latter half of the nineteenth century.

[6.1] A fleet of eighty-odd coasters at anchor, apparently in the early seventies. Most are two-masters —some of ancient silhouette—intermixed with several three-masters and sloops. Note the monster of a sloop lying directly beyond the foremast of the steamer *Forest City,* the white side-wheeler to the right. A full-rigged naval brig lies off the end of Central Wharf (the middle wharf). The scene demonstrates something of the visual effect of coastal sail in the port.

In the foreground we see the slash of Atlantic Avenue, cutting through Central Wharf. To the left, a half-brig, a small Down Easter bark, and a Boston & Philadelphia Line steamer lie at Long Wharf. The twin-stacked steamer facing outward at the end of Central Wharf is the Metropolitan Line steamer *Nereus,* running to New York. The Central Wharf berth in the foreground was occupied during the night by the Gloucester steamer. By rights, the steamer lying on the southern side of Central Wharf should be a Merchants' & Miners' Liner for Baltimore, but neither her general appearance nor her stack design is familiar to me. The *Forest City,* lying at India Wharf, ran between Boston and Portland (her namesake) for nearly forty years.

[6.2] 1905. The topsail schooner *Bessie,* of Yarmouth, Nova Scotia, is becalmed while trying to tack off "the Castle" (Fort Independence, on Castle Island). A poor Nova Scotia vessel could not casually hire a tow, and she may spend the rest of the day trying to work out of the harbor. Her people have concepts of time and distance far different from our own, and might appear to be blessed with saintly patience. In fact, all is relative, and the master of the *Bessie* would probably be just as upset by missing the tide into Broad Sound as a modern businessman is by missing a jet to Los Angeles.

Previous to the Civil War, the American marine claimed many topsail schooners, brigs, and half-brigs. After the war their numbers declined steadily, and by 1900 they were quite rare. Some from the Maritimes, however, lived on into the new century, their square sails earning their keep in the ancient salt fish trade to the Caribbean.

Although Caribbean trades were offshore and international, they were dominated by coasting vessels. Practically speaking, a Caribbean voyage was a coasting voyage, and certain trades of colonial origin survived to the last days of coasting sail. It was not uncommon for schooners and brigs to make extensive voyages to Europe, Africa, and the Mediterranean. Prior to the late eighties, many small two-masters, usually of fisherman design, made annual voyages to England with cargoes of apples packed in barrels.[17]

[6.3] 1894. The little *Eugenie,* of Machias, Maine, arriving from the eastward with lumber, heels to a November squall. Both the foresail and the mainsail are reefed. Forward, a jib halyard has apparently parted, and the thrashing sail may soon be in tatters. To ease the situation, the helmsman may be trying to put her off the wind a bit, but the schooner would be slow to respond in the puff. She sails in the wake of thousands of sisters from the east who arrived at Boston over hundreds of years.

Many small coasters had the good sense to lay up for the winter, hibernating in a snug cove. In January 1885, 157 schooners were reported arrived at Boston; in July of that year, reported schooner arrivals would exceed 940.[18] When a vessel got into trouble it was usually during the winter (life-saving stations were not even open in summer). Shipping journals and newspapers from the winter months were seemingly never without a column of short, matter-of-fact accounts of coastal casualties.

Brig A. S. H., Cap. Lee Marchland from St. Pierre, Miq., Dec. 15, with a cargo of dry fish for Boston on Friday night during a gale, was dashed to pieces on Sable Island. Only one man was saved, the first mate. All hands had previously suffered much from the cold. The steward, in a frenzy, cut his throat from ear to ear and jumped into the surf.[19]

Dry fish, lathing, lime, lumber, granite, and coal were common causes for which thousands of coasting men, over many winters, froze and drowned. The little *Eugenie*, however, enjoyed a long life, and was still enrolled in 1920, thirty-eight years after her launch from Albert Strout's yard at Millbridge, Maine.

Beyond her jibboom the U.S.S. *Columbia* appears on the horizon.

[6.4] The "lime coaster" *E. Arcularius*, of Rockland, Maine, runs wing-and-wing down Massachusetts Bay before the afternoon southwester. She is light, and must be running back to the kilns of the Penobscot. Lime was of great importance to the construction industry and was also heavily used by farmers to temper the acidity of their harsh New England soils.

Photographed in 1904, the *E. Arcularius* was built at South Thomaston, Maine, in 1851. The ideal lime coaster was old but tight, since spontaneous ignition would occur if the cargo were wet. The quicklime was carried in casks held above the bilge on platforms. Despite precautions, fire was common. When the smell of slacking lime came from below, the only hope lay in smothering the combustion. All cracks were hastily sealed with lime plaster. If the burning limer made port, she was banished to an isolated and unimportant anchorage to wait it out. Stripped of gear, many sealed-up limers smoldered for months. If opened too soon, they would be consumed by flames.[20] Scuttling was a drastic cure at best, since the pressure of expanding casks (slacked lime is two or three times the volume of quicklime) almost always ruined the hull.

[6.5] Mid-eighties. With a tug fast to her quarter, a small schooner loaded with spruce lumber heads toward Fort Point Channel. Spruce, a cheap wood, was largely used for scaffolding and other temporay purposes. Similar little coasters lie at anchor, the rather plain one to the left setting the others off to advantage. All probably hail from Maine or the Maritimes, and their people may spend more of the year farming or logging than coasting. On any summer's day twenty or thirty small coasters might arrive at the port; on July 14, 1885, fifty-nine schooners and two sloops arrived, twenty-six hailing from Maine ports.[21]

The prevailing craft [of Boston Harbor] is the "Down East" schooner, commanded by Captain Overalls, which takes about two days to work in from Boston Light. By the "Down East schooner" I refer not only to those from Maine ports, but those from New Brunswick, Nova Scotia, and Prince Edward Island coast towns. These vessels bring everything—hay, produce, wood, lime, paving stone, etc., and one of these takes as long to come from Prince Edward Island to Boston as it would take an ocean greyhound to cross the Atlantic. Besides the Captain, there is a mate, carpenter and crew, who is usually a triplet all by himself. Frequently the Captain's wife comes along too and acts as cook. The Captain from the Provincial ports generally wears a red shirt, with a colored cotton handkerchief knotted about his throat. His vessel drifts into port in an unconcerned way, both ends ahead, usually, and he knows just as much about customs, rules and regulations of the port as he does about usages in the drawing room of Lord Aberdeen. Our Customs officers require every craft of whatever name or nature, immediately upon dropping anchor in the harbor, to display their colors as a guidance to boarding officers, because it is oftentimes impossible to tell a Yankee from a "Johnnie" schooner any other way, without going out to it. But usually the "johnnie" shows nothing more than the galley dish cloth which the skipper's wife hangs over the rail, until the revenue officer goes out and orders him to run up his colors, when he saunters leisurely into the cabin and fumbles around under the bunks for it. Perhaps he finds it in the course of half an hour and it takes him another half hour to get the knots and tangles out of the halyards.

C. W. Willis, *Industrial Journal* (Bangor, Me.), June 14, 1895.

[6.6] A hay schooner arrives in the eighties. Her cargo of bales is probably "Prime Eastern Hay" from farms on Maine rivers and bays. No doubt much of the hay which arrived by schooner was saltmarsh hay, used chiefly for bedding. Sails are reefed to clear the deckload. Ladders help her people move about. An old-fashioned "bonnet" is laced to the foot of her jumbo, or forestaysail.

In a sense Boston ran on coal, cordwood, and hay. Most of the hay seems to have come to town by rail or wagon, and from the seventies onward great quantities left in British steamships to feed the cargoes of cattle. Great amounts of hay were consumed by the thousands of horses of the street railway industry.

It is commonly recognized that one of the most dramatic and important economic and social changes of our own century has been the replacement of the beast of burden. We are forced to be aware of the very mixed blessings of the motor vehicle, but we tend to forget the wretched role served by the horse for thousands of years. There was little romanticism and a great deal of suffering and cruelty in the long age of the horse. Teamsters in the city were often ignorant and brutal, being underpaid and overworked recruits from society's lower elements. The sight of a stricken horse down in its harness was not uncommon. Horse-drawn transport was perhaps the most overextended component of the modern economy—and modern warfare—of the later decades of the nineteenth century. In 1864, during an eight-month period, the cavalry alone of the Army of the Potomac required two complete remounts, involving 40,000 horses.[22] In 1906, 15,000 horses were worked to death clearing the rubble of the San Francisco earthquake.[23] Boston's dead horses were removed by barge to Spectacle Island, where an odoriferous rendering plant, the bane of Nantasket-bound steamer passengers, converted them to fertilizer called "tankage".

[6.7] The "Rockport stone-sloop" *Albert Baldwin,* of Gloucester, on the Charles sometime before 1904, when the construction of the new West Boston Bridge closed the upper reaches of the river to masted vessels. Big sloops had colonial bloodlines. Throughout the late nineteenth century several distinct types of big sloops were still being built in New England; most were intended for fishing, or for the carriage of stone or cordwood. The *Albert Baldwin* was the largest member of a superior class of sloop built by Ipswich Bay yards and employed carrying granite coastwise.[24] (Granite was a building material of major importance.) The *Baldwin* was listed as measuring eighty-six feet between perpendiculars; her boom could not have been much shorter. Although the run from Cape Ann is "outside," her deck is nearly awash.

A light breeze at length sprang up, and we laid our course for Rockport, on the outside of Cape Ann. Off Thatcher's Island, at the extreme end of the Cape, we encountered a fleet of large sloops laden with granite from Rockport, which they were taking to Boston. They were very deeply laden, and as they rolled along they dipped a volume of water which immediately poured out again in great streams from their scuppers.—*Robert Carter* [25] (*c. 1858*)

[6.8] A stone sloop, probably the Quincy-built *William P. Hunt,* of Gloucester, coming up harbor in the nineties. Her derrick boom is lowered onto the cabin. Many of the big sloops were slippery sailers, especially when running home to Maine or Cape Ann empty, "flying light," before a healthy southwester.

Probably the largest fleet of stone sloops hailed from Chebeague Island, Maine. Sloops were preferred in the stone trade since their rigs permitted the big derrick booms to be freely worked. In later years granite was sailed in schooners that were specially rigged, with their mainmasts stepped far aft.[26]

[6.9] The packet *Sarah Louise,* of York, Maine, loads for Calais, Maine, at T Wharf. The box-like structure aft of the mainmast is the galley, called the "caboose." A sister packet, having her foremast scraped down, lies alongside. All of the other vessels in the dock are fishermen, for by the mid-eighties sailing packets were becoming rare birds.

Packets—meaning vessels plying regular routes, often on some sort of a schedule—dated from colonial times. Their most prosperous era occurred in the middle decades of the nineteenth century, when hundreds of small sailing vessels—mostly schooners—connected the coastal, river, and Cape Cod communities. In 1860 there were at least twenty packet lines between Boston and Down East ports alone.[27] East of Cape Cod the lines converged to Boston, and at Boston many of the packets congregated at T Wharf, which, along with Mercantile Wharf, supported the bulk of the eastern business.

By the end of the Civil War the mammoth transportation revolution engendered by the steam engine succeeded in altering the age-old laws of geography and patterns of commerce. Sailing packets were generally replaced by railroads and steamboats, although some stragglers, like the *Sarah Louise,* serving by-passed eastern backwaters, hung on for many years.

[6.9] Detail

[6.10] 1891. The *Frank W. Howe,* of Boston, admirably displays the economical grace of the East Coast three-masted schooner. She is pictured newly built by William McKie of East Boston. She was intended for the southern hard pine trade.

In December 1889 the British bark *Mertola,* Captain Alfred Green, loaded a cargo of hard pine up the St. Mary's River, on the border between Florida and Georgia. Captain Green wrote home:

I haven't told you that a neighbor arrived a few days ago, a handsome "down east" schooner (three masted) called the Susie P. Oliver. Please to note the initial letter, without which an American name would be incomplete. Almost all American vessels are named after some individual (an abominably tasteless fashion), as Joel F. Hopkins, Amanda K. Jones. They are great institutions, these same schooners, for, owing to their simplicity of rig, they can sail a vessel of 900 tons capacity with eight hands all told. They sail well, shift without ballast, use but little gear, and rarely exceed 13 feet in draught. Perhaps the first thing that strikes a stranger's eye is their enormous beam. This schooner alongside of us is of much less tonnage than the Mertola but her beam is 35 feet, the Mertola's being 29 feet. One would think that so much breadth with so little depth would make them very skittish in a seaway, and be terribly severe upon the masts, but they seem to get along all right, and undoubtedly sail like foam balls. . . The skipper of the Susie proves to be a great acquisition. He is an elderly individual, of the decided "Daun East" pattern . . . with a lean, leathery visage, as impassive as the back of a ledger . . . As it turns out, this solemn-visaged, slow-of-speech, old Yankee salt is as full of fun as a kitten and as tender hearted as a child.[28]

The American method of name selection may have occasionally been as tasteless as Captain Green judged it, since often a big investor in a vessel was rewarded (attracted?) by the honor of having it named for him. On the other hand, the common practice of naming the new vessel after a shareholder's small and thrilled daughter seems a perfectly delightful custom. As with most merchant vessels, schooners were usually financed through the sale of shares representing $\frac{1}{64}$ interest— a peculiar division of ancient origin. Most owners spread their investments over several vessels. Managing owners both recruited the capital and operated the vessels.

[6.11] About 1890. Two three-masters—the *Messenger*, of Saco, Maine, is at left—lie at George B. McQuesten & Company's East Boston lumber yard. Both vessels were employed in the southern hard pine trade. The port is experiencing a stretch of unusually cold weather. The Navy Yard, Charlestown, lies across the stream.

The standard three-masted schooner rig, with equal mast heights and spacing, appears to have developed in the fifties. Early three-masters were commonly either shoal centerboarders or of deep-keel model. From the seventies into the nineties a large number of compromise deep-centerboarders were built. It should be remembered that vessel design was strongly affected by the intended trades. For example, schooners built for the hard pine trade had to be of shoal draft to cross southern river bars. Schooners intended for sugar carriage often were fitted with long poops, or "sugar decks," extending forward of the mainmast, for cask storage.[29]

[6.12] The long-pooped three-master *Rachel &
Maud,* of Providence, Rhode Island, was extremely
fortunate to survive this 1884 dismasting. Note
the great size of the mast lying on the forward
house. Her people have erected a jury rig from lesser
spars, setting a variety of sails.

A schooner was most likely to be dismasted in
either a severe gale or a dead rolling calm. Newly
rigged vessels were often in danger of dismasting
when their shrouds and lanyards received their
initial stretch. The strains put on the rigging when
the vessel was sailing heavily laden, or rolling
badly, were enormous. Some builders experimented
with bar-iron shrouds, and most big schooners of
the nineties were fitted with turnbuckles. The angle
of staying on a big schooner was greatly inferior
to that of a square-rigger. Frederick S. Laurence,
referring to a four-master, wrote:

Going aloft on one of them is not as easy as on a
square rigger. There are no intermediate tops to break
the long ladder-like stretch of steep shrouds running
about a hundred feet and coming so close together near
the crosstrees that toe hold can scarcely be had within
ten feet of the top. One has to reach up and pull himself into the crosstrees with main strength of the arms.
I wondered how they did it in winter, encumbered with
heavy clothing and boots, in oilskins and sometimes
with ice on the shrouds. It is disconcerting halfway up
since the shrouds there, unless blowing hard, swing and
sway with each step, and there is always the chance
that the rope ratlines may give away underfoot from
undiscovered rot. In addition the shrouds are so thick
that a firm grip with the hands is difficult.[30]

The small schooner beyond is a "Johnny wood-
boat" from the St. John River, New Brunswick.
These roughly built little vessels, often lacking
headsails, were employed in great number carrying
cordwood to New England cities and kilns. They are
representative of various types of small workboats
which were so common that they were rarely
photographed by themselves, and usually appear in
backgrounds, if at all.

[6.13] About 1890. Mr. George B. McQuesten, far right, a prominent Boston lumber shipper and schooner owner, inspects a new schooner anchored in the harbor. Sails slat in the light morning breeze, while one man enjoys his coffee, hot from the galley range.

George B. McQuesten & Company dealt largely in southern hard, or "yellow," pine, brought by schooner from river ports of Florida and Georgia. Although often overlooked, the southern lumber industry after the Civil War was extensive and important. The seventies and eighties, in particular, were decades of expansion for northern industry, cities, and suburbs. This growth consumed immense quantities of timber supplied from great forests via cheap rail and water transportation. Nationally, white pine dominated the markets until 1890, and Wisconsin, Michigan, and Minnesota led the states in value of timber production through 1900.[31] But probably most of the lumber used on the Atlantic coast was schooner-delivered hard pine—especially in the fast-growing suburbs of northern cities.[32] Many oversized and heavily ornamented houses were built largely of hard pine, while stone and brick-faced buildings were often framed in pine, and contained much in their interiors. Great quantities were used for wharves, bridges, shipbuilding, and railroad ties. Many cargoes of pine were exported.

The hard pine trade was a very important factor in the postwar growth of the coastwise sailing fleet, and as a result was of real significance to the New England shipbuilding industry. The hard pine industry perpetuated a state of virtual slavery in the southern forests for many years after Emancipation. Research would likely reveal that most southern lumber barons were once carpet-bagging Northerners.

[6.14] About 1890. The office of the Boston lumber merchants, George B. McQuesten & Company. In addition to supplying great quantities of southern hard pine for general use, McQuesten's carried oak, hackmatack, and locust and white oak treenails for shipbuilding and repairing. Mr. McQuesten was a very savvy and successful businessman.

[6.15] 1890. The schooner *J. E. du Bignon,* built
and managed at Boston, tows down the harbor for
her trial sail in Boston Bay. Castle Island is to the
left, Governor's Island is to the right. Forward, several hands prepare to set the headsails; one casts
off stops from the jibs. No doubt someone aft is
upset about the ripped ensign, what with taking
pictures and all. The breeze is brisk from the north,
and about all that the tug has to do at this point
is to stay ahead.

[6.16] The hawser has been dropped, and the *J. E. du Bignon* sails on her own for the first time. The tug ranges alongside to pass compliments and to photograph the cheerful party aft. With the relative silence of sail and steam, conversation is easy. The ladies and children are warmly dressed against the chill. A busy clatter is likely coming from the galley where lunch is being prepared for the guests. The man standing farthest aft may be the mate, watching activity aloft. Something seems to be amiss with the leeward spanker lift—perhaps the tackle is being rereeved. A vessel's first sail invariably exposed many incorrect rigging leads which had to be set to rights. Following good practice, the new cotton spanker has been rather loosely set up, to protect it from stretching before it has been properly broken in by wind and water. Notice the taper of the boom.

[6.17] Clear of the harbor, the *J. E. du Bignon* thrashes along in fine style. The head of the fore-topsail is being hoisted preparatory to sheeting the sail home. The *du Bignon* was primarily employed in the southern hard pine trade—indicatively, J. E. du Bignon himself was the president of a Brunswick, Georgia, towboat company. The schooner proved fast and successful and sailed until 1918. She was said to have once made the passage from Fernandina, Florida, to Perth Amboy, New Jersey, in 101 hours, and then to have returned in ninety-eight. One of her later owners wrote: "One time I was loading this *du Bignon* in Savannah when three Negro sailors came by and one exclaimed "Why there's the old *du Bignon*. I used to sail in her and she *p'ints five p'ints to windward of de' wind!*" [33]

[6.18] Loaded with coal, covered with ice, the
Augustus Hunt, of Bath, Maine, discharges at
the Boston Gas Light Company's North End Works,
in the mid-eighties.

Coasting schooner development closely paralleled
the growth of the bituminous coal industry. Prior
to the post-Civil War decades of industrial expansion, New England's coal needs were largely
met by shipments of Pennsylvania anthracite,
supplemented by Pennsylvania, Maryland, and
Cape Breton bituminous. Initially, a vast fleet of
small schooners carried the anthracite to New
England from the coal ports of Pennsylvania, New
York, and New Jersey.[34] Beginning in the seventies,
the anthracite railroads attempted to take control
of the water trade, and by 1890 the railroad-owned
steam colliers and barge lines effectively monopolized the business.[35]

Through the seventies, increasingly large
quantities of bituminous were required by New
England railroads, textile mills, and gas works,
and shipments of bituminous from Baltimore,
Philadelphia, and Georgetown steadily increased.
The business was revolutionized in the early eighties
when the Chesapeake & Ohio and the Norfolk
& Western railroads linked the incomparably rich
West Virginia fields with tidewater, creating great
bituminous ports at Newport News and Norfolk,
respectively.[36] For the next thirty-odd years the
bulk of the enormous trade from these Hampton
Roads ports was carried in New England schooners
of steadily increasing size. The *Augustus Hunt,* built
in 1882, the year following the opening of the
Newport News facilities, was one of the first half-
dozen four-masters launched. Although big three-
masters continued to dominate the trade through
the eighties, in 1890 at least thirty-five four-
masters were built at East Coast yards, with at
least thirty-seven following in 1891. Sixty of these
are known to have been built at New England yards,
primarily in Maine.[37]

[6.19] The handsome bow of the Bath-built four-masted schooner *Augustus Hunt.* The carved trailboard, above the hawse pipe, is highlighted by ice. Her graceful entrance was typical of many schooners of the eighties, before serious barge competition caused vessels of fuller model to be built. The *Hunt* is fitted with "built masts," probably consisting of sections of hard pine. Douglas fir spars were apparently not available when she was rigged. The masts of the big schooners were the largest wooden spars ever placed in sailing ships.

The photograph well illustrates the inconvenience of shifting headsails when tacking into a strong northerly breeze while deeply loaded in the dead of winter—especially at night. Sailors are removing the remnants of a blown-out jib. In 1886, about the date of this scene, coasting sailors shipped at Boston were receiving between $15 and $18 per month during the winter. Ironically, because of supply and demand, wages were $20 in the summer months.[38]

It is impossible to convey to anyone who has not experienced it the contrast between the care of a ship and crew at sea in winter off the New England coast, and being ashore with the responsibilities all gone, able to lay down at night with no thought of being called, no listening for sounds on deck telling of a shift of wind . . . Some people think all a captain has to do is to pick his finger-nails, but at the present time it is the hardest job for the poorest pay that I know of, and any boy in America who starts on sea life is making a great mistake.—*Captain W. L. Josselyn* (*probably written in the early 1900s*) [39]

By the mid-eighties relatively few American-born boys were making the "great mistake." Although native Americans retained command, the fore-castles of the coasting fleet were filled largely with Scandinavians, Germans, Provincials, and other foreign-born.

[6.20] 1884. A rare portrait of the *Weybosset,* of Boston, one of the earliest four-masted schooners. Built at Mystic, Connecticut, in 1863 as a Civil War transport steamer, she was converted to sail at East Boston in 1879. The result was queer-looking, with short lowermasts, long topmasts, a strange midships house, and a round stern. One wonders why her owners went to the expense of fitting her with carved trailboards. Despite appearances, she was successfully employed in the coal trade until July 1886, when she stranded in Pollock Rip Slue after striking the wreck of the Vanderbilt yacht *Alva.* The *Alva* had been run down and sunk by a Metropolitan liner while anchored in fog.[40]

[6.21] The *Haroldine*, of Providence, R.I., was a notable early four-master, launched at North Weymouth in 1884. Symbolic of the shift from deep-water sail to coasting, she had originally been intended for a square-rigger—note the indicatively high bulwarks. She is rigged with one yard, from which a square sail was set, bent to hoops. A triangular raffee was set above. This rig was especially common in the seventies, and was often found on schooners employed in offshore trades. The foot of the square sail, brailed in and stopped, shows in the photograph. These sails must have been useful, but were apparently not considered worth the bother, and were rarely seen in the eighties and nineties.[41]

The photograph was taken prior to the *Haroldine*'s unusual maiden voyage to Melbourne and Hong Kong. Subsequently she was primarily employed in the coastwise coal trade and made three voyages to the River Plate as well as a second voyage to China.[42] Although square-rig was better suited to conditions offshore, the big schooners successfully engaged in considerable deep-water voyaging.

[6.22] April, 1890. The big centerboarder *Tecumseh,* of Taunton, flying light, heads back for the coal ports. Her artfully balanced proportions make her appear deceptively small, although close inspection reveals the mate and helmsman rendered insignificant by her great size. The yawlboat hoisted on the stern davits is likely over twenty-five feet long. The breeze is freshening, and the topmast staysails and the jibtopsail have recently been taken in. Furling a headsail out on that great lance of a jibboom, high above the water, far ahead of the charging vessel, must have been an exhilarating task.

Under such conditions the big schooners could make remarkably fast passages. One of their cardinal virtues was their ability to sail without ballast, due chiefly to the flatness of their bottoms and the great weight of their scantlings. Outsized keelsons, sister keelsons, and waterways were necessitated by the inherent longitudinal weakness of the big shoal hulls. Centerboard trunks contributed to structural stiffness, but diminished carrying capacity, and often developed bad leaks.

Taunton shipowners were pioneers in the development of big schooners for the New England coal trade. Many Taunton vessels were modeled by the gifted Albert Winslow, and were distinguished by their raked masts, handsome ends, low deck houses, and sweeping sheer. The *Tecumseh,* built at Bath in 1889, was one of a number of superior schooners managed by members of the Phillips family.[43]

[6.23] January, 1893. Although this photograph was probably taken off Monomoy Point, or in Nantucket Sound, it is appropriate to this collection because it says so much about the business of coasting, especially about carrying coal to Boston.

The East Boston-built *Peter H. Crowell*, of Dennis, lies at anchor awaiting a breeze. Ice sweeps by on the flood, parting at her sheathed bows. Salt streaks her topsides. The white ice on her bulwarks, forward, indicates that not long ago she had all the breeze she wanted, probably a numbing cold northwester. She is almost certainly loaded with coal. In summer, northbound coal schooners usually ran before the prevailing southwesters through Vineyard Sound and out Pollock Rip Channel. In winter, the prevailing winds are easterly or northeasterly, punctuated by bitter, clearing westerlies. During a long spell of easterly weather huge fleets of coal-laden vessels accumulated at Vineyard Sound anchorages—Boston religious interests maintained a seaman's bethel at Vineyard Haven and a reading room at Tarpaulin Cove for the use of windbound sailors. Southbound and flying light, the colliers commonly went by way of the Great South Channel between Nantucket Shoals and George's Bank, which they could usually fetch on the starboard tack with a summer southwester.[44]

Good ground tackle was absolutely essential for navigation along the difficult and dangerous coast. The big five- and six-masters had anchors of battleship proportions. The waters off the back sides of Cape Cod and Nantucket are especially treacherous, and served historically to separate the coastal domains of Boston and New York. Here there are strong and varying tides, narrow channels through shifting shoals, much fog, and a long lee shore during easterly gales. From 1875 to 1914 almost six hundred vessels were lost on Cape Cod alone.[45] In addition to natural perils, there was frequent danger of collision with other vessels. Coasting demanded great skill and knowledge, good judgment, and physical and mental fortitude. Day for day it was usually a much more dangerous and exacting business than was deep-water voyaging.

Anchored in the Ice.
4265
N.L. Stebbins Photo.

[6.24] 1892. Coasting offered certain psychic compensations for all its danger and discomfort. Witness the *Cox & Green,* of Greenport, New York, snoring happily along before an April southerly. Boom tackles are rigged, but still the helmsman must be alert and steer with a sensitive hand lest the leeches luff. The three-master off to port provides the added interest of a contest, although the *Green* appears to be a slippery customer and is probably walking right by. A fast schooner was the object of great pride and respect, and racing was taken seriously—especially if a berth at the coal docks hung on the outcome.

The mainsail has likely only recently been set wing-and-wing, as the topsail has been left ready to set again on the starboard tack. The maintopmast staysail has been partially clewed-up to prevent it from chafing on the spring stay. The yawlboat is on deck, probably as a precaution—when a schooner was deeply loaded a yawl on the stern davits was likely to be lost or damaged in bad weather. The *Cox & Green* has lovely carving on her stern. She was Newburyport-built, and her fine finish shows it.

The hailing port of a vessel can speak much to us. In this instance, "Greenport" (on Long Island) speaks of the loss of the coaster's world, the destruction of the physical and social seaboard that he knew. Eighty years ago a Long Island schooner hailed from a gentle land of pastures and hay fields, of fresh ponds and salt bays, of oysters and wild duck, and pounding surf on barren beaches. The island climate was tempered by the sea, and the natives spoke an ancient variety of English. Today, even the pattern of the winds has been changed by urbanization, and the coaster's afternoon southwester on the Sound is diminished. But we should remember that we are our fathers' children, and that eighty years ago the natural devastation of the island—and of much of the seaboard—was well advanced. It is unlikely that the logger and the shipbuilder had spared any but token stands of Long Island's chestnut, oak, and locust, and on the bays the market hunter decimated the great rafts of waterfowl.

[6.25] The Commercial tug *William Wooley* tows the Boston schooner *Charles L. Jeffrey* into Fort Point Channel. Both vessels were East Boston-built. The *Jeffrey* is deeply loaded with coal, and her sheets are removed and her sail covers in place in expectation of the dust and grime of discharging. A boy sits on the fore gaff, out of the way. The yawl-boat has been lowered to clear the tug's stern line. Wood fenders drag alongside. The large size of the "spanker," or aftermost sail, was characteristic of East Coast schooners of all types. Although it was unhandy in a breeze, it improved tacking ability and it made a schooner look like a proper vessel. The *Jeffrey*'s single spanker lift was less common on coasters.

Harbor tugs, like locomotives, were commonly not fitted with condensers for exhausted steam, and therefore were always followed by a white plume. Most were powered by a relatively high-pressure vertical single-cylinder engine and had to replenish boiler water after four hours or so of hard steaming. For coastwise towing, engines were "compounded" by the addition of a low-pressure cylinder and a condenser, which allowed boiler water to recirculate.[46]

[6.26] 1883. The mechanics of discharging coal. Dozens of steam hoists at numerous "coal pockets" were required to handle the millions of tons arriving at the port annually. At the southern coal ports vessels were loaded and trimmed by Negroes. It is likely that the whites who discharged coal at northern ports were immigrants of similar social status. Note the schooner mast, upper right.

[6.27] The *Lucinda G. Potter,* of Greenport, discharges coal at the new Commercial Point plant of the Boston Gas Light Company. Both holds are being worked. The relatively small hatches of wooden schooners hindered loading and discharging and necessitated much hand shoveling and trimming in the dusty holds. Masts and rigging were dockside nuisances. Barges and steam colliers were not so disadvantaged.

The *Potter*'s mainmast is stepped slightly to port of the centerline so as to accommodate the centerboard trunk. The centerboard tackle and the iron centerboard rod may be seen just beneath the flying coal bucket, alongside the mast. The carpenters in the foreground are constructing another gantry.

Notice the *Potter*'s fine-looking yawl-boat, partially lowered to clear the stern lines. With a couple of huskies at the oars it must have moved out smartly.

Nothing ever gave me more delight and a vivid sense of anticipation than the schooner's yawl-boat, waiting at the wharf. There she lay, buoyant as a duck in her simple lines of shapely beauty, rising and falling on the glassy, sunlit water which swelled up through the swishing seaweed on the piles of the wharf. . . . Our boatbuilders were fine modelers and there was so much that they could put into the simple structure of these boats.—*A. E. Averill* [47]

[6.28] August 13, 1894, a still Sunday afternoon at Medford, a good day to take out the camera and snap the view from Craddock Bridge, what with a coaster lying at the coal pocket. A schooner-man relaxes in the shade of the foresail, while the wheelbarrows and the steam hoisting engine also enjoy a day of rest. The *Emma M. Fox,* of Bangor, Maine, is nearly empty, but the cargo block hoisted on the fore throat halyard indicates that there are still a few licks left for morning, before a tug comes up the Mystic to fetch her. When towing in narrow channels small schooners commonly secured their yawl boat forward, beneath the bowsprit, to be clear of the tug at work aft.

The stacked lumber at the river bend was also brought by small schooners, which were essential to the economic life of many coastal communities. By the nineties, especially in the coal trade, small schooners could not compete with bigger vessels in the major ports. But the markets up winding, shoal rivers, and beyond narrow bridge piers remained secure until the arrival of the motor truck.

[6.29] Spring in the late nineties. Two coal schooners and a coastal coal barge lie at the Chelsea pocket of the Metropolitan Coal Company. The far schooner is the *William H. Clifford,* of Bath, Maine. The near schooner is unidentified. The barge was once the small medium clipper *Mary Whitridge,* built at Baltimore in 1855. On her maiden voyage she made a record transatlantic crossing. The ferry *City of Boston,* upper right, heading into Chelsea Creek, is on the Winnisimmet Line from Hanover Street to Chelsea. In the right foreground, an ambitious soul has begun to fit out the sloop *Rosie.* In the center background, between the two coal towers, the Kennebec Steamboat Company's white steamers *Kennebec* and *Sagadahoc* are being readied for the new season, which commences after the ice breaks up in the river.

The photograph affords a good view of the great size and "steeve" (angle) of the schooner's head gear. The jibbooms are probably over seventy feet long, and twenty inches in diameter. The ends are perhaps fifty feet above the water. It is not surprising that in steamer–schooner collisions the steamer often came off the worse for the experience. No doubt jibbooms cleaned out more than a few pilothouses.

[6.30] October 1900. A singularly satisfying photograph of the new white *William C. Carnegie,* of Portland, Maine; and the year-old *Jennie French Potter,* of New York, anchored in President Roads awaiting berths at the coal docks. Men working on the *Potter*'s starboard bow may be repairing minor collision damage. To the left, a tug brings in a little American bark.

The first East Coast five-master, the *Gov. Ames* (a centerboarder), was built in 1888. The next was not built for ten years, although by 1910 forty-five had been launched. The overwhelming majority came from Maine yards.

All of the big schooners were built with bold sheerlines, although that of the handsome *Carnegie* is especially noble. This was an attempt to reduce the visual effect of their eventual "hogging," or humping, and to create islands above the wet for when they were sailing heavily loaded in a seaway. The critical problem of building sufficient longitudinal strength into the long, shoal hulls was never completely solved. When light, there was great buoyancy in their midsections, with relatively little in the heavy ends. Loaded, the hulls were subjected to severe strains when hard-driven or allowed to ground at low water when discharging. Probably all of the big schooners which lasted any length of time became very limber and leaked badly, relying upon their steam pumps to remain afloat. B. B. Crowninshield reported:

Captain John Crowley once told me that the most joyful sound he ever heard was when the pumps *sucked,* coming across Massachusetts Bay in the *Wells* with fifty-four hundred tons of coal, in the teeth of a nor'wester.[48]

The *George W. Wells* was the first six-masted schooner.

[6.31] A striking photograph of the *Edward B. Winslow,* of Portland, Maine, towing past the Castle on a blustery day in October 1910. The tug is ahead, out of the picture. Between 1900 and 1910 ten six-masters were built for the New England coal trade. With the exception of the steel *William L. Douglas,* built at Quincy, all were products of the state of Maine. Seven, including the *Winslow,* were built by the Bath firm of Percy & Small. The *Winslow* was launched in 1908, and measured 3,425 gross tons, with a registered length of 318 feet. Only one larger wooden schooner was built, that being the magnificent *Wyoming* built by Percy & Small in 1909. The *Wyoming* was surpassed only by McKay's four-masted bark *Great Republic* as first built, the largest wooden sailing vessel.[49]

The *Winslow* was a member of the J. S. Winslow & Company fleet, which in 1910 included five six-masters. The history of this Portland firm is instructive of the great changes occurring in New England shipping, for into the mid-eighties the Winslow fleet consisted of square-riggers engaged in ocean freighting.

The big schooners could operate only with the aid of steam power, which was used for getting the anchors, making sail, trimming sheets, and pumping out. At least two schooners were fitted with steering engines. The schooner rig was ideally suited for steam, unlike the square-rig. The *Winslow* sailed with a crew of fourteen, compared with the crew of thirty-eight required aboard the *Shenandoah,* a 3,406-gross ton four-masted Bath bark.[50]

[6.32] 1903. The new *Dorothy Palmer,* of Boston, displays the striking white paint which was the trademark of the Palmer Fleet. Between 1900 and 1909 William F. Palmer, a former schoolmaster from Taunton, managed a fleet of thirteen five-masters and two four-masters employed in the bituminous trade. With the exception of the five-master *Jane Palmer,* built by Brooks at East Boston, the entire fleet was Maine-built. Mr. Palmer designed all but one of the schooners himself.[51]

In the early 1900s there was a great expansion of the bituminous industry, aided by the 1902 anthracite strike. In that year bituminous receipts at Boston were 2,100,000 tons, compared to less than one million tons of anthracite,[52] and the Palmer Fleet earned an average 21 percent on investment.[53] The earnings of 11 percent in 1905 and 1906 were the more usual.[54]

In 1905 the schooners of the Palmer Fleet delivered 123 coal cargoes to New England.[55] Under ideal conditions it was possible for a big collier to make the round voyage between Boston and a Hampton Roads port in two weeks, although with loading delays the average was closer to three weeks.

[6.33] October 1907. The *Mertie B. Crowley,* of
Boston, dresses ship in celebration of her first
visit to her home port. She was built at Rockland,
Maine. Beyond, a Leyland liner puts to sea. To the
left, a Cunarder, either the *Ivernia* or the *Saxonia,*
lies at her East Boston wharf. The funnels of these
well-liked sisters were the tallest ever to go to sea.

The *Crowley* was a member of the important fleet
of big coal schooners managed by Captain John
Crowley, and incorporated in 1903 as the Coastwise
Transportation Company. Crowley was yet another
Taunton man engaged in the bituminous trade.
He was an innovator and brought out the first
six-masted, and the only seven-masted schooner.

[6.34] 1907. Her holds empty, the *Mertie B. Crowley* stands out from Boston, headed back to a coal port. All five of her topmast staysails are set—a rare sight. New vessels were usually equipped with the staysails, but often the first suit was not replaced when it had worn out.

The *Crowley* was short-lived, stranding two years later on Wasque Shoal. As the coal schooners grew in size the difficulties of piloting them increased in geometric proportion. Since earnings were determined by the number of cargoes delivered, masters had to "strike a nice balance between prudence and daring." [56] The business required, and attracted, shipmasters of exceptionally high ability. Probably more than half were State of Mainers, with many from Cape Cod, Boston, and the Maritimes.[57] The average life span of the great schooners was on the order of twelve years.[58]

The average for the entire sail coasting fleet was much better. Although the *Boston Transcript* could cleverly editorialize after a costly November gale: "Don't give up the ship. If you must give up anything, give up the schooner," [59] the average age of the sixty-four eastern coasting schooners lost for all reasons in 1903 was twenty-three years.[60] Given the hazards of the business, this average was commendably high. Victims ranged from the *Washington B. Thomas,* a five-master only sixty days old, to the *Ira Bliss,* a two-master fifty-six years old.

[6.35] The third great Boston schooner fleet sailed under the houseflag of Crowell & Thurlow. The member pictured here is the *Stanley M. Seaman,* slipping along nicely in 1908. The firm was created soon after 1900 with the partnership of two managing owners, Captain Peter H. Crowell and Lewis K. Thurlow. Their vessels were engaged in all the usual schooner trades, often venturing to the Caribbean, South America, and Africa.

The *Seaman*'s fore, main, and mizzen gaff topsails have not been set, perhaps indicating that she is soon going to tack. These sails were something of a nuisance when tacking, as they had to be clewed up, and sailors had to go aloft to shift the sheets and the tacks to the other side of the spring and topmast stays. Frederick S. Laurence described the scene:

They were setting the topsails, and I watched the proceedings with interest. The captain was wrathfully shouting to a man standing on the head of the lower mainmast with his back against the topmast and wrestling with a heavy chain.

"Right over everything!" the captain was shouting. "Can't you understand? Right over everything!" He meant the springstay, over which the chain had to be passed.

"He's a square rigger man and don't understand fore and aft," the captain explained. "And they don't know anything anyway. Right over everything!" he continued, "Get the chain over the other side of the stay!"

The man, a slightly built youth, finally did, lugging and heaving the heavy mass up and over the stay, and the topsail was then sheeted home. How he ever did it without falling to the deck a hundred feet below I don't yet understand.[61]

[7] Coastal Steam

From the latter decades of the nineteenth century until well into the twentieth, Boston was a major center of coastal steam navigation. In addition to supporting local traffic, Boston stood as the port of demarcation between distinctively different services to the south and the east. Reflecting Boston's preeminence on the Gulf of Maine, some regular services to the eastward were established in the thirties. Direct (outside Cape Cod) services to New York and southern ports, which consolidated Boston's coastal steam role, were not established until after mid-century. The heavy post-Civil War steamer traffic which rounded Race Point and boomed through Vineyard Sound was a reflection of the great commercial prominence of Boston and its industrial environs.

According to the best available information, in 1850 135 steamers arrived at Boston from domestic ports.[1] In 1860 domestic steamer arrivals were reported at 807;[2] by 1880 they had grown to 1,695.[3] Of course, these figures do not include arrivals from the Maritime Provinces, which were listed as foreign entries.

The detailed figures compiled in 1900 are more illuminating. In that year the recorded arrivals from southern domestic ports included 1,083 steamers; 1,235 tugs; 2,817 barges; and 1,339 schooners. Arrivals from the east included 1,104 steamers; 958 tugs; 553 barges; and 1,327 schooners.[4] The extent of the barge traffic, constituting one-third of the total arrivals, is striking. The gross tonnage of barges arriving from the south was three times that of schooners from the south, reflecting the paramount position barge lines had gained in the coal trade.[5] Although the data from other ports are not all comparable, it appears fairly certain that Boston was then the second most active coastwise port in the nation, surpassed only by New York.

In 1895 Boston received about 8,000,000 tons of waterborne freight. Of this total, 2,000,000 tons were delivered by coastwise line steamers; 3,500,000 tons were coal, primarily carried by barge and schooner; 1,500,000 tons arrived by foreign line steamships. The balance was accounted for by tramp steamers and sailing vessels.[6] Considering that the coastal steamers generally carried cargoes of at least comparable grade to those delivered by foreign liners, and since it appears certain that over half of the coal arrived in the tow of steam tugs, it may be concluded that the coastal steam services delivered the greatest tonnage and value of goods received at the port.

The institutions of coastal steam and coastal sail shared little beyond the waters in which they traded. Underlying their differences was the inordinately high cost of steel shipbuilding in America.[7] (Although it was possible to build successful large wooden sailing vessels, wood was not suited for the construction of profitable seagoing screw steamers. Coastal steamers, like all American-flag vessels, were required to be of domestic origin.) Whereas the sailing marine was composed primarily of unscheduled tramp vessels, the steam marine consisted almost entirely of scheduled liners. Steamers carried high-grade freight and passengers; sailers were predominant carrying low grade bulk cargoes. Sailing vessels were usually financed by the ancient system of shares, whereby the owners invested directly in individual vessels; most coastal steamship lines required far more capital and were modern joint stock corporations. Many participated in the activities of the world of high finance and became deeply involved with railroads.

The injurious effects of the shipbuilding restriction were more than compensated for by the total exclusion of foreign competition from the coastal trades. Higher costs were passed along to the customer. Many steamer lines were attractive and profitable properties. It should be remembered, when viewing the entire spectrum of coastal shipping, that throughout the nineteenth century the average speed of freight trains probably did not exceed ten miles per hour.[8] Many steamer lines could thus provide services comparable or superior to those of railroads without investing funds in such fixed items as right-of-way, track, and bridges. If revenues fell, steamers could usually be placed on other routes. In many cases where steamer lines and railroads vitally complemented each other the potentially mobile steamer line held a bargaining advantage over the fixed road when the time came to decide upon joint freight rates. Understandably, railroads developed great interest in coastal steam. Many railroads became the owners of steamer lines—to cite the outstanding example, by the early 1900s the New Haven Railroad controlled virtually all of the many Long Island Sound steamboat companies. Whether in collusion or collision, the influence of railroads made the coastal steamer business highly volatile. Coastal sail, on the other hand, by process of elimination, was chiefly employed in trades the railroads could not profitably enter and generally ignored.

Steamer lines to Maine and the Maritime Provinces—unlike some of the lines running to the south—were very much involved in the passenger business. The geography and economies of the eastern coastal regions did not suit the construction of railroads able to compete with the swift and comfortable steamers. Separate services from Boston ran to Portland, the Kennebec, and Bangor. From the early 1840s until the Civil War intense

competition prevailed on these routes—at one point in the fifties the fare from the Kennebec to Boston was driven down to 12½ cents, inspiring most of the valley's residents to go and view Boston.[9] Eventually the routes fell under dominant powers—the Portland Steam Packet Company prospered by its tie-in with the Grand Trunk Railroad; Bangor and Penobscot Bay were captured by the Sanford Independent Line (later changed to Boston & Bangor Steamboat Company); after intense skirmishing involving the Sanfords and railroad steamer lines from Portland, the Kennebec Steamboat Company emerged as the ruler of its territory.[10]

Although long deprived of rail connections, the Maritimes did not acquire dependable steamer service to Boston until after mid-century. In the late fifties Nova Scotians promoted their own line from Yarmouth. In 1860 the International Steamship Company, which had close ties with the Portland Steam Packet Company, was organized to link Boston and Portland with St. John, New Brunswick. From 1840 until 1868 Halifax was a waystop for the Boston Cunarders; in the seventies a regular line from Boston was established. Halifax's own Canada, Atlantic & Plant Steamship Company (founded in 1888 as the Canada Atlantic Steamship Company, known after 1892 simply as the "Plant Line") provided varying degrees of service for nearly thirty years.[11]

The prevailing post-Civil War tendency for steamer routes to fall under the control of monopolies and duopolies reached its logical conclusion in 1901 when lines from Boston to Portland, Bangor, the Kennebec, and St. John were combined into the Eastern Steamship Company. In 1912 the Nova Scotian-managed Boston & Yarmouth Steamship Company was added to the fold. In 1914 it was disclosed that the New Haven Railroad owned a substantial minority interest in Eastern.

Early steamer services between Boston and New York and points south were effected via rail connections to Narragansett Bay and Long Island Sound ports. Providence, Fall River, Norwich, and Stonington all profited from the existence of great, hooked Cape Cod to the east. In the fifties regular direct lines were establishd to New York (Metropolitan), Philadelphia (Sprague, Soule),

Baltimore (Merchants' and Miners'), Charleston (Boston & Southern), and New Orleans (Union). Soon after the Civil War was over Boston interests resumed or inaugurated steamer services to New Orleans, Charleston, and Savannah. Most were short-lived enterprises, and only the line to Savannah—under various managements—survived.[12]

The establishment of direct outside services by no means separated steamer lines from railroad involvements. New England roads viewed lines as connections to the South; southern roads desired outlets to the North. Connecting trunk roads saw coastal lines as competitors. Symbiotic agreements between steamer lines and the major roads of the Southeast gave Boston low rates to the South, although the traditional direct water route to New Orleans was eliminated by the carriage of cotton by rail to southern Atlantic Coast ports.

Coastal sail learned to coexist with regular coastal steamer lines, but met its match in the coastal caravans of tugs and barges. Coastal towing of coal began in the seventies and grew rapidly. Most of the barge lines were owned by the coal-carrying railroads that they served, especially in the anthracite trade. Barge lines themselves declined with the development of regular steam collier service after the First World War.

After 1918 practically all coastal steamer lines, other than the collier lines, entered a protracted period of instability. Harried by railroad and highway competition, labor difficulties, high costs, and old tonnage, coastal steam effectively died with the nation's entry into the Second World War.

[7.1] The *Star of the East* was operated by the Kennebec Steamboat Company and usually ran up to Gardiner (here, she is apparently employed as a spectator craft for some nautical extravaganza). Built in 1866, the steamer was renovated and re-named *Sagadohoc* in 1899, and continued in service for many more years. At Boston, the Kennebec steamers sailed from Lincoln Wharf. Service on the fresh water Kennebec could not be maintained during the winter. (Steamer names painted on paddle-boxes were always ended by a period.)

The sociological impact of the Down East steamers was of lasting effect. Boston and its coastal hinterlands were cross-fertilized by steamers. Fast, convenient, and inexpensive steamboat transportation profoundly changed the lives of natives of many small Maine and Maritime villages. Eastern girls came to Boston by steamer to learn nursing or teaching, or to work as domestics or seamstresses. Carpenters and fishermen came seeking seasonal employment. Just as the railroads populated interior New England towns with French Canadians from Quebec, the steamers delivered a migration of folk from the Maritime Provinces who eventually constituted a considerable proportion of the population of Greater Boston. In the summer the steamers were crowded by thousands of tourists who became increasingly important to the eastern economies.[13] Steamers made Boston truly the Hub of the Gulf of Maine.

[7.2] The East Boston-built *City of Bangor* leaves Jeffries' Point astern as she heads down for the Castle. The walking beam, aft of the twin stacks, is modestly housed. Her feathering paddle-wheels are strikingly smaller than the static radial wheels of the *Star of the East,* previously illustrated.

The design of the Down East paddle steamers offered certain advantages. The vessels were roomy, while still shoal enough for low-tide river navigation. They had commodious main decks, convenient for quick freight transfer at way stops. They were fast—the *City of Bangor* was capable of an honest sixteen knots. Paddle-wheels could back down strongly in emergencies, and could be powered by simple and reliable machinery which was easily accommodated in a shoal hull. Wooden construction was inexpensive.

But the disadvantages were serious. Windage was great. In cross seas some of the steamers were notorious rollers, and no doubt many seasick passengers, watching the arc described by the clothes on the coat hook, became convinced that the only force preventing the steamer from going completely over was the fragile buoyancy of the overhanging "sponsons." It is said that in rough weather it was often necessary to shift cargo to leeward in order to elevate the windward sponson away from the smashing seas, although this procedure rendered the windward wheel nearly useless. In severe weather it was often impossible to keep a steamer head to wind.[14] One candid Boston–Bangor skipper admitted:

> She is only fit for smooth water, and my greatest care is not to get caught out with her on the first part of this route. If I do, it means getting out of the wet at the first chance and favoring her in every way, shape or manner. Once let a sea strike full force under those infernal sponsons and it would start the whole tophamper [superstructure].[15]

That weakness alone might explain the deeply felt loss of the steamer *Portland* in the terrible gale of November 1898. This disaster caused much soul-searching in the Down East steamboating fraternity, and greatly sped the adoption of steel screw vessels for eastern runs. Additionally, wooden steamers afforded the constant peril of catastrophic conflagration, although, with great good fortune, few steamers burned while underway. When the *City of Bangor* burned in 1913 she was lying at Foster's Wharf and was rebuilt.

[7.3]

The eastward voyage on these great steamships affords a very refreshing change from the summer temperatures of Boston . . . and removes one . . . from the torrid zone to the cool air of the ocean, enriched by the intense vitality which comes pulsing in from the distant plains of the outer Atlantic . . . [With] no care but the coming dinner hour . . . he must be a very unreasonable American who returns from such a voyage without feeling himself a better man.—*M. F. Sweetser, 1882* [16]

5 P.M., August 1906. The passengers aboard the *City of Bangor* experience the magical sensation as the big steamer draws effortlessly away from Foster's Wharf. Those bound home already feel that they are on Maine soil. Aft, a crew member bends the ensign. The steamer will arrive at Tillson's Wharf, Rockland, in the light of early morning. Later she will push on for Bangor, making several intermediate stops.

The relaxation enveloping the passengers came at the expense of the officers in the pilothouse. At the completion of a difficult run a steamer captain was often nervously exhausted. Schedules were maintained through nights of fog and snow, since the effects of wind and tide were reduced by running at high speed. Skewering schooners was an occupational hazard. Whistle blasts bounced off landmarks served as primitive radar (the *Bangor*'s whistle, mounted between her stacks, was a relic from the beloved *Katahdin*). Few steamers escaped occasional groundings, but the accidents often occurred after time had run out on a course—when the pilot was proceeding with caution—and damage was rarely severe. Given the countless opportunities for disaster, the safety records of most lines were remarkably good.

[7.3] Detail

[7.4] Colored stewards (in casual dress, between trips) on the *City of Bangor*. Negroes appear to have replaced native whites in the steward departments of the Maine boats towards the end of the century. Black or white, stewards on coastal steamers were known for their helpfulness, their memories for names and faces, and for loyalty to their vessels. Many of the steamers were only seasonally employed, but often the same crew members returned year after year.

Negroes, many from the West Indies, were employed on steamers and sailing vessels in large numbers as cooks, stewards, and seamen. On steamers the races were likely to be segregated by ratings. Though black officers could probably have been found in some of the surviving whale ships, in other trades they were practically nonexistent. Although blacks were the mainstay of southern fisheries, probably few were so employed in New England.

The rounded roof of the walking beam house, behind the stewards, is worth notice. It must have been extremely difficult to construct; the general standards of carpentry in the nineteenth century were very high. Howard S. Buck recalled the walking (or "rocking") beam house from his childhood:

My Uncle Lee had joined us in Boston for the trip down East. He was fond of boats, and had a store of fascinating incidents and facts concerning *City of Bangor* and her predecessor *Penobscot*. And he knew engines. We were standing looking down into the well of the rocking beam house. My uncle said, "Now we'll feel the steam push her. Stand on your tip toes—high as you can—so you can just balance. Now keep your eye on the piston-rod. As it goes up, see what you feel!" I did as I was told—and sure enough, as the rod rose under the upward thrust, there was just a perceptible lurch to the whole boat—the deck beneath me shivered and moved foreward—ever so faintly but unmistakably in my precarious position.[17]

[7.5] The big East Boston-built *City of Rockland* was accident-prone. In 1904, when only four years old, she was nearly lost on Grindstone Ledge in Penobscot Bay. In 1906 she was seriously damaged in a collision with the *City of Bangor*. In 1923 she received her fatal injury on a ledge off the mouth of the Kennebec. On the occasion pictured here, in 1912, she has been in collision with the steam collier *William Chisholm* off Boone Island. Her passengers were removed by her running mate, the *Belfast*, and the collier towed her stern-first to Boston.[18]

When new, the 274-foot *City of Rockland* was the queen of the Boston–Bangor fleet. Her thunder was greatly diminished by the appearance of the steel turbine-driven triple-screw *Belfast* and *Camden*—truly modern vessels—in 1907 and 1909. After 1909 she served primarily on the lesser Kennebec Division.

[7.6] 1884. The hierarchy of the big side-wheeler *State of Maine* (II) poses for a portrait. Sitting in front, from left, are the mate, the master (probably Captain Colby), and the chief engineer. The engineer ranked just below the captain. The pilot stands at right—coastwise steamers were required to carry one first-class pilot in addition to the master. Mates would have pilotage through practical necessity rather than regulation.

Those standing look far more comfortable than those sitting, since officers of big coastwise steamers were not programmed for sitting when aboard the vessel. This type of steamer combined shoal draft with considerable windage, and piloting one amongst ledges and schooners on a black night of blowing fog and running tide, before electronics, demanded the highest degree of competence. These gentlemen look equal to the task. All were probably born east of the Piscataqua.

The *State of Maine* was brought out by the International Steamship Company in 1882, and spent most of her life running from Boston to Portland, Lubec, Eastport, and St. John, New Brunswick. She was designed for open-sea service, and featured narrow sponsons and very heavy framing. She was a successful and fortunate vessel.

The view is forward, from the port side of her hurricane deck. The white structure directly beyond the officers is the top of her port paddle-box. The top of her pilothouse shows between the twin stacks. The massive walking beam is well displayed.

[7.7] A view of the forward end of the 1200 indicated horsepower beam engine of the *State of Maine*. In the nineteenth century machinery was enjoyed and admired for its own sake. On passenger steamers the engine room could often be viewed through windows, and the symphony of shining movement was often enhanced by mirrors. Engines looked like engines, and many displayed great craftsmanship. Here, the Portland Company has prominently included the building date, "1882," beneath their name plate, as though confident that their work would stand the measure of time. Gleaming with polish and varnish, wrenches all in order, the *State of Maine*'s engine room was a worthy domain for the man who had mastered the mysteries of the New Age, the Engineer. It is the image of pride and care.

The two turned columns, or "side-pipes," connect the two steam chests, steam entering the engine through the left-hand pipe, and exhausting through the right. The huge single cylinder is behind them, obscured. The upper steam chest is visible, the lower is beneath the floor plates. Valve mechanism is in front. The four vertical valve lifters (the left two steam, the right two exhaust) are activated when their "lifting toes" are struck by the moving "wipers" attached to the prominent horizontal "rock shafts" (there are two, separated at the central bearings). The two shafts are normally rocked by "eccentric rods" driven by eccentrics on the crankshaft—the hooked ends of the two rods are clearly visible on both sides of the engine. Neither is presently "hooked" onto the rock shaft "arms," since the engine is stopped, and they cannot be engaged when the engine is started or reversed. When starting or reversing, it is necessary for the engineer to activate the valve lifters independently with the "starting bar," center foreground, which connects to a smaller rock shaft (called a "trip shaft") located beneath the floor plates.[19] Beam engine operation was not something which could be learned from a book. If an engine were stopped on dead center it was "hung up," and had to be laboriously advanced by turning a paddle-wheel with a heavy timber pry-bar, inserted through an opening on the inside of a paddle-box, before it could be started again.

The left-hand horizontal valve wheel is likely the throttle (on most engines the throttle was lever-controlled). The wheel to the right probably regulates the flow of cooling water into the condenser. The large indicator on the right-hand bulkhead shows the all-important crankshaft position. Gauges on the engine count revolutions, show steam pressure and vacuum. Over the right-hand door is the half model of a vessel's hull—very likely it is the designer's model of the *State of Maine*, from which her hull lines were taken. Not visible is the large brass gong which announced the desires of the pilot. The gong system was far more expressive—and open to misinterpretation—than the telegraph system of later years. Some engine rooms were also fitted with a cow bell, and a sign which read:[20]

> THE COW BELL MEANS
> only one thing
> Whether Engine is Working Ahead
> is Stopped, or Backing
> BACK STRONG

[7.8] The forward saloon of the *State of Maine*. Compared with the furnishings of some of the big Long Island Sound flyers this was perhaps embarrassingly austere, but no doubt it had the desired effect on innocent Down Easters.

Figures on the extent of the Down East steamer traffic are scarce. The Census of 1880 recorded that in that year 113,500 passengers traveled by steamer between Boston and the Maritime Provinces (excluding Newfoundland). Freight carried by steamer from Boston to Maine amounted to 188,500 tons; freight to the Maritimes totaled 100,000 tons.[21] The totals landed at Boston were not reported. A manifest for the *State of Maine* on a trip to the eastward would have listed predominantly general freight. Boston-bound cargo from St. John was heavy with herring, mackerel, lobster, and other sea and country products.[22]

[7.9] 1899. Breaking "white ice" on the International Steamship Company's wooden screw steamer *St. Croix*, lying at Commercial Wharf. White ice is generally formed from sea spray; ice from freezing rain or fog is generally clear, or "black." The *St. Croix* must have been hard-driven into some very sloppy going to have encased her pilothouse—the center window was lowered to maintain visibility (in a properly run pilothouse a window was always open when underway in darkness or poor visibility). On the crack and able steel screw steamers of the Dominion Atlantic Railway stewards often had to break ice from exposed stateroom doors to release passengers after a wild night on the Bay of Fundy (the marine division of the D.A.R. was later called the Boston & Yarmouth Steamship Company).[23] Most coastal steamer services were reduced or suspended during winter.

Built at Bath, Maine, in 1895, the *St. Croix* proved a disappointment. Like many other large wooden screw steamers (including the hundreds built by the federal government during World War I), she leaked badly and could not carry enough freight. She was sold to the West Coast after 1906.

[7.10] The steamer *Carroll* lying at T Wharf in the seventies. Boys fish from the wharf caplog. The *Carroll, ex-Proteus,* was one of five similar wooden screw steamers built by a New York yard in 1863. Before any of the five had been completed they were purchased by the government for war service. After the war four of the sisters were sold to the Baltimore & Ohio Railroad, which renamed them after Maryland counties, and placed three, including the *Carroll,* in transatlantic service to Liverpool. The trio proved too small and slow to compete on the North Atlantic, and about 1872 they were sold to F. Nickerson & Company, of Boston, and placed in service between Boston and Halifax, Nova Scotia. For this work they proved well suited, and they spent the rest of their days on the run. The *Somerset* was scrapped about 1887; the *Carroll* and the *Worcester* were scrapped side by side at Nut Island, Quincy, in 1894.[24] They must have been exceptionally well built, since the usual "working" of big wooden hulls interfered with engine and shaft alignments.

The identity of the European-looking sailing vessel in the foreground remains an intriguing mystery. Her bluff bows and log windlass are reminiscent of vessels built in the early decades of the century. A Bentinck yard is rigged to the foot of her foresail; the purpose of the slender spar atop the foreyard escapes me. The rake of her dolphin striker, and the separated forestay, were not characteristic of American vessels. Despite her ancient appearance, she has double topsails.

[7.11] A wooden screw steamer, probably the *Somerset,* sister and running mate to the *Carroll* and the *Worcester* on the Boston–Halifax run, lying at T Wharf in the early seventies. The pipes fastened along the deck contain the tiller lines. Early coastal steamers often set some canvas in a fair breeze, especially if the captain were an old sailing ship man. Notice the rigging of the little full-rigged brig lying across the dock at Long Wharf.

[7.12] 1884. The *City of Gloucester* was widely regarded as the ugliest and most dependable steamer on the coast. She operated daily between Boston and Gloucester, and is pictured in President Roads on an afternoon run to the eastward. The steamer entered the service in 1883 and continued on the line for forty-two years, serving, with her successive running mates, as an important link between the fishermen of Gloucester and the fish dealers of Boston. After leaving Massachusetts Bay she was operated on Long Island Sound under the name *Thames*.[25]

Over the years numerous other "local outside" steamer services were established, although most were short-lived or seasonal. At various times, steamers ran to Piscataqua River, Merrimac River, North Shore, South Shore, and Cape Cod ports. The most enduring service was to Provincetown. Water transportation to Provincetown was more efficient than the railroad, but since the only suitable wharf at Provincetown was owned by the New Haven, the later steamer lines were allowed to carry freight only at railroad rates.[26]

[7.13] 1884. The Metropolitan Line's iron *General Whitney* runs through harbor ice. The Providence-based Neptune Steamship Company, the first regular direct Boston–New York steamer line, failed in 1866 after less than two years service (owing to disasters on its separate Providence–New York division). The Boston business, which had been so popular that the Worcester Railroad was once forced to declare a ten-day embargo to clear the glut of freight,[27] was left to the more recently organized Metropolitan Steamship Company, of Boston.

Metropolitan's original fleet was a motley collection of vessels released from war service, enhanced by two ex-Neptune Line steamers. The *General Whitney*, built in 1873 and named for the line's moving spirit and president, symbolized Metropolitan's rapid success. In the seventies the line became the Erie Railroad's freight outlet to New England; later, it became the Boston & Maine's principal connection with New York. In 1880 Metropolitan was considered the most profitable line running out of the port.[28] It not only became the major carrier for the Boston grocers, but, reflecting New York's heavy southern steamer trade, delivered large quantities of cotton.[29] The *General Whitney* was equipped with cribs to secure her cotton deck loads, since bales allowed movement could spontaneously ignite.

[7.14] The Metropolitan liner *H. M. Whitney* rests on the bottom of the upper harbor, sometime in the nineties. Research has failed to discover the date or details of the accident, but the smashed rail would indicate that the *Whitney* was involved in a collision. The other party to the mishap must have been a steamer, for the headrigging of a sailing vessel would have made quick work of the *Whitney's* pilothouse, which seems to have afforded the best view of the event. The pilot of the *Whitney* apparently had the coolness of mind to search out a shoal spot to let her settle on. It is most likely that the accident occurred in fog.

The *Whitney*, built at Philadelphia in 1890, lived an exciting life and was sunk several times. The foggy waters between Boston and New York were the most congested coastal waters west of the English Channel. The difficulties of the run were probably surpassed on this seaboard only by the direct run from Portland to New York. In Massachusetts Bay, in the waters off the Cape, in Nantucket, Vineyard, Block Island, and Long Island sounds steamers daily ran risk of collision with other steamers, schooners, yachts, fishing vessels, and tugs with mile-long tows.

[7.15] Summer 1908. A part of the daily 5 P.M. exodus. The *City of Rockland,* leaving the broad wake of a side-wheeler, is headed for Bangor. The handsome *Yale,* with two stacks, will round Cape Cod for New York. In New York, her twin, the *Harvard,* is leaving for Boston. Steel, turbine-powered, and triple screw, the two "white flyers" were capable of twenty-three knots and were among the finest steamers in the world. They provided the first direct Boston–New York passenger service. On the left, a "narrow gauge" ferry (mostly obscured) and the Nantasket steamer *Myles Standish* load rush hour crowds.

The *Rockland* and the *Yale* were both parts of the tottering empire built by the irrepressible and unscrupulous Bath financier, C. W. Morse. The entangled corporate structure of the New England steamship establishment in 1908 would have confused Samuel Insull himself, and Morse deserved much of the credit. Bowdoin, Class of '77, Morse became heavily involved in ice and shipping while still an undergraduate. By 1899 he controlled the American Ice Company, a huge trust monopolizing ice shipments to East Coast cities. The company collapsed in scandal in 1900, partly as the result of C. W.'s characteristic decision to double the New York prices on a particularly sweltering day. Morse escaped from the wreckage with $12,000,000, and directed his considerable abilities toward monopolizing East Coast shipping.[30] By 1907 he controlled many of the important steamship lines between Bangor and Galveston. All of the Boston–Maine lines were included in his Eastern Steamship Company.

Conflict developed between Morse and J. P. Morgan over the domination of the heavy Boston–New York water traffic. Morse intended his new pets, the *Harvard* and the *Yale,* to win passengers away from the Fall River Line, a subsidiary of the Old Colony Railroad, which, in turn, was controlled by Morgan's New Haven Railroad. (The Old Colony provided rail service between South Station and the Fall River pier.) The New Haven was already fortifying the Fall River Line by the construction of the giant *Commonwealth,* but added additional fuel to the fray by building the fast freighters *Massachusetts, Old Colony,* and *Bunker Hill.* These vessels were designed to be easily converted to passenger service; as freighters, they competed handily with the Morse-controlled Metropolitan Line for Boston–New York cargoes.[31]

Morse's downfall began in the panic of 1907. An investigation of his banking practices sent him to Atlanta Penitentiary in 1910 with a fifteen-year sentence. Never one to lose heart, C. W. worked steadily for release through various political and legal channels. When all other attempts failed, he swallowed a combination of soap and chemicals which gave him the temporary symptoms of Bright's disease and won him a presidential pardon after little more than two years' imprisonment.[32] In the meantime, the New Haven had deviously caused the banishment of the *Harvard* and the *Yale* around Cape Horn to the West Coast. Typically, more than seven different corporations, most of them dummies, were involved in the deal. And, odd as it may seem, the New Haven's three fast freighters, converted to passenger use, were running Boston–New York under the flag of the Metropolitan Line, which was by then a division of the reorganized Eastern Steamship Corporation.

[7.16] Probably 1867 or 1868. Two Sprague, Soule & Company steamers for Philadelphia lie at Long Wharf (the nearest steamer is practically hidden by the bark, the brig, and the schooner, in the left foreground). Across the dock, a small Merchants' & Miners' steamer lies at Central Wharf (the square-rigged masts belong to a brig lying astern). A lofty sloop is fast alongside the steamer.

Sprague, Soule & Company's steamer service to Philadelphia began in 1852. The firm was reorganized in 1873 as the Boston & Philadelphia Steamship Company, known locally as the "Winsor Line." A separate all-freight service was maintained between Philadelphia and Providence. The interests behind the line also controlled the Boston Tow Boat Company and the Boston Steamship Company, which operated steamers from the West Coast to the Orient.[33]

The Merchants' & Miners' Transportation Company was chartered in Maryland in 1852, although service between Baltimore, Norfolk, and Boston did not begin for two years. Services to Providence and Savannah were soon added. The line was intended to transport raw materials from Baltimore to the manufacturers of New England, and to carry the products of New England south for distribution. Indicatively, the major power behind the creation of the line was a Baltimore tanner and railroad investor; his chief Boston ally was a shoe manufacturer.[34]

In addition to hides, steamers northbound from Middle Atlantic ports carried flour, corn, whiskey, soap, peanuts, glassware, and iron. New England provided return cargoes of boots, shoes, textiles, provisions, hardware, and machinery.

Steamer lines running to the south from Boston operated vessels of ocean-going design and adopted iron construction and screw propulsion earlier than transatlantic steamer lines. Paddle-wheels were vulnerable at sea, and, since ocean-going vessels could not be sponsoned out, the protruding paddle-boxes were a great nuisance at dockside. When too deeply loaded, early low-powered steamers had to "reef" their paddles, disconnecting them from the paddle-arms and securing them again nearer to the center of the wheel.[35] Screw propellers could be powered by compact machinery, thereby conserving cargo space. Most of the vessels on the southern steamer lines were built at Middle Atlantic shipyards.

[7.17] 1907. The Merchants' & Miners' Transportation Company's *Kershaw* making knots on a cold and blustery day. A solitary figure stands aft. By 1914 the company's fleet numbered twenty-six steamers operating from Baltimore and Philadelphia to Norfolk, Newport News, Boston, Fall River, Providence, Savannah, and Jacksonville.[36] The vessels were handsome, fast, and able. The *Kershaw*, built of steel by Harlan & Hollingsworth at Philadelphia in 1899, and powered by a triple-expansion engine, averaged thirty-six hours between Boston and Norfolk in good weather. Bad weather might add an hour or two, but rarely more.[37]

Considering the modern and seaworthy characteristics of the southern steamers, it is shocking to realize that only four years before the *Kershaw* came out the Portland Steam Packet Company took delivery of the wooden radial-paddle steamer *Bay State,* which was a near sister to their steamer *Portland,* lost in the famous gale of November 1898. During the height of the "*Portland* Gale" the Merchants' & Miners' steel propeller *Gloucester* took a terrific beating off Cape Cod, but arrived safely at Norfolk, two days late.[38]

In 1907 Merchants' & Miners' purchased the Boston & Philadelphia Steamship Company; in a closely related deal, the New Haven Railroad purchased a controlling interest in Merchants' & Miners'. The steamship line thus became the railroads' Middle Atlantic and southern outlet. In 1914 the I.C.C. ordered the New Haven to divest itself of its Merchants' & Miners' stock, which it did only at enormous loss.[39]

[7.18] The *City of Columbus* was operated by the Boston & Savannah Steamship Company. She is shown lying at the Fort Point Channel terminal of the New York & New England Railroad. The *City of Columbus* entered the Boston–Savannah service in 1882 and was wrecked two years later. She was built by John Roach at Chester, Pennsylvania, in 1878; her hull was iron, her houses wood. The *City of Columbus* could load 2,500 tons of cargo, which, in terms of cotton-carrying capacity, was equivalent to a 122-car freight train of the day. She was licensed to carry 200 passengers. The steamer was powered by a compound engine; top speed was 12½ knots; and she was capable of making the run in seventy-five hours.[40]

The Boston & Savannah Steamship Company was tied in with the famous Southern Railway and Steamship Association. The Association established joint rail-water rates from the Southeast to the Northeast that were lower than the all-rail trunk line rates. These rates gave Boston a trading position to the South comparable to those of New York and Philadelphia. The arrangement also succeeded in squeezing out sail competition from several trades.[41]

The *City of Columbus* and her sister, the *Gate City*, maintained weekly sailings. Northbound, the steamers carried cotton, vegetables (many potatoes), fruit (oranges, watermelons), and naval stores (primarily rosin and turpentine). Steamers departed Boston laden with fish, shoes, boots, bacon, furniture, carriages, gunny sacking (to wrap cotton bales), and other products of New England.[42]

The *City of Columbus* was wrecked on Devil's Bridge, a ledge off Gay Head, Martha's Vineyard, as the result of a gross error of piloting which was never satisfactorily explained. One hundred and three persons drowned or froze to death in what was perhaps the most unnecessary major marine disaster in American history.

[7.19] The big, rakish Boston–Savannah steamer *Tallahassee* blows off steam while posing for her portrait in the mid-nineties. The *Tallahassee* was operated by the Ocean Steamship Company of Savannah—more commonly known as the "Savannah Line"—which was owned by the Central of Georgia Railroad. She was built by Roach in 1882.

The Boston & Savannah Steamship Company was incorporated in 1882 as an outgrowth of the Savannah steamer service established in 1869 by F. W. Nickerson & Company of Boston. The new line purchased two vessels, the *Gate City*, and the *City of Columbus*, from the Ocean Steamship Company, which maintained extensive service to New York. It appears likely that interests behind the Central of Georgia were also involved in the creation of the Boston line. The loss of the *City of Columbus* ruined Nickerson, and in 1887 the line, its name changed to the New England & Savannah Steamship Company, came under the management of the Ocean Steamship Company. Several years later the new name was dropped and the line was included in the regular "Savannah Line."[43]

In 1905 the Boston & Philadelphia Steamship Company instituted triweekly service, and the *Tallahassee*, renamed *Persian*, was one of several steamers added to the fleet. Two years later, the Boston & Philadelphia Line passed to the ownership of the Merchants' & Miners' Transportation Company. Thus, the *Persian*, ex *Tallahassee*, was operated to Boston by three major coastal lines. She was scrapped in 1928. The Savannah Line, like Merchants' & Miners', died in World War II.

[7.20] 1902. The coastal freighter *Carib,* of New York, passes a line of coasting schooners anchored off Bird Island Flats. The schooners are headed into the flood tide. The *Carib* was a member of the Clyde Steamship Company's fleet. Her cargo booms are hoisted preparatory to working cargo—with hatches on deck, she little resembles the characteristic American coastal liner. Coastal steamers generally worked cargo through side ports, reflecting both the requirement of large passenger deckhouses and the high quality of the freights. Coastal steamer freight traveled in bales, boxes, or barrels—and not in bulk. Indicative of their trade, many coastal steamers shipped a cooper who inspected and repaired containers.

Nevertheless, the *Carib* could claim thousands of look-alike sisters steadfastly plodding the oceans of the world, driving the last fleets of deep-water sail before them, for she was a typical Scots-built "three island" cargo steamer, probably intended for a tramp. She was built at Port Glasgow in 1882 as the British steamship *President Garfield;* later she sailed under the Austrian flag as the *Kimon.* She was probably admitted to American registry after undergoing repairs at an American yard equal to three-quarters of her value, or by a special act of Congress. In 1903 there were 132 forcign-built vessels (including barges) employed in the American coastwise marine.[44]

The Clyde Line instituted service from Boston to Charleston, Brunswick, and Jacksonville, via New York, in the nineties. Previously the line had operated between Fall River and Philadelphia, connecting with the Old Colony Railroad to Boston.[45]

[7.21] The wooden tug *Cyclops*, of New York, lying at a coal pocket in the mid-eighties. The *Cyclops* was built at Tottenville, New York, in 1878—the Hudson Valley was the source of many handsome, big towboats. Her low freeboard probably indicates that she was primarily intended for river towing. She is painted in the customary fashion for big tugs of the day.

The employment of tugs towing barges coastwise was the inevitable outgrowth of the development of big, seaworthy towboats capable of handling large sailing vessels in exposed waters.[46] Instead of remaining welcome helpmates to the coastal sailing marine, tugs became their bitterest rivals. The principal cargoes carried by barge were ice (although no ice arrived at Boston) and coal (by far the larger of the two trades). The towage of these particular commodities directly competed with coastal sail.

The practice of towing coal began in the seventies, primarily involving traffic from the anthracite railroad terminals at Philadelphia, Hoboken, Perth Amboy, Port Reading, and Elizabethport to southern New England. It was not long before extensive traffic was risking the perils of Cape Cod. Economically, coastal towing was very attractive. Several shiploads of coal could be transferred quickly with a small total crew (aboard tugs and barges), including only one pair of licensed navigating officers. When in port, barges accumulated minimal expense, while the high-cost tugs, like locomotives, were kept otherwise employed. Tugs running on big barge lines seldom paused longer than was necessary to take on coal and water. Barges could be shuttled like freight cars; single barges could be removed from passing tows by waiting harbor tugs.

Additionally, there was a generous supply of old sailing vessels, primarily deep-water square-riggers, which were suitable for conversion to barges and which could be purchased cheaply. Such barges, called "ship barges," were favored by their crews, as they offered splendid accommodations in the cabin, steered well, and were gentle in a seaway.[47] Barges constructed for service in unprotected waters, unlike the scow-shaped barges of Long Island Sound, were variations on the standard big four- or five-masted schooner hull. They were fitted with stump schooner rigs and usually featured a raised house aft.

[7.22] 1891. The tug *Wrestler,* of New Bedford, was built at East Boston in 1889. In later years she hailed from Boston. Sails provided a steadying influence in a seaway. Her engine (probably a compound) was rated at 490 indicated horsepower.

It is probably accurate to say that almost anyone with business in coastal waters—except, presumably, a towboat man—was critical of the practice of coastal towing. A schooner captain speaks his mind:

> Picture it then, on a foggy night, when you can not see a thing. A tow boat is along ahead. The law prescribes one long and two short blasts, indicating that she has a tow. It does not say anything about the length of the tow. You do not know whether the tow is 300 feet long or 6,000. I have repeatedly seen tows on this coast 6,000 feet long. Take a vessel when it encounters a lot of these tows. The captain does not know what to do. If he makes a mistake, there is a collision, and the vessel or the barge goes to the bottom. Four or five weeks afterward it is reported that a vessel was lost. You do not know what became of her.—*Captain Frank Houghton, 1904* [48]

The coastal towing business was hardly more protective of its own people or property. Barges were often leaky, poorly maintained, and manned by inferior and small crews. There were no loading restrictions. Tows were so long (to make the process of towing more efficient) that often the last barges could not be seen from the tug. Occasionally barges broke loose, or had to be cut free. Although provided with some sail, most barges were practically helpless as independent vessels, especially since it was only in extreme conditions that they were likely to have to fend for themselves. On one occasion a tug caught off Point Judith in a severe gale was forced to abandon five barges, all of which perished with their crews.[49] Between 1890 and 1903, 472 barges were lost on the Atlantic and Gulf coasts.[50]

[7.23] 1902. The triple-expansion powered tug *Lykens* pays out steel hawser while making up a tow off Governor's Island. Barges were towed in a line, from bitts aft of the tug's deckhouse. Strangely, few American coastal tugs were fitted with towing machines. The *Lykens* is typical of the superb big steel tugs built around the turn of the century which were capable of towing seagoing barges offshore in any season.

The *Lykens* was operated by the Philadelphia & Reading Railroad, an anthracite road possessing mines, port facilities, steam colliers, tugs, and barges. It was perhaps the biggest coal carrier serving New England. A determined effort by the company to invade the New England anthracite market by rail, over the Poughkeepsie Bridge, was shot down by a vigorous financial barrage mounted by J. P. Morgan of the New Haven.[51]

The command of a big coastal tug was no sinecure. The captain ruled as commodore of the flotilla, signaling all orders—even as to what sails to set—by means of whistle blasts. In confined coastal waters it was often very difficult to turn a long tow—to "snap the whip"—without standing in too close to danger with the tug, or clipping a lightship or obstruction with the last barge. Tows raised havoc with coastal buoyage. In prolonged westerly gales even the most powerful tugs were often blown far to sea with their charges.

Dark, squat, smoking, efficient, dangerous, and scheduled as closely as weather would permit, the coastal caravans must have appeared ugly and ominous interlopers from the decks of graceful schooners. W. J. Alward, a fine marine artist, traveled from Philadelphia to Boston aboard a coal barge in the early 1900s. Although he greatly ad-mired the skill of the tug pilots, he was less enthusiastic toward his vessel:

In the bald blue daylight that hangs above open water the utilitarian character of the craft was uncompromisingly revealed—the scarred decks smeared with coal-tar, the bulwarks, hatches, and deck-houses an iron-ore red and dun snuffy brown; while over all—houses, decks, rails, sails, masts, and even the scant rigging—the smutty touch of her sable cargo . . . The whole effect was quite as forlornly ugly and forsaken as a railroad yard on a hot Sunday afternoon.

Off Handkerchief Shoal (southwest of Monomoy) the tow was forced to anchor with a large fleet of schooners in dense fog. When the weather broke with a spanking fair breeze, the sailing fleet was off with the sound of slatting canvas.

. . . out to sea there was a battle royal between a score of huge five and six masters deep laden, who stood up to it like so many churches under all sail, till we wondered how long the gear would stand the strain.[52]

Despite the grandness of the show, the future lay more with the burly tug and her dour train than with the great schooners of wind and wood and canvas. Data from 1902 are deceptive, due to the anthracite strike. In 1903, however, 2,538 barges arrived at Boston from the south, compared with 1,103 schooners.[53] Slightly more bituminous than anthracite arrived—the total receipts of domestic coal by sea exceeded 4,100,000 tons. The greatest single coal port was Philadelphia, which accounted for 800,000 tons of anthracite and nearly 600,000 tons of bituminous [54]—thereby indicating a not inconsiderable participation by barges in the traditionally sail-dominated bituminous business.

[7.24] 1908. The Mystic Steam Ship Company's steam collier *Malden* lies at anchor, her hatch covers raised preparatory to discharging. Owned by the New England Gas & Coke Company, the *Malden* and her sisters *Everett* and *Melrose* were the first modern-type steam colliers built for the bituminous trade, long the stronghold of big schooners. They entered service in 1907, fared poorly during the depression of 1908 and 1909, but survived to prosper.[55] They contributed greatly to the overdue elimination of the sailing collier and to the eventual reduction of coastal towing.

The design of the *Malden* was probably inspired by the Great Lakes ore carriers. She carried about 7,000 tons and could load or discharge in less time than was required by a schooner of much smaller capacity. Steamers could complete forty to fifty round trips in a year, compared to about eleven for a big schooner. Steamer building costs, per ton, were about double schooner building costs; steamer crews were about twice the size of crews carried on six-masted schooners; yet when all was accounted for, a steamer was considered to be three or four times as efficient as a comparably sized schooner.[56]

The Philadelphia & Reading first introduced steam colliers into the anthracite trade about 1870, although barges were subsequently favored. The anthracite roads owned the mines, railways, docks, and vessels, and this tight control was very amenable to steam carriage. It took more than thirty years, however, for steam colliers to enter the bituminous trade, since the mines, railways, and vessels were owned independently. Owing to the consequent disorganization, vessels were often subject to lengthy delays at the coal ports. During the decades of rapid bituminous expansion, loading facilities were always inadequate. The expenses incurred by idle sailing ships, or barges, were far less than those of idle steamers, which represented larger investments, shipped larger crews, and had to maintain steam. The schooner operators' lobby, the Atlantic Carriers' Association, successfully prevented steamers from loading ahead of their turn.[57] Schooners were thus able generally to hold their own until the opening of the giant Virginian Railway loading facilities at Norfolk in 1909 eased the congestion. Subsequently, two of Boston's major schooner fleets, Crowell & Thurlow and the Coastwise Transportation Company, added steam colliers. By 1915 sixteen steamers were employed in the bituminous trade. The fate of the schooner was sealed, although the war postponed execution.[58]

[8] Deep-Water Sail

The story of deep-water sail at Boston in the second half of the nineteenth century must be considered in two general categories, since it is probable that after the Civil War the majority of the sailing ocean carriers owned in Boston were not the deep-water sailing vessels which more regularly entered and cleared the port. On July 4, 1855, there were forty-five ships, sixty-five barks, and seventy-eight brigs present in the port. Twenty-six of the ships, forty-one of the barks, and thirty-five of the brigs hailed from Boston.[1] On July 3, 1875, the vessels in the port included seven ships, thirty-seven barks, and thirty-three brigs. Three of the ships, fifteen of the barks, and only ten of the brigs were from Boston.[2] On July 4, 1885, there were six ships, thirty-six barks, and seventeen brigs in the port. Three of the ships, and only nine of the barks and one of the brigs were from Boston.[3]

Most of Boston's post-Civil War ocean freighters were involved in long-distance trades between other ports, continuing for several decades a semblance of the old shipping traditions. Although Boston was a party to several deep-water sail trades, none approached the great traffic of sail involved in the trades of Puget Sound, San Francisco, Melbourne, New York, and many other ports. Nor did any, after about 1880, compare with Boston's deep-water steam trades. Indicatively, the best photographs of Boston vessels of the period were taken at New York and San Francisco.

In 1860, 320,449 tons (old measure) of foreign-going shipping were permanently registered at Boston.[4] In 1870 Boston's registered tonnage was 220,348.[5] By 1880 it had fallen to 153,342,[6] and by 1890 it was only 69,792.[7] These figures almost entirely represent sailing tonnage. Despite decline, through the seventies and early eighties Boston remained a relatively important center of deep-water sail ownership. Of the 690-odd square-riggers built on the ocean coasts of the United States from 1870 to 1885, at least 140 were first registered at Boston.[8] The greatest yearly addition was forty-one vessels in 1874, corresponding to the production of 120 square-riggers, the highest of any post-Civil War year.[9] By the nineties, vessel sales without replacement caused the virtual disappearance of Boston's square-riggers.

Of course, square-riggers had no monopoly on deep-water commerce—many schooners made regular voyages to South America, Africa, and Europe. But the number of active square-riggers is perhaps the best relative measure of deep-water sail trading, since the square-rig was always preferred for long voyaging. It was the only rig which could consistently perform satisfactorily on the important Cape Horn route. It was structurally far stronger than the fore-and-aft rig and could spread more sail area, divided into more manageable units. It was ideal for trade wind sailing and could be carried in rolling calms. Schooners, when becalmed, often had to lower sails lest they slat to destruction.

The history of square-sail in the seventies, eighties, and early nineties, on both sides of the Atlantic, is of considerable interest. While steam navigation developed on the shorter sea routes—particularly transatlantic—sailing vessels of improved design dominated the long-distance carrying trades. The great distances of these trades, combined with the low grade of cargoes, the difficulties of obtaining bunkering coal, and the delays in port discouraged steamer participation. And whereas American shipowners were hopelessly handicapped in steam navigation by the primitive and expensive state of American metal shipbuilding, they were able to obtain wooden sailing tonnage at competitive cost from the shipyards of New England, particularly Maine.

The most important post-Civil War sail trade was the carriage of grain from the West Coast to Europe. In the four-year period ending July, 1885, 1,521 grain-laden sailing vessels cleared San Francisco, compared with only twelve steamers. Participating American sailing ships numbered 423.[10] The Americans usually discharged at a European port, then sailed to the East Coast—usually to New York— with low-grade cargoes (often salt), or in ballast. At East Coast ports they often loaded barreled oil for Europe; or coal or tinned "case" oil for the West Coast or the East Indies. Boston was likely to be the recipient of cargoes of sugar and jute loaded in the Indies. The story of the ship *Great Admiral*, the pride of the leading Boston shipping firm of William F. Weld & Company, however, was all too typical. In her twenty-eight years' service with the Welds she returned to Boston only four times.[11]

The grain trade was exceedingly rugged, and the American grain ships were among the finest classes of wooden vessel ever built. Known as "Down Easters," they were of good capacity, fairly fast, moderately canvassed, moderately manned, and well constructed. Most were ship-rigged. Their rates of depreciation, however, were faster than those of foreign iron and steel vessels. Insurance rates were higher for wooden hulls. American crew costs were higher despite greater efficiency. As a result, when the Down Easters of New England grew old they were generally sold to Scandinavia and Germany, to the West Coast coal, lumber, and cannery

trades, or for conversion into East Coast coal barges. They were not replaced.

The deep-water sailing vessels actually entering Boston were a mixed lot. Into the late eighties, at least, prime Down Easters trading to Australia and the East Indies entered and cleared with some frequency. Possibly the last American sailing vessel to enter Boston from the Indies was the ship *John Currier,* of Boston, which completed a voyage from the Philippines in April 1899. Although greatly reduced from previous levels, some Mediterranean and African trading continued under sail. The most consistent sail trades, employing a variety of American and foreign vessels, were to South America and the Caribbean. Vessels cleared with lumber, manufactures, and machinery, and entered with wool, hides, pitch, nitrates, and dye woods. In 1871 entries at Boston included 130 ships, 499 barks, 787 brigs, and 2200 schooners.[12] Most of the schooners and many of the brigs may be dropped from consideration, since 2,359 vessels entered from the Maritime Provinces and Newfoundland alone, to say nothing of near-Caribbean ports.[13] Comparing only ships and barks with steamers (although foreign steam entries include steamers running to Provincial ports) in 1880 there were 388 sail entries to 442 steam.[14] In 1888, American-flag entries included six ships, ninety-two barks, and 116 steamers. Foreign-flag entries included six ships, 124 barks, and 547 steamers.[15] The gaps between sail and steam, American-flag and foreign-flag, would steadily widen. The only deep-water sail trade from Boston of any importance to last into the twentieth century was the lumber trade to the River Plate.

Most of the available photographs of sailing vessels at Boston were taken by professional photographers, presumably for local customers. It is not surprising therefore, that the following collection is weighted heavily in favor of home town vessels. They are fine photographs of worthy vessels, and deserve to be shown, but they do not present a fully balanced portrait of deep-water sail at Boston.

[8.1] Central and India wharves in 1857, at the height of Boston's shipping industry. In that year 122 vessels loaded at Calcutta for the United States; ninety-six entered Boston. Other Boston-owned Calcutta traders discharged at New York.[16] The resulting glut of eastern goods at Boston and New York contributed greatly to the shipping panic of the fall. The big black ship in the center distance may be the McKay medium clipper *Defender*, named for Daniel Webster (as was the *Expounder*, built at Medford in 1856). The Portland steamer lies to the left, at the end of Central Wharf. The schooners to the far right are probably New York packets. The brigs, barks, and half-brigs along Central Wharf are Mediterranean fruiters; most are likely owned and commanded by South Shore men, many from Kingston and Duxbury. The trade supported a large fleet of little square-riggers, necessarily fast because of the perishability of their return cargoes. It is likely that some were sailing into the eighties.

Captain Walter Josselyn, born at Duxbury in 1841, was employed as seaman aboard a fruiter in the fifties:

Our homeward passage was very long, and Captain Dawes was out of his head. First we were a long time getting out of the Mediterranean, then when up to the Grand Banks we had four days dead calm. And all the time our oranges were rotting. Captain Dawes would froth at the mouth, then when we had headwinds he would steer the ship himself for eighteen hours at a stretch, allowing only the Second Mate or me to relieve him for his meals. I believe he had considerable money invested in the cargo. Six days after we reached home he was taken ill at Kingston Depot and only lived a few days. He was a large man, and so goodhearted, it seemed a pity he should die.

As soon as we arrived off Cape Cod we hoisted a signal. The tug was sent from Boston for us with a crowd of stevedores on board. They made all ready and before the barque was fast to the wharf they were putting oranges out.[17]

DINING SALOON.

[8.2] About 1870. The ships *Anahuac, Lucy S. Wills,* and *Anna Decatur* load ice at the Tudor Wharves, Charlestown. The *Anahuac* and the *Wills* were both East Boston-built and Boston-registered. Both cross mainskysail yards. The *Decatur* was built and registered at Portsmouth, New Hampshire. Ice for export was cut largely from Fresh Pond, Cambridge, and was stored in area ice houses. The Fitchburg Railroad had connections to the dock. The ice was packed in the holds with insulating sawdust, much of which was delivered by schooner from the mills of the Penobscot. Charlestown Bridge, crossing the Charles River, is in the foreground.

Frederick Tudor, the "Ice King," was a Boston phenomenon. Combining two nearly worthless commodities, ice and sawdust, he created a valuable export trade and a major New England industry. He was ridiculed when he sent out his first ice cargo, cut from his father's Saugus pond, to Martinique in 1805. The sceptics enjoyed the first laugh, but Tudor persevered, and eventually built up a thriving trade to the West Indies and the southern states. In 1833 he sent his first cargo to Calcutta, followed in 1834 by a cargo to Brazil. Buried in the ice were thousands of Baldwin apples—which remained a Charlestown export for many years.

Of Tudor's six East Indies depots, Calcutta was the most important. After an often tedious 16,000-mile voyage of three or four months, about half the ice loaded at Charlestown remained. The buyers were mostly the English residents, for whom American ice had quickly passed from a luxury to a necessity.

Other firms joined the business (the wharf of Hittenger, Gage & Company may be seen to the right) and ice saved Boston's badly faltering East Indies trade. Cargoes were sent to Japan, China, and Australia. Returning ships carried hides, jute, bagging, dyestuffs, saltpetre, linseed, and shellac. They arrived infested with huge cockroaches that chewed the fingernails of sleeping sailors to the quick, sounded like the report of a pistol when stepped upon, and, it was said, sent the tough waterfront dogs of Boston yapping up State Street. (The brick building to the left, with the stack, was Tudor's linseed oil plant).

In 1856 Boston's ice exports reached 146,000 tons. Cargoes were sent to London, where Boston ice predominated.[18] By 1870 export shipments were reduced to about 63,000 tons, with another 43,000 tons being shipped coastwise.[19] In 1869, 17,000 tons were shipped to Indian ports.[20] By 1880 the competition of artificial icemakers caused Tudor to terminate shipments to the Far East.

The ice industry was developed most extensively in Maine, where it became of very considerable importance to the coastal sailing marine. In the twenty years after 1870 only twice was the annual cut under 1,000,000 tons.[21] Boston, however, was the only major exporter of ice to the Far East. With the development of economical ice plants at the end of the century the natural ice industry disappeared like the proverbial snowball.

[8.3] A fascinating glimpse of a little pre-Civil War ocean freighter, the bark *Acacia,* of Boston, lying at a North End wharf in the mid-seventies. She was built at Harpswell, Maine, in 1858, and was probably employed in South American and Mediterranean trades. Previous to the mid-seventies she was registered at Portland. Note the early three-masted schooner lying in the stream.

[8.4] October 1884. The little full-rigger *Sooloo*, of Salem, W. F. Powers, master, is bound out for Manila. Point Allerton is astern, Nantasket lies low to the left. The *Sooloo* has made sixteen previous voyages to the East Indies, and Captain Powers will write home from Manila:

I almost believe that the *Sooloo* could find her own way out here alone, so many times has she been over the route. We have had fine weather all the way and I have had to settle the topsail yards but once.[22]

The *Sooloo* was built at East Boston in 1861 by John and Justin Taylor for the old Salem house of Silsbee, Pickman & Allen, who owned her until 1887. She is a fine example of a pre-War East India trader of the first water.

There is frequently in port, from Manila and the East Indies, a ship of the old-time kind . . . or else a bark. They bring skins, cutch, gambier and other products to Boston. Sometimes they have several Sumatra goats on deck, or a lot of Java monkeys. I frequently go on board these East Indiamen, and many is the fragrant Manila cheroot that I smoke in the cabin, perhaps with a little of something which a long sea voyage of thousands of miles is said to improve.

C. W. Willis, a Boston fruit merchant, in the *Industrial Journal* (Bangor, Me.), August 6, 1897.

[8.5] In May 1887, while returning from her eighteenth voyage to the Indies, the ship *Sooloo*, of Salem, W. F. Powers, master, collided with the schooner *Messenger*, of Salem, in fog seventy miles ESE of South Shoals Lightship. The *Sooloo* was substantially dismasted, and was towed first to Vineyard Haven, and then to Boston. At Boston, she was purchased by the Boston Tow Boat Company and converted into a coal barge. So ended the independent career of the ship *Sooloo*, of Salem. In twenty-six years she made nineteen successful long-distance voyages for her owners.[23]

Here we see the *Sooloo* being towed to a berth at Boston by the Boston Tow Boat Company's tugs *Vim* and *William Sprague*. The ship appears strikingly small without her tophamper. The pulling boat towing astern of the *Sprague*, on the right, may well belong to North End boarding house runners, eager to acquire the sailors' long voyage pay.

[8.6] June 6, 1887. The ship *Panay*, of Salem, tows down the harbor, followed by a fisherman. She is bound for Ilolio and Manila with 33,000 cases of oil, and will return in eleven months with 1437.5 tons of sugar. This will be her eighth voyage to the Far East.[24]

The departure of a sailing vessel for a long voyage was often a social occasion, and a group of well-wishers and relatives usually towed down the harbor on the vessel, to return with the tug. The departure of a Salem-owned vessel to the Indies in the eighties was a special occurrence, no doubt giving rise to much nostalgia for all concerned. By this date deep-water vessels could no longer put into shoal Salem.

Several of the personages posing in the front row are identifiable. The bearded gentleman standing to the left appears to be Captain Charles Allen Jr., of Salem, the retired master of the Salem ships *Mindoro, Sooloo, Formosa,* and *Derby.* He commanded the *Sooloo* from 1876 to 1884.[25]

The man standing next to Captain Allen, with his hands by his sides, is probably Captain William Beadle, of Salem. Captain Beadle previously commanded the Salem barks *Glide* and *Taria Topan.*[26]

Standing third from left, holding a cheroot, is Captain Joseph W. Luscomb, of Salem, who was commanding the *Panay* on this voyage. Subsequently he was master of the *Mindoro* and the *Taria Topan.*[27]

The gentleman with the windblown beard and the prosperous paunch (notice how its prominence is enhanced by the fashion of fastening only the top coat button) is Captain Stephan Bray Jr., of Newburyport. With the exception of this voyage, Captain Bray commanded the *Panay* from her first voyage in 1877 through her tenth voyage in 1889, when the ship was lost through the error of a tug captain. Captain Bray was a gentleman and a mariner of high reputation.[28]

The slightly blurred man immediately to the right of Captain Bray is probably Mr. George Allen, the youngest partner of the old trading firm of Stone, Silsbee, Pickman & Allen, the owners of the ship.[29]

Frederick Cleaveland, the *Panay*'s mate, was later mate of the great Sewall wooden four-masted bark *Shenandoah.* He is probably not in this group, likely being occupied with the crowd of drunken sailors forward. Also, despite their great responsibilities, mates were often not held in high social regard by masters and owners.

The identity of the young gentleman in the front row, at right, wearing the striped tie, has escaped detection, but, at the risk of making a hasty judgment, it would seem a pity that he is not making this voyage with Captain Luscomb, before the mast. Perhaps the two other young gentlemen, wearing glasses in the back row, could similarly profit. At present they appear to share lamentably few interests or experiences with the seaman at the wheel.

Notice the fine joinerwork of the compass housing, and the absolute simplicity of the steering gear.

[8.7] The departing *Panay* as viewed from the homeward-headed tug. Free at last from the inevitable problems of departure, Captain Luscomb surveys his first command. The same seaman is still at the wheel—perhaps, by deftly catching the mate's eye back at the wharf, he has avoided all the labor of setting sail. The weather clews of the crossjack and the mainsail have been left hoisted to provide a better draft for the foresail.

The *Panay* was a handsomely proportioned vessel worthy of a second glance. Every subtle curve and detail appears to have been perfectly executed. She was a small full-rigger to have been under American register in the eighties, and must have been expensive to operate; nevertheless, she was always maintained like a yacht. She was built by Justin Taylor at East Boston in 1877 and was constructed in the finest Boston traditions. She was the last of the great fleet of Salem East Indiamen.[30]

[8.8] Charles Brewer & Company, of Boston, was the pioneer shipping firm trading from Boston and New York to Honolulu. The company was founded in 1826 by Captain Brewer, a whaling master, and, to its end in 1914, was managed by family members. Captain Brewer also founded C. Brewer & Company, one of the original "big five" Hawaiian sugar and plantation powers. The shipping company owned and operated sailing vessels, including the fine Scots-built barks *Nuuanu* and *Foohng Suey,* into the early twentieth century.[31] Previously the fleet was composed of wooden Down Easters, including the little bark *Amy Turner,* shown lying at Lewis Wharf in the eighties. The *Turner* was built at East Boston in 1877. Fishing schooners lie in the foreground.

In the present day of electronic communication and mass air transportation it is difficult to appreciate the economic and social importance of a shipping house such as Brewer's to an isolated and distant island community.

The sign on the wharf shed advertises Peabody's Australasian Packets—the full-rigger lying in the next dock is no doubt chartered to the line. Henry W. Peabody & Company, of Boston, for many years provided an Australian service (via Capetown) with chartered sailing vessels, trading needed supplies and manufactures for wool, hides, and tallow. Later the firm imported copra, cocoanut oil, hemp, and manila. In 1890 the head office was transferred to New York.

[8.9] Towing out of Nantasket Roads aboard the bark *Martha Davis*, of Boston, the smallest member of Charles Brewer & Company's fleet of Honolulu packets. Guests mill about the decks, while sailors are at work on the forecastle head. Spare spars are stowed on the forward house. The black stack is a manifestation of the steam donkey engine. The *Davis* was East Boston-built. From the perspective of the present it seems incredible that such a short time ago it was profitable to send this small, slow vessel on the long, rugged voyage from Boston, on the North Atlantic, around Cape Horn, to islands in the North Pacific Ocean.

In July 1880, sixteen-year-old L. V. Briggs made the voyage from Boston to Honolulu as a passenger aboard the Brewer's bark *Amy Turner*. He later described the departure:

My friends had come to see me off, and a gay party of forty-three accompanied me on board the bark as far as Boston Lower Light . . . At 6 p.m. after many hand-shakings and farewells my friends boarded a tugboat and steamed away with the pilot, leaving the bark to proceed on her journey under sail.

After watching the little tug fade away to a mere speck, my eyes wandered towards the shore, resting first on Boston for a long, last look, and a little later on the beaches of the South Shore. Then I went down to the cabin to supper. Returning to the quarterdeck at twilight, I could see Boston's revolving light, electric lights at Nantasket, especially its brilliantly-lighted hotel, Minot's light . . . and other familiar points.[32]

[8.10] The charming little Boston barks *Kennard* and *Sarah* traded to the Western Islands (the Azores) into the nineties under the flag of E. A. Adams. They were reputed to be the last Atlantic sailing packets, although the term was used loosely, and they should not be confused with the hard-driven Atlantic packets of the forties.

The pair were engaged in an ancient and honorable trade, for the Western Islands had long enjoyed a special relationship with New England. Whalers regularly put into the islands to recruit men, reprovision, and leave oil to be shipped home. Mediterranean traders stopped to load fruit and wine. Many islanders had emigrated to New England aboard American vessels. The principal merchants at Fayal for most of the nineteenth century were Dabneys from Boston.

Here, in November 1888, the *Kennard* is the picture of trim good order, despite the crowd. Most of the people are likely guests, as the barks probably carried few passengers to the eastward. The four flags set from the mizzen are her signal letters, J S L P. Boston Light, on Little Brewster Island, is to port.

[8.11] The 135-foot *Sarah* was almost a Down Easter in miniature. Nevertheless, she was reputed to have had accommodations for 250 passengers. As unlikely as that figure might at first appear, it should be remembered that into the twentieth century crack Scots coolie ships—sailing vessels of between three and four times the *Sarah*'s tonnage —were regularly carrying as many as eight hundred passengers on voyages halfway around the world under remarkably civilized conditions.[33]

Do not dismiss the little *Sarah* too quickly, for thousands of forgotten *Sarah*s were in many ways centrally responsible for the nature of our lives today. The present population patterns of much of the world were determined by vast fleets of little square-riggers carrying millions of persons in the great transoceanic migrations of four centuries.

[8.12] 1884. A small bark, the *Clara Eaton*, of Portland, Maine, under tow with a tug on each quarter. A South ferry for East Boston scuttles across her bows; the Boston & Albany's Grand Junction grain elevator looms in the background. The trim tug on her port quarter is the Boston Tow Boat Company's *Active*. The ensign flying from the bark's mizzen truck completes the picture. Little square-riggers of the *Eaton*'s class were often employed in the South American trades.

[8.13] The Boston ship *John Currier* at a North End wharf in the nineties. The poor stow of her sails may be the work of shoreside riggers hired to fit the vessel for sea—at the outset of a voyage most sailors did not come aboard until just before sailing time. As a rule, American deep-water vessels were maintained in the finest manner.

The *Currier* was built in 1882 at the Newburyport yard of her namesake, a yard noted for its high standards. Notice the star on the butt of her foretopmast; the golden balls at her mastheads; and the general crispness of her finish. She is a fine example of the superior class of big and powerful Down Easters built from the seventies into the nineties, intended for the California grain trade. They were possibly the finest class of wooden vessels ever constructed.

A study by Captain W. W. Bates of the performances of all the vessels employed in the California trade from 1881 to 1885 indicated that on a per ship average the Down Easters carried more grain faster, cheaper, and in better condition than did any other class of vessel of any nationality. Additionally, he found the Down Easters to be superior in "efficiency of navigation, escape from disasters, preservation from loss both of life and property." [34] Bates's conclusion was that American wooden ships were being unjustly discriminated against by English insurance companies, which granted much more favorable rates to British vessels, built mostly of iron and steel, and of inferior performance.

Even granting that all of Bates's extensive data are correct, he seems to have overstated his case. In basic design the Down Easters were conceivably superior to the British vessels, many of which appear to have suffered from insufficient beam and freeboard. Despite basic differences in their general design, American and British vessels appear to have been of comparable speed. Bates maintained that American vessels were the fastest in the grain fleet—if so, this was likely due to their clean coppered bottoms. British iron and steel vessels, of course, could not be coppered, and often were quite foul on their homeward passage. It could be argued, therefore, that a new Down Easter was superior to her British counterpart *while* she was new—but a dozen years in the Cape Horn trade would have caused far greater depreciation to the wooden hull than to a metal hull.

The sign on the sail of the catboat to the left of the *Currier*'s stem advertises linament—after the Civil War advertising became brashly exhibitionistic. The catboat is possibly a "waterboat," employed supplying vessels with fresh water.

[8.14] The ship *Sea Witch*, of Boston, was built at East Boston in 1872 for William F. Weld & Company. Although she remained with the Welds for only three years, she was owned in Boston until 1901. She was primarily employed in Far Eastern trades. The ship is pictured lying at the end of Union Wharf on a wet and foggy day in the eighties.

In the left foreground a kedge anchor is stowed against the forecastle break. Capstan bars stand in the rack on the foremast, which grows between the heavy main and maintopmast stays. The belaying pins have been removed from the pinrails along the bulwarks, apparently to facilitate repair work. The running rigging is stopped to the shrouds.

The foremast and mainmast are "built" spars, constructed from separate timbers. The sections, probably hard pine, are doweled and banded together. Mast-building was an intricate and exacting art, and the particular plan of assembly varied with the species and size of the timbers.[35] New England had once possessed an abundance of white pine big enough to form large masts from single trees, but most had been cut long before the *Sea Witch* was built. The need for built masts ended with the availability of West Coast fir toward the end of the century. The *Sea Witch* has likely just received a new mizzenmast—it looks bright; yards are set up as shears; no spanker boom is fitted—and it is probably a West Coast spar.

[8.15] The ship *Joseph B. Thomas*, of Thomaston, Maine, lying at Fiske Wharf, probably after discharging a cargo of sugar in 1896. Slabs of white Italian marble are stacked on the wharf—no doubt the wharf's heavy-lift derricks are being used for the *Thomas*'s rerigging job. The ship's foretopgallant mast and foretopmast have been sent down, and spars have been erected as shears preparatory to lifting out the foremast. Observe the great length of the foreyard, which forms the right-hand leg of the shears. Judging by the proportions of her main rigging, the *Thomas* was a handsomely sparred vessel. American square-riggers usually had loftier rigs, with narrower and deeper sails, than did comparable British and European vessels. Few American vessels were fitted with double topgallants, a popular foreign fashion.

The master and part owner of the *Thomas* was Captain William Lermond, a gentleman and a highly regarded shipmaster, who tolerated no hazing by his mates at sea. Captain Lermond commanded the *Thomas* with great success for over fifteen years. In 1900, reflecting the demise of deep-water sail, he became master of a big Thomaston four-masted schooner. In 1903 he moved to the command of the new five-master *Washington B. Thomas*, in which he had invested heavily. In June 1903 the *Thomas* was wrecked on ledges off Stratten Island, south of Cape Elizabeth, while attempting to make Portland at the end of her second coastal coal voyage. The big schooner had anchored in thick fog and was unable to get underway when caught by a sudden and violent storm. A lifeboat did not reach the vessel until nearly a day after the grounding, by which time Captain Lermond's young wife had been killed in the wrecked cabin, and the old captain had been seriously injured.[36] During Captain Lermond's recuperation it was discovered that his share of the schooner—representing his life savings—had not been covered by insurance, due to another person's oversight.[37]

The large naval vessel across the river is the frigate *Wabash*, serving as a receiving ship at the Navy Yard. The tug disappearing behind the bow of the *Thomas* nearly escaped capture by the camera.

[8.16] 1893. The ship *Great Admiral,* of Boston, discharging salt from Trapani, Sicily, at Battery Wharf. The schooner *Hattie Weston,* of Provincetown, loads alongside. Astern, the *Willie L. Smith,* also of Provincetown, and an unidentified schooner apparently wait their turns. The *Weston* and the *Smith* were usually employed in the West Indies salt-fish and fruit trade, but here they are probably loading salt for the Provincetown cod fishery. Trapani salt had qualities especially desired by banks fishermen. In the foreground, the crooked old *Mail,* of Boston, built in 1850, is laden with tile. Astern of her lies the *Mary Lee Newton,* a coaster from Calais, Maine.

The *Great Admiral*'s jibboom has been "housed" so as to clear the wharf. Below the bowsprit the fine figurehead of David Farragut shows well. At sea, the Admiral was removed and kept in a special locker, safe from the elements. Beneath the shed roof a longshoreman tends a steam hoisting engine working the salt.

The *Great Admiral* was a superior vessel, built of selected materials by Robert Jackson at East Boston for the Boston firm of William F. Weld & Company. All of her exterior fastenings were copper. She was always excellently maintained, and retained her first-class insurance rating after her twenty-year survey.[38] She had the lines of a medium clipper, and being her owner's great favorite, was called "the Weld yacht." She was a happy ship, and her last master under the Weld house flag commanded her for seventeen years.

In 1869, the year that the *Great Admiral* was built, Weld & Company owned perhaps the largest American-flag deep-water sailing fleet; when the *Great Admiral* was reluctantly sold in 1897, she was the firm's sole remaining vessel. The Welds were prospering, however, having invested shrewdly in railroads and real estate. The story of William F. Weld & Company is instructive of the great shift of Boston capital from the sea to the land. Before the railroad boom the firm imported much of the hemp and manila required by the large American merchant marine for cordage. As shipping declined and railroads grew, Weld & Company became the sole agent for Messrs. Thompson & Forman, leading English rail founders.[39] William F. Weld was one of the powers behind the growth of the Boston & Maine, and served as director for other New England railroads.

[8.16] Detail

[8.17] The carpenter (holding a plane) and the chief mate of the Boston ship *Great Admiral* at sea in 1887 during a voyage from New York to Melbourne.

The chief mate of a big sailing vessel was usually a man to reckon with. As the officer most directly concerned with the management of the vessel his standards were apt to be high, and his opinions strongly held. Ideally, a good mate reduced the master's role to a minimum. Most of the masters and probably most of the mates of the Down Easters were native New Englanders, although the passage of a prohibition against the employment of foreign officers on American ships in 1884 was one indication that the deteriorating merchant marine was no longer attracting native sons to its officer ranks. Seamen could be admitted to American citizenship after only three years of service on American ships, and after 1884 there was a large increase in the number of naturalized officers.

As a class, American mates were renowned for their fine seamanship, and for cruelty and brutality which lost nothing in the telling. By law, American foreign-going vessels were required to sign their crews for the entire round voyage. This regulation both raised labor costs on American ships and contributed to the incidence of "hazing" as the mates tried to drive the men to desert the vessel—and their pay—in foreign ports.[40] Nevertheless, despite the economic incentives, and despite the certainty that the profession attracted and produced more than its share of "hard cases," there were many just and reasonable officers running happy ships, ships such as the *Great Admiral*. Successful voyages under these men were relatively uneventful, would have made dull reading, and were easily forgotten.

According to contemporary complaints, old sailormen of the carpenter's cut were becoming distressingly rare in the late decades of the century. A good ship's carpenter was a man of many skills, and in an emergency he might be called upon to shape and fit a replacement spar from the spare lashed in the waterway (behind the mate).

Notice the *Great Admiral*'s high man-of-war style bulwarks in the background. They are painted a brilliant white, in proper Yankee fashion.

My pals and I did a good deal of roaming through
downtown Boston and along the waterfront. We would
take the penny ferry to East Boston, call at a wharf
where a Cunarder or Leyland liner was lying, and ask to
be allowed aboard. On one memorable occasion we
climbed all over the full-rigged, three-skysail yard ship
Aryan, then in the lumber trade to the river Plate.—
Samuel Eliot Morison [41]

The *Aryan* discharges Puget Sound timber
through bow ports at National Docks, East Boston.
Schooners were commonly built with bow ports to
facilitate the handling of big timbers—the *Aryan*'s
ports were probably cut after she was sold into the
West Coast lumber trade. Before putting to sea,
ports were closed and caulked.

Even a moderately sized vessel held an astonishing
amount of tightly and skillfully stowed lumber. Every
cargo required appropriate handling; improper loading
damaged property and sometimes sank ships. The
stevedoring industry depended on an army of tough
longshoremen who, whether loading heavy blocks of
ice or discharging reeking hides, were unsung heros
of commerce. Hazards of the profession included both
rupture and temptation.

Photographed in 1911, the *Aryan* was no longer
a three-skysail yarder, but she was still a fine
specimen of a latter-day Down Easter. Built at
Phippsburg, Maine, in 1893, she proved to be the
last full-rigger built in the United States.

The quantity and quality of shipcarving declined
in the final days of sail—some vessels were perhaps
the handsomer for the absence of distracting
decoration. By the old standards, the *Aryan*'s
diminutive eagle's head would have been an embarrassment.

[8.19] Pumping the bilges of the ship *Aryan,* at National Docks. The men, typically, are a mixed lot dressed in varied fashion. No doubt they represent several nationalities. The native American seaman was fast disappearing by mid-century, and by 1911 he was a positive rarity. Native American seamen of ability were quickly promoted aft. Americans were replaced largely by northern Europeans from the great tribe of wandering seamen. By international standards, American ships paid well and were good "feeders," but featured harsh discipline.

The crew which signed aboard the Boston bark *Amy Turner* in 1880 for a voyage to Honolulu was representative. The captain and the mates were native Americans. The cook was a Negro from Maine; his wife served as steward. The carpenter was German. The gang before the mast consisted of two Germans, two Norwegians, two Swedes, two Prince Edward Islanders, one Englishman, one Kanaka, and one American.[42]

The *Aryan*'s pump works are mounted on the main fiferail, which traditionally was an impressive member of a vessel's deck furniture. The small fresh-water pump stands center aft, with a tin cup near by. The mizzen braces, staysail downhauls, and the mainyard lifts are led to belaying pins in the rail. The big fir mast is probably a relatively recent West Coast replacement. Capstan bars are held in a rack. The heavy band fastens the mizzen stay. From the great size of the spar one can gain at least a notion of the danger and destruction experienced when a vessel was dismasted.

[8.20] Had three particularly gruesome and mysterious murders not been committed aboard the barkentine *Herbert Fuller*, of Harrington, Maine, in July 1896, we would not now be enjoying this fine photograph, which was taken by a post card printer during the subsequent sensational trial. The *Fuller* was on a voyage from Boston to the River Plate with lumber when the captain, his wife, and the second mate were found dead, apparently killed with an axe while they slept. The first mate was found guilty, although some years later he was pardoned by President Wilson.

The *Fuller* was a fine example of the East Coast barkentines which were commonly employed toward the end of the century in both coastwise and deepwater trades—especially to the Caribbean and the River Plate. Unlike the Great Lakes and European versions of the rig, East Coast barkentines were fitted with main and mizzenmasts of equal height, connected by a spring stay. Unlike the West Coast rig, a triangular mizzen supplemented by a queer-looking topsail was not substituted for a proper gaff-headed spanker. In most cases, the barkentine was a happy compromise, possessing more of the respective advantages than disadvantages of the combined square- and fore-and-aft rigs.

The *Fuller* is shown fast to Pigeon's and Poole's Wharf, East Boston. The Pigeon sparmaking firm was established in 1830 and continues in the business today at Quincy. To the left of the *Fuller*, spar timber seasons in a boom. The Lockwood Manufacturing Company (beyond the *Fuller*'s masts) made marine engines and propellers.

[8.21] The Little Mystic Channel, Charlestown, in the nineties. From right to left, the schooner *George V. Jordan,* of Saco, Maine; the barkentine *Altona,* of Windsor, Nova Scotia; the barkentine *Rachel S. Emery,* of Boston; the bark *Auburndale,* of Boston; and two unidentified schooners load lumber for the River Plate. The little fisherman-type schooner in the left foreground is the *Peerless,* of Southport, Maine. The steam in the far right distance is from locomotives of the Boston & Maine. The Little Mystic Channel formed the southern boundary of the extensive Boston & Maine Mystic Terminal.

In the eighties, heavy British and European investment and immigration created a boom in the Argentine. The demand for lumber was great, and Boston and Portland became centers of the trade. Return cargoes of wool and hides, or Caribbean sugar, were perfect complements to Boston's industry and commerce. Although the trade to the River was deep-water, it attracted many coasters. The high shipping rates to the River in the late eighties drained off much of the American coastwise tonnage; the shortage of tonnage on the coast, in turn, raised rates, and inspired a great burst of schooner construction. In the early nineties the River Plate bubble became temporarily deflated, contributing to the shipping depression of the mid-nineties.[43]

[8.22] 1890. J. S. Emery & Company's new barken-tine *John S. Emery* puts to sea with a cold northerly breeze. The *Emery* was built at East Boston. Yesterday's snow lies on the islands, and on the vessel's forward house and furled headsails. J. S. Emery & Company, a Boston firm, was for many years a major trader to South America, the Carib-bean, and Africa. Outward bound, their vessels carried lumber and manufactured goods. Returning, they brought sugar, pitch, rum, molasses, ma-hogany, bones, wool, hides, guano, and palm oil.

In 1904 Daniel S. Emery testified before the Merchant Marine Commission at a hearing held in the Chamber of Commerce Building:

I have been in the business of owning vessels fifty years. Forty-seven years the present firm has been in business. We have owned in about two-hundred vessels in that time, and at the present time we may have perhaps thirty, mostly engaged in the coastwise trade . . . Within my experience, from where this build-ing stands down to the end of the wharf, vessels have come bringing cargoes from all parts of the world . . . Now there is not a sailing vessel that comes here or a vessel under the American flag, hardly. There was some business left in the river Plata, but that is monopolized mostly by foreign vessels which can be sailed so much cheaper than our own vessels that we have about given it up. I have men in my employ who began as boys and who have been in only two vessels . . . one man who has been in only two vessels . . . has been master for thirty years. He has grown up in the business. He was making a good living at one time. Now that man makes but very little.[44]

[8.23] 1904. The bark *Helen A. Wyman,* of New York, lies to her port anchor off Bird Island Flats. A light southerly breeze carries her up on her chain against the ebbing tide. Crew members are apparently bending sail—two hands stand on the bowsprit hanking-on headsails. Built at Bath in 1881 as the ship *William J. Rotch,* of New Bedford, she is shown without her original mainskysail and mizzen yards. A deckload of lumber, probably for the River Plate, hides her forward house.

In the final decades of the nineteenth century the American deep-water sailing fleet shrank drastically. In 1870 there were 731 ships, 889 barks and barkentines, and 675 brigs under American registry. By 1903 their numbers had been reduced to 96 ships, 230 barks and barkentines, and only 24 brigs.[45] The lost sailing tonnage was not, for the most part, replaced by steamers.

The surviving deep-water sailing vessels occupied an awkward position in the maritime community. American seamen avoided them like the plague; enterprising officers were more interested in steam. Wise fathers directed their adventurous sons toward other outlets, since shipboard conditions were often shockingly bad, even by contemporary standards. Nevertheless, there is a certain nobility about this old vessel which is enhanced by her reduced circumstances and which cannot be attained by yachts or steamers. Constructed of the elemental timber of the American forests, quietly living out her last years of freedom, she still earns her keep wandering about the planet with the ocean winds. In several years the *Wyman* will be cut down for a coal barge, joining many old ocean sisters at the end of a towing hawser.

[8.24] In the nineties. The German bark *Maria,* of Pappenburg, outward bound, approaches Castle Island. Ahead, a little puff brings a coaster to starboard while the helmsman is away attending to other matters. The bark's yards are too squarely braced, but after another mile she will be able to head farther off the wind as she runs out the ship channel.

The *Maria* is beginning to show some "hog"— her ends are beginning to droop—and she is no longer young. Small, with an elaborate stern, bluff bows, and deep topgallants, she is reminiscent of thousands of predecessors under many flags which for centuries carried the bulk of the commerce of the world.

[8.25] East Boston, in the nineties. The bark *Arracan* and the ship *Scottish Lochs,* both of Liverpool, lie at the Boston & Albany's Grand Junction Pier 2. The *Arracan,* built of steel in 1892, and the iron *Scottish Lochs,* built in 1888, were both products of the last great boom of British sailing ship construction, from 1888 to 1893. They were big vessels, reflecting the pressure of growing steam competition. The *Lochs* was a member of the "Scottish Line" fleet of W. H. Ross & Company, one of many Liverpool shipping houses of Canadian origin. Previously the firm owned numerous wooden vessels, built and often manned by Nova Scotians. Many Nova Scotians were employed in the iron fleet as well. A vessel with a Provincial master or mate which was run in the traditional firm Down East fashion was generally known as a "Bluenose" vessel despite the legend "Liverpool" on her stern.[46]

The *Arracan* has a lighter alongside and is apparently discharging or loading ballast. Many sailing vessels had to be handled with great caution when they were empty, as there was danger of capsizing.[47] Steel hulls were lighter than iron hulls, while both were lighter—and therefore more unstable—than wooden hulls. Additionally, British designers favored narrower beam than was thought wise in America. For example, the *Arracan*'s beam of 42.1 feet was actually several inches less than that of the American ship *John Currier,* although with a registered length of 291.3 feet the *Arracan* was the longer vessel by more than fifty-five feet. An American sailing vessel of similar length, the bark *Shenandoah,* had a beam of 49.1 feet, and even that was less than the customary Down Easter proportions would have had it. Even a small variation in beam could affect performance.

Some British vessels were reasonably stable even with swept holds. Some had at least to send down their upper yards, or even their topgallant masts, when lying empty. Many could not shift berths without some stiffening ballast, and when lying empty had to be supported by heavy ballast logs chained alongside. The *Arracan* has sent down her royal yards, which are lashed vertically alongside her lower masts.

PIER. 3

[8.26]

Word was received in the city this morning that the British barque *Corryvrechan* was at anchor between Harding's Ledge and Minot's Light with the entire crew so frostbitten that they were unable to do anything towards working the vessel. The *Corryvrechan* came to anchor in the storm last night, and let go both anchors, paying out all her cable in order to make sure of holding, and the crew were suffering so from frostbite that this morning they were unable even to raise the anchors. A passing tug was spoken by Captain Hammond of the *Corryvrechan,* who sent word to Messrs. J. G. Hall & Co., the agents of the vessel in this city, of the plight in which they were. The Boston Towboat Company was immediately communicated with, and the tugs *Vesta* and *Juno* were dispatched to the vessel with men enough to raise the anchors and handle the vessel while she is being towed up . . . The men on board the vessel are suffering fearfully, and are absolutely helpless to do anything towards helping the men on the tugs. It is not expected that the vessel will arrive up much before sunset, as she has a tremendous amount of chain out, and it will take four or five hours to weigh the anchors. Nearly all the barque's sails were blown to shreds in yesterday's storm. The *Corryvrechan* is consigned to the American Sugar Refining Company of this city, with a cargo of 7760 baskets of sugar, and is from Sourabaya, Java, Aug. 26, and Besoki, Sept. 20, via Delaware Breakwater.—*Boston Evening Transcript,* January 29, 1897

Despite the *Corryvrechan*'s experience, and the indisputable severity of the weather, there were few casualties along the coast. The coasting schooners *J. E. du Bignon* and *Agnes E. Manson* entered the harbor safely during the night of the storm; the *Lizzie Babcock* arrived in the morning. No doubt the men on the *Corryvrechan* were quite unprepared for the cold weather, and were without proper clothing. After months of tropical flying fish weather, the shock of winter off the New England coast very nearly proved fatal.

[8.27] 1910. Foreign square-riggers load lumber for the River Plate in the Little Mystic Channel, Charlestown. The lumber came by rail from Maine, Michigan, and Canada.[48] As British steam steadily overspread the ocean world, taking many of the long-distance, bulk cargo trades from sail, some very fine British and European sailing vessels sought refuge in the Boston–River Plate business. By 1910 even ex-crack Scots coolie ships could be found loading pine in the Little Mystic. Although the fleet was largely foreign-flag, it represented not a little Boston capital.

From right to left we see three Glasgow-registered vessels—the steel bark *Gael*, the ship *Pass of Balmaha* (almost obscured), and the light-hulled ship *Timandra*. The *Gael*, full-ended, wall-sided, and "bald headed," represents the final effort of British sailing ship builders and owners to compete with steam. Her short rig reflects the owners' concern for cutting crews to a bare minimum. The fore and mainmasts are rigged to similar dimensions, reducing construction, replacement, and sail costs. This rig—with double topgallants, but no royals—was termed the "Jubilee Rig" on account of its introduction in 1887, Queen Victoria's Jubilee.

At the outbreak of the First World War, many British vessels were allowed American registration by an act of Congress. Boston thereby gained a fine little fleet of square-riggers, including these three. While under the American flag the *Pass of Balmaha* was captured by the Germans and converted into the famous armed raider *Seeadler*, commanded by Count von Luckner.

Photographs of the Little Mystic are perhaps deceptive indicators of sailing ship activity in the port. In 1910 a total of thirty barks and nine ships cleared Boston.[49] From January through June 1906, four ships, twenty-two barks, one schooner, and one barkentine cleared Boston for the River Plate.[50] In 1900 a Boston pilot stated that he had not boarded an incoming sailing vessel in over two years.[51]

[8.28] The lovely *Timandra,* of Glasgow, drives across Massachusetts Bay, bound for the River Plate. Lumber covers her decks, piled higher than the bulwarks. A temporary railing is fastened to timber stanchions. Running rigging is fastened to temporary pinrails, the regular pinrails being inaccessible. The watch is aft, on the lee side, sweating-in the main sheet. When everything is drawing well, and when the master is certain of his offing, the men will go forward and hoist the anchors onto the forecastle deck.

The photograph well illustrates the "screw of the sails," a fashion of bracing the yards when sailing on the wind. With the lower yards "pointed" higher than the upper yards, the helmsman was able to judge how high on the wind he was sailing by watching the weather leeches of the upper sails.[52]

The record passage from Boston to the River Plate was thirty-four days, made in 1901 by the ship *Pass of Balmaha,* while under the command of Captain Dick Lee, a Bluenose driver.

[9] Deep-Water Steam

The outstanding period of deep-water steam navigation at Boston occurred between the late seventies and the First World War. Despite the depressed business conditions and the surfeit of North Atlantic tonnage in the nineties the foreign steamship business at Boston remained sound, and was centrally responsible for the port's remarkable growth through this period.

Data from an unexceptional year illustrate something of the extent of steamship activity. In 1896 at least 361 line steamships cleared Boston for British and European ports. Liverpool, as always, headed the list with 199 sailings. London followed with eighty-two; Glasgow and Hull received twenty-eight and twenty, respectively. The only non-British port represented by a comparable number of sailings was Antwerp with twenty-three—but this service, by the Belgian-flag, American-owned Red Star Line was via Baltimore, and not direct. The most active steamship lines using the port were Warren, Leyland, and Cunard to Liverpool, and Furness to London.[1]

On November 3, 1896, the Leyland Line steamer *Armenian,* of Liverpool, cleared Boston for Liverpool. Her cargo included 799 head of cattle; 18,157 barrels of apples; 5,730 bales of cotton; 30,378 bushels of corn; 111,377 bushels of wheat; 3,760 quarters of beef; and one hundred barrels of rum.[2] (Reflecting a taste acquired in an earlier age, much New England rum was still being shipped to the West Coast of Africa via Liverpool).

On November 25, 1896, the Cunard Line steamer *Pavonia,* of Liverpool, entered the port of Boston from Liverpool. In addition to passengers, she carried brandy, ale, tin, caustic soda, iron, mackerel, sardines, wool, wine, oranges, grapes, figs, machinery, emery ore, clay crockery, rat traps, and barreled sheep guts.[3]

As indicated above deep-water steamship service to Boston was overwhelmingly provided by British-flag scheduled "liners" running to British ports. Boston's traffic of unscheduled tramp steamships was insignificant, reflecting the port's traditional difficulty providing export cargoes of sufficient bulk —Baltimore, by contrast, was a great wheat port and a great tramp port. At Boston return cargoes for scheduled liners were provided through special agreements with the port's railroads.

The story of the ocean commerce of the world in the second half of the nineteenth century is primarily the story of the British steam merchant marine. Great Britain's domination of the oceans was the outgrowth of an advanced industrial society, with great capital resources, combined with a vital need for markets and raw materials, and centuries of seafaring tradition. In 1870 Great Britain possessed 1,652,000 gross tons of seagoing steam shipping, compared with 514,000 tons under United States registry. The world total was 2,800,000, or, typically, less than twice the British figure.[4] In 1886 the total of British steam seagoing tonnage had risen to 6,500,000, compared with a world total of 10,500,000.[5] Of the 12,000,000 tons of steam shipping built in the world from 1890 to 1900, 9,790,000 tons—or 4,638 vessels out of a total of 6,213—were launched from yards in the

United Kingdom.[6] By 1900 the United Kingdom and its colonies possessed 12,150,000 tons of steam shipping of over 100 gross tons; the seagoing steam tonnage of the United States, by contrast, had still not exceeded 600,000.[7] Throughout this period the United States and Great Britain engaged in heavy mutual trading—it is not be considered odd, therefore, that the deep-water steamship business out of the port of Boston was virtually monopolized by British steamship companies.

The North Atlantic Ocean figured prominently in the development of ocean-going steamships. The transatlantic route was short enough for navigation by early steamships, featured strong westerly winds which greatly hindered sail service to America, and connected the two most important and complementary economic areas of the world—western Europe and America. Owing to harsh winter weather conditions and the pressures of fierce competition, the run compelled rapid improvements in ship design. In America, New York was the port privileged to receive the highest quality transatlantic steamers, but even a casual inspection of the steamers calling at Boston over relatively few years reveals considerable technological improvements.

The history of regularly scheduled transatlantic steam navigation to Boston predates even that of New York. Boston was selected as the American terminus for the pioneering steam service inaugurated by Britain's Cunard Line in 1840. No doubt Boston's relative proximity to Halifax, Cunard's Canadian port, figured in the decision. Service was semimonthly for eight months of the year, and monthly during the winter. In 1844 the unusual freezing of Boston harbor threatened to delay indefinitely the departure of the Cunarder *Britannia*, thereby jeopardizing Boston's future with Cunard. Aroused merchants engaged the professional ice cutters of Fresh Pond, under the direction of Jacob Hittinger, a Charlestown ice shipper, to cut a five-mile channel to open water. The *Britannia* departed on schedule to the cheers of the large crowd assembled along her path. (A severe winter in 1857 necessitated similar action.) [8]

Despite this display of civic enterprise, Boston was unable to hold the Cunard Line's exclusive attentions. By 1848 Samuel Cunard had won a new subsidy permitting him to double his fleet to eight ships and had instituted a separate service to New York. During the first year of this run the customs duties collected on Cunard cargoes at New York exceeded those at Boston by one-third. By 1850 they were three times as great.[9]

In 1864 a group of Bostonians interested in entering the transatlantic steamship business formed the American Steamship Company. In 1866 and 1867 two impressive iron-strapped wooden screw steamships were built for the company at Newburyport. The vessels, named the *Ontario* and the *Erie*, were designed by the talented Samuel Hartt Pook, measured 325 feet in length, and were powered by machinery built at South Boston. They were probably the equal of the best of the Cunarders. The cost of their construction, however, was much greater than anticipated and nearly exhausted the company's resources. Unlike the Cunard Line, the American Steamship Company stood to collect no subsidy from its government, and in 1868 the firm failed. The *Ontario* had made only a few trips; the *Erie* had not left Boston.[10]

The port's problems continued to mount. In 1868 Cunard suspended its mail steamer service to Boston in order to concentrate on its New York business, and because of the difficulty of obtaining outbound cargoes at Boston sufficient to fill the newer, larger steamers entering service. The lesser Cunarders that were sent to Boston called on their way to New York.

In the end, the net effects of the Cunard cutbacks and the American Steamship Company's failure were beneficial to the port, as they inspired the establishment of an arrangement which would prove to be the foundation for the rebirth of Boston as a major deep-water port. In 1870 Cunard agreed to revive the Boston service subject to the guarantee of the Boston & Albany Railroad, acting in concert with the New York Central, to provide outward cargoes of grain. All parties stood to gain by this arrangement, and it served as the model for future alliances between other railroads and steamship lines.

The port's situation improved dramatically. Whereas in 1869 there was not one direct steamer sailing from Boston to Europe,[11] in 1880 there were nearly two hundred sailings to Liverpool alone. With close cooperation between railroad and shipping companies Boston was developed into the major North American cattle port, while the related provisions trade made the Boston area a major packing center. Despite high rail rates, Boston gained a respectable portion of the important North American grain trade, and by most standards regained its status as the nation's second port. In 1870 the port of Boston was still surpassed only by New York in terms of the value of goods imported, although in terms of the value of exports, it was surpassed or equaled by New York, Philadelphia, Baltimore, Savannah, Mobile, New Orleans, Galveston, and San Francisco. By 1896 the value of Boston's exports totaled $95,850,000, which was second only to the value of those of New York, worth $334,300,000. Baltimore, in third place, had exports worth $88,400,000.[12]

The line traffic in the port became so heavy that at times it was virtually impossible for an unscheduled steamer to obtain wharfage. In December 1895 Henry W. Peabody, a prominent old-time Boston shipper, described such a situation in a letter to the chairman of the State Board on Docks and Terminal Facilities.

I beg to call to your attention the case of the steamer "Blackheath," arrived here this morning with a cargo of 7,236 bales of sisal to my firm's consignment. We desired to store 5,000 bales and to ship off the balance, and have been working for the past week to secure a berth for the steamer, and found it impossible to accomodate her at any wharf in the harbor below bridges. . . . The only other alternative to us was to send her up to Boston wharf through the bridges. The New York & New England refused to authorize us to send any boat through their railroad draw of more than forty-one feet beam, and the "Blackheath" is forty-one feet six inches.

We, however, succeeded in getting her through by the aid of two tugs, although she scraped in so doing. Had this steamer, then, been of one or two inches more beam, she could not have been discharged in all Boston harbor.[13]

In 1913 there were over two hundred steamer sailings from Boston to ports of the United Kingdom (Cunard, Leyland, White Star, Furness-Withy, Warren, and Allan Lines); over 140 sailings to Scandinavian, Dutch, French, German, and Mediterranean ports (Red Star, Holland-America, Hamburg-American, Scandinavian-American, White Star, and Italian Lines); 125 sailings to the West Indies and Central America (United Fruit Company); forty-six sailings to the Far East (American-Indian Line); and seventeen sailings to South America (Barber, Norton, Houston, and Furness-Withy Lines). Over 450 additional "foreign" sailings to the Canadian Provinces, Cuba, and Puerto Rico more fittingly belong under the classification of coastal navigation.[14]

Despite this impressive listing, the decline of deep-water steam at Boston was well underway. The cattle and provisions (mostly dressed meat) trades were dying out; the traffic of the declining North American grain trade was shifting away from Boston. After 1900 Boston's relative share of imports and exports fell steadily. The trend in the shipping industry toward mergers and combinations worked to the disadvantage of Boston and her steamship lines. World War I, like the Civil War, served to advance the processes contributing to decline. Many "Boston" ships were lost in the war; in the great shipping depression that followed, many "Boston" lines failed or were absorbed. With improved rail and highway transportation in the Northeast and New England, Boston was at last undeniably within the growing sphere of influence of the giant port of New York.

[9.1] About 1855. A fascinating daguerreotype of an early Cunarder, probably the *Niagara,* lying in the Atlantic Dock, East Boston. Her protruding paddle-wheels and paddle-boxes were severely punished at sea, and were of the most substantial construction. They were apparently also something of a dockside nuisance—witness the special derricks. Oddly, the steamer is rigged with studdingsail booms on her foreyard. Perhaps it was thought that studdingsails provided the best means by which sail area could be increased in a fair breeze while adding the least amount of windage in a head wind; or perhaps it was simply a matter of status—even on a steamship. Horses pull carloads of freight discharged from the vessel.

Snow lies on the northern slopes of the shed roofs. South Cove lies across the channel, beyond the heights of Fort Hill. The Boston waterfront is jammed with shipping—the square-riggers with painted ports are likely Boston cotton ships and immigrant packets. The lofty vessel with the skysail yard (above the right-hand derrick) may well be a California clipper. The cotton ships were of central importance to the development of the English and New England textile industries, the agricultural South, and many local fortunes. In 1855, 175 vessels cleared Boston for New Orleans alone.[15] Many vessels carried cotton to the eastward and immigrants to the westward.

The *Niagara* and her sisters were of less immediate importance. Although early steamers were a great novelty, and were consistently faster than sailing vessels, they could carry relatively little cargo and were expensive to operate. They earned a reputation for dirt, noise, and crowded discomfort —one disgruntled customer described a Cunarder as resembling nothing so much as a lump of Nova Scotia coal.[16] (Of course, since these Cunarders carried only cabin-class passengers, the conditions were being compared with cabin-class accommodations on first-rate sailing packets, and not to the horrible immigrant steerages.)

The Cunard Company (short for British & North American Royal Mail Steam Packet Company) was founded in 1840 to take advantage of subsidy offered by the British government, and was for many years dependent on subsidized mail contracts. From its beginning it displayed a curious blending of progressiveness and conservatism which served it well. These characteristics perhaps reflected the firm's origin as the amalgamation of the interests of an energetic young Nova Scotian, Samuel Cunard, with the established Glasgow packet company of Burns & McIver. In the second half of the century the line emerged as the foremost transatlantic shipping concern, important to the port of Boston, and far more important to New York port.

The *Niagara* was one of four standardized steamers built for Cunard in 1848. Their construction permitted the line to maintain separate fortnightly services from Liverpool to Boston and New York via Halifax. They were powered by Napier side-lever engines, and averaged thirteen days to New York, via Halifax.[17] They were definitely steamers rather than auxiliary sailing vessels. Each had berths for 140 passengers. The *Niagara* was sold in 1862 and, like two of her sisters, was converted to sail by her new owners. It was the iron screw steamers of the next generation, and not the pioneer wooden paddlers, which drove sail from the North Atlantic.

[9.2] The Cunarder *Russia*. This photograph was thought to have been taken at Boston, but was evidently taken at New York. It is no less interesting, however, and has been allowed to remain. From 1868 to 1870 Cunard's Boston service was provided by steamers calling on passage to New York, although the *Russia,* admittedly, was several cuts above the steamers that usually came to Boston. The *Russia* was registered at Glasgow under the firm of Burns & McIver—hence the legend on the stern of the lifeboat. The combination skylight-and-bench was a common furnishing on British and European vessels. A cargo whip is rigged from the port main-yardarm.

Built in 1867, the iron 358-foot *Russia* was a pioneer screw transatlantic liner. She was powered by a two-cylinder vertical direct-acting engine and was capable of nearly fourteen knots. She was actually no faster than the last Cunard paddler, the *Scotia* of 1862, but her coal consumption was much reduced and her machinery occupied less space. The *Russia* carried a boiler pressure of twenty-five pounds per square inch, which was considered very daring at sea (even the *Niagara*'s thirteen pounds had been considered high-pressure in 1848). By the end of the century transatlantic liners were carrying boiler pressures of two hundred pounds. The machinery of the *Niagara* developed 2000 indicated horse-power (that is, horse-power developed in the cylinders, with no losses for friction); the two five-cylinder triple-expansion engines of the 1892 Cunarder *Campania* were rated at 30,000 i.h.p. By the end of the century a pound of coal was doing four times the work at sea that it had done fifty years previously.[18]

The story of the improvement of the reciprocating steam engine is the story of increasingly higher steam pressure with correspondingly advanced rates of the steam's expansion. In 1827 Jacob Perkins, of London (a native of Newburyport, Massachusetts), was experimenting with working pressures of eight hundred pounds, and had cut-off steam to the cylinder at one-eighth the stroke.[19] Owing to a combination of conservatism and technological limitations British marine engineers were slow to utilize the advantages of high pressure —perhaps the frequently explosive results accompanying high-pressure engineering on American waters was a factor. The practice of using salt water in boilers persisted into the sixties, and even at the relatively low pressures of the time the frequent chore of "blowing off" boilers to remove brine was attended with danger. Additionally, the craft and science of boiler-making lagged considerably behind the progress in engine-building.[20]

The compound marine engine, in which the steam expanded successively in a high-pressure cylinder and a larger low-pressure cylinder, became popular in the seventies. The higher pressures demanded by the compound forced the improvement of boiler design and construction. The manifold advantages of expansion inspired increased engineering activity in many areas. Triple and quadruple expansion engines were introduced in the eighties. In the days of low-pressure engineering, horsepower was gained by increasing the size of the engine; high pressure made possible increased power and efficiency with a reduction in machinery weight and size.[21]

[9.3] February 1885. The "B Type" Cunarder *Pavonia* is headed down the ship channel by the tugs *Camilla* and *Curlew*. The *Pavonia* was for many years the favorite of traveling Bostonians. She and her sisters, the *Cephalonia* and the *Catalonia* (known locally as the *Cattle-only*), were built for the Liverpool-Queenstown-Boston service in the early eighties, as part of Cunard's massive fleet rebuilding program. During the seventies Cunard's Boston service, in particular, had been badly outclassed. Joined by several New York-run veterans and (in 1895) two all cargo-cattle steamers, the *Pavonia* and her sisters remained on the Boston run until 1900.[22] Their replacements were the splendid new twins *Ivernia* and *Saxonia,* the largest members of the Cunard fleet. The new *Ultonia,* which entered service in 1899, carried third-class passengers only. After 1911 the new liners *Franconia* and *Laconia* became the Boston regulars. Cunarders built especially for the Boston trade were slower and more economical than the flyers operated to New York and gave the total fleet more balance.

Cunard played a major role in the carriage of immigrants to Boston. The *Pavonia* and her sisters each had accommodations for 200 cabin passengers and 1500 "third-class," or steerage passengers. In 1884, 35,000 immigrants entered at Boston, the largest single group being 14,000 Irish.[23] No doubt many of the Irish arrived on Cunarders.

[9.4] A brisk westerly breeze helps the Cunarder *Pavonia* along on her way to Liverpool—the square sails on the foremast are taut and pulling. The passengers are warmly dressed, for this is the age of the well-prepared traveler. Boston is several days astern; seasickness has been met and, for the most part, conquered. It is pleasant on deck, as the coal smoke is blowing off to leeward, and there is no cinder problem. Everyone feels chipper, and camaraderie runs rampant. This delightful photograph perfectly captures the novel spirit of an Atlantic crossing in the eighties, when the first-class passenger list appeared on the front page of the *Transcript*.

The protected pipe in the foreground is a steam-line connected to the capstan at the far right.

The sailing rigs carried by steamers created great windage, and on balance probably contributed little to propulsion. No doubt they added something to the physical comfort of shipboard life by lengthening the moment of roll. Their primary function, however, was in the realm of psychic security and ticket sales. Passengers would have felt unduly imperiled venturing to sea without some sail to be used in the event of a breakdown, and passenger steamers did not wholly discard sail until twin engines and screws were introduced. In most cases the amount of sail actually carried was insufficient for much progress in any conditions short of a strong fair breeze.

The notorious conservatism of mariners (especially marine superintendents) was certainly an additional factor explaining the survival of sail on steamers. It would simply not have occurred to many seamen that there was any possibility of building a seagoing vessel that was without some vestiges of the network of masts, yards, and rigging that had always loomed overhead when one stood on the deck of a ship. Most steamship men, of course, came out of sail. The emotional need for tangible links with the past was perhaps partially satisfied by the fact that steamers were the last commercial vessels to be rigged with single topsails, and steamship sailors were the last merchant seamen to stow square sails in the traditional and obsolete manner with the clews hoisted to the bunt.

[9.5] Aboard the *Pavonia,* steaming to the eastward in the eighties. A number of first-class passengers have gathered for a group portrait on the boat deck—perhaps they are traveling together—but it is more likely that they are simply cooperating with the active photographer in their company, Mr. Nathaniel Stebbins, of Boston. The camera rests on the forecastle deck and is aimed aft toward the deck house. The officers standing on the flying bridge above are apparently far more conscious of the camera's presence than are the relaxed steerage passengers on the main deck, at the bottom of the picture. Weather cloths, called "dodgers," are rigged to protect the watch officers from the wind. Ironically, the main deck looks to be a better sheltered and more comfortable location than the first class's boat deck above.

The pleasant world of the deck is a world apart from the hot iron depths of the stokehold and the dark, dust-laden labyrinth of the coal bunkers. While the passengers revel in the fresh air, streaming firemen tend the roaring furnaces, skillfully spreading shovelfuls of coal across the almost white hot combustion. When cleaning fires, they bend into the searing heat, choked and half-roasted, drawing out fiercely hot clinkers. Meanwhile, coal passers, called "trimmers," aided only by the rays of a miner's safety lamp, crawl about the black bunkers, which, like an afterthought, occupy the odd and crooked crevices of the steamer's hull. They work continually, wary always of being buried under a suffocating avalanche. Danger, darkness, and sickening dust are their miserable lot.

Most of the men of the *Pavonia*'s "black gang" are probably Liverpool Irish, the lineal and spiritual descendants of the notoriously rough Atlantic packet crews of an earlier generation. Few are likely to die in bed.

[9.6] A group of the *Pavonia*'s officers, photographed at Boston in 1892. Standing, from left to right, are Hughes, fourth officer; Allsop, an engineer; Grindley, an engineer; Campbell, third engineer; Paynton, an engineer; and Kidley, third officer. Seated, from left, are Milliken, purser; Hatchwell, second officer; Cresser, first officer; Inman, chief officer; Foulds, chief engineer; and Coutts, second engineer. Kidley and Coutts make a charming couple.

To anyone who, like the writer, was in the habit of sailing on these ships, it was evident from the first that some one at the head of the [Cunard] company was an excellent judge of character. This was seen in the captains, engineers, and officers, and even in the stewards. Never was discipline more perfect or order more complete. Such men . . . were the very *créme de la créme* of the British mercantile service. Brave, bold, watchful, cautious, and stern, they were also, with perhaps one or two exceptions, accomplished gentlemen.—*Henry Fry, 1896* [24]

The growth of steam navigation precipitated a social revolution at sea of major proportions. On a sailing ship the master and the mates (primarily the chief mate) ruled with lordly power. They were concerned with all aspects of the vessel's management and were responsible for its very propulsion. The business of successfully sailing a windship about the waters of the planet demanded of officers a high order of skill, knowledge, and nerve, and the status and power of the positions were commensurate. The steam engine transferred the vital area of propulsion to the engineer, and in short order the chief engineer rose to a position only slightly below that occupied by the captain himself. Deck officers—to use engineers' jargon—became "bridge ornaments" at sea. In fact, the fast passages, quick turn-arounds, and great hold capacity of steamships introduced problems of cargo stowage, cargo handling, maintenance, and port affairs which sailing ship officers never dreamed of—but these were problems demanding the attentions of administrators, not sail carriers. Whereas in sail a good chief mate knew in detail the rigging and performance characteristics of his vessel, in steam the chief engineer was likely to know more about the structure and mechanical workings of the ship than all the deck officers and the master combined. The deck officers of a big liner, like the *Pavonia*, were men of indisputed ability, and enjoyed considerably more professional prestige than many of their brother officers, but the status enjoyed by a liner engineer was relatively even greater.[25]

[9.7] The big Cunarder *Servia* normally operated on the New York run, but she came to Boston in June 1896, to embark several hundred stalwarts of the Ancient & Honorable Artillery Company, and members of their families, bound for a European tour.

The departure of an ocean liner is always full of interest to the friends of the passengers. But the leaving of the *Servia* was a spectacular event. The huge . . . steamer . . . was surmounted by flags and a crowd of men in resplendent uniforms and women in bright dresses . . . Bells strike and a warning gun is fired. The friends . . . make a nervous rush for the gang-plank . . . Another gun is fired, and the after gang-plank is cast off.—*Boston Evening Transcript,* June 29, 1896

Were it not for the uniformed foppery of the Ancients in the foreground, I might suggest that the contrast on the flying bridge between the master's calculated seafaring appearance and the casual street clothes of the Boston pilot was a reflection of national styles. The small helm below, standing absurdly unprotected, was such a reflection. British seafaring opinion long held that the only proper way to stand a watch was to be out in the open. The *Servia* was a fast ship, and wheel watch on "Mount Misery" in the winter must have been a sobering experience. On British tramps an exposed steering station was wryly called a "West Hartlepool wheelhouse." Many writers have stated or implied that cruelty toward the sailor was a general characteristic of life aboard American sailing ships—it is interesting, therefore, to note that many of these "hell ships" were at least furnished with enclosed wheel houses.

One wonders whether the men standing on the bridge were deafened and scalded every time the siren blew, as it was mounted only several feet above their heads.

Despite these inconsiderations, the *Servia* was a highly advanced vessel in her youth. Built of steel in 1881, she was 515 feet long, powered by compound engines, and capable of nearly seventeen knots. Her launching marked the beginning of the dramatic improvement of the Cunard fleet in the eighties.

[9.8] The departing *Servia* is held against a fresh northerly breeze by four Boston Tow Boat Company tugs. The bow line has just been cast off from the shore and is being hauled in. Her old-fashioned stocked anchors must have been terrible nuisances to "cat" after they were used. The white tower at the break of the forecastle deck contains the starboard running light. When hard driven into the North Atlantic "purlers," the plumb-bowed Cunarders shipped so much water that the canvas bridge dodgers had to be furled lest the railings be damaged.

The indomitable Ancients were well provisioned for their seven-day sea epic. The *Transcript* reported that the *Servia* had loaded 11,000 lbs. of beef; 4000 lbs. of mutton; quantities of duck, fowl, chicken, broilers, pigeons, plover, squab, quail, partridge, prairie hens, geese, spring lamb, green turtle, lobster, ox tails, pigs heads, frog legs, roasting pigs, as well as proportionate supplies of numerous varieties of vegetables, fish, fruits, baked goods, and treats.

> What the Ancients will drink is a much more important matter . . . Most of the strong waters have been provided by the command itself. Colonel Hedges absolutely refuses to reveal to the vulgar gaze the quantity or kind of liquids which will wash the salt out of the throats of himself and his comrades. However . . . almost all the boxes going down into the steward's department of the *Servia* for the last two or three days have something inside of them which gurgles . . . The Cunard Co. has provided only a few sundries . . . 2740 bottles of wines, 930 bottles of spirits, 19,500 bottles of ale, porter, and beer, but these, of course, amount to nothing, and will probably be used only in case of shipwreck or other disaster.—*Boston Evening Transcript,* June 29, 1896

In awe, we can only wonder how many hungry, hard-case sailing vessels the Ancients observed from their sagging deck chairs; how many of our heroes were too seasick to do battle with the sixty pounds of cod tongues; and how crisply they marched onto the landing stage at Liverpool.

[9.9] A splendid view of a Leyland cargo liner, probably the *Istrian,* lying at East Boston. The photograph was probably taken in 1876, the year Leyland began its Liverpool-Boston service. The *Istrian* was built at Belfast in 1867, and—if this is she—admirably displays the characteristics of her type. She is as slender as she looks. With registered dimensions of 390′ × 37.2′ × 29′, she has a beam-to-length ratio of better than ten to one. The principal theory behind these proportions was the mistaken notion that a hull's resistance depended upon the wetted surface of its midship sections. Although some radical designers argued that with proper fairing of lines a hull of wider beam would create no greater resistance, the average shipowner was not interested in making expensive experiments. There was also some fear that a beamy vessel would prove too "stiff," or stable, in a seaway, resulting in excessive hull strains.[26]

The steamer's small deckhouse reflects unwise tonnage regulations which taxed enclosed deck space, and the open-deck tradition of sailing ships. Notice the after whaleback. Sails are bent; the rigging is set up with lanyards.

The photograph was taken from the Boston & Albany Railroad's Grand Junction grain elevator. Fast-loading American grain elevators suited steamer economics by allowing prompt turn-arounds. The major disadvantage of the method was that it made hand trimming of the grain in the wings and under the stringers impossible, due to the thick dust. Although it was understood that sailing ships had to be loaded with extreme care, steamers often put to sea with grain cargoes that would settle several feet, thus greatly increasing the chances of its shifting. Shifting elevator-loaded grain was probably responsible for the high steamer losses on the North Atlantic in the seventies, before more stringent loading procedures were instituted at the American grain ports.[27]

Looking beyond the steamer, toward the south-east, Jeffries' Point is to the left, Governor's Island is seen to the right, surmounted by Fort Winthrop. The long building beyond the ferry "above" the *Istrian*'s stack is the Boston, Revere Beach & Lynn Railroad's train shed. A "narrow guage" ferry is in the slip at the outer end of the wharf. Simpson's Dry Dock is hidden beyond the train shed. The vessel-in-frame at the end of the point is probably the ship *Sachem,* built in 1876 by Sampson (not Simpson). If it is not the *Sachem,* then it almost certainly is the bark *Great Surgeon,* built by D. D. Kelly in 1878 at approximately the same location. The *Istrian* was out of service for most of 1877 having her engine compounded.

[9.10] 1904. The handsome "four-masted" steel Leyland liner *Columbian* was built at Belfast by Harland & Wolff in 1890 for the Boston trade. She was powered by a triple expansion engine, and could carry 1,000 live cattle in addition to 7,000 tons of dead-weight cargo.[28] In 1904 Leyland Line steamers cleared Boston forty-four times for Liverpool, nineteen times for London, and twenty-six times for Manchester. They carried off a healthy portion of the 131,002 head of cattle, 87,616 sheep, 282 horses, and 563,961 beef quarters exported from Boston that year.[29]

The North American live cattle trade, centered at Boston, Montreal, and New York, was a big, brutal, and unnecessary business. It flourished long after mechanical refrigeration should have ended it entirely, owing, apparently, to the premium paid for domestically dressed meat on the British markets. With live American animals middlemen could realize the British farmer's profit, as well as their own. At its best the trade was cruel; at its worst it was horrible. The common practice was to force the tightly packed and seasick cattle to stand during the entire passage, since a downed animal allowed the penmates dangerous movement. During gales the frenzied cattle suffered from gorings, broken legs, thirst, and wholesale suffocation when hatches were battened.

The unfortunates who shipped as "cattle-handlers" were among the hardest working and lowest paid men on the North Atlantic. The positions were usually filled by single-trippers — often college students — desiring transportation to Britain. Many probably completed the trip in little better condition than the cattle.

A story is told of two college students who signed aboard a steamer as cattle-handlers in the early 1900s. One, an artist, was so unnerved by the conditions that he jumped overboard off Boston Light, to be picked up by a tug. No one on the steamer had witnessed his departure, and he was soon booking passage to England aboard a liner in order to appear as the star witness for the defense at the murder trial of his classmate.

The high mortality rates of the seventies and the eighties were reduced in later years by improved handling techniques and more stringent regulations. In 1895 losses of all cattle shipped from the United States to Great Britain were only 0.62 percent; losses of sheep were 2.6 percent. The losses of animals shipped from Boston were much lower, the mortality rate for cattle being one-quarter the general average, the rate for sheep being one-half the average.[30] No doubt Boston's superior record resulted from its nearness to Europe, its temperate climate, and the extensive cattle-handling experience of its railroad and steamship lines. The New York cattle trade, by contrast, included tramp steamers as well as some regular lines of notoriously brutal record.[31]

Leyland Line (Frederick Leyland & Company) was founded in 1873 as an outgrowth of the Bibby Line. Although Leyland maintained Bibby's Mediterranean service, the line's success was primarily founded upon the Boston–Liverpool cargo trade, which in the early seventies included only Warren Line and Cunard as half-hearted participants. After the death of founder Frederick Leyland in 1892 the firm became a limited company, and soon was closely associated with Furness Line. From 1896 to 1914 the London–Boston operations of both lines were largely joined in the separate Wilson's & Furness-Leyland Line. (In 1904 Wilson's & Furness-Leyland Line effected thirty-three sailings from Boston to London). Between 1895 and 1902 Leyland added eight single-class passenger-cargo liners to its fleet. In the early 1900s the company inaugurated services to New York, New Orleans, and the Caribbean; in 1901 Leyland's Atlantic operations were acquired by J. P. Morgan's giant International Mercantile Marine Company. Although the line retained its identity, it was one of the I.M.M. members destined to slowly wither away. An important factor in its decline was the loss of twenty out of forty-three ships during World War I.[32]

[9.11] On March 2, 1895, the "Furness Line" (Wilson's & Furness-Leyland Line, to be exact) steamer *Venetian,* outward bound from the Hoosac Tunnel Piers for London, drove hard aground on Slate Ledge, located off Governor's Island about one hundred feet outside the channel. Her pilot claimed that a buoy was out of position; that a fishing schooner had tacked under his bows, causing him to change course; and that he had been blinded by a snow squall. Since buoys were quite commonly dragged out of position by tows and could not be relied upon, his explanation was not sufficient to save the pilots from great embarrassment. When the tide fell the *Venetian* broke her back and was a total loss.

The 423-foot *Venetian* was built in 1881 on the Tyne for the Leyland Line. She was intended for the Boston–Liverpool cargo-cattle trade, and was fitted with a reefer compartment and large condensers for manufacturing fresh water for the livestock. She carried a crew of forty-nine. When she hit Slate Ledge she was carrying general merchandise, including shoes, machinery, Canadian whiskey, and flour; 16,000 bushels of wheat; 3000 quarters of beef; 845 sheep; and 645 head of cattle. Most of the animals were successfully lightered off and returned to the Fitchburg Railroad's big Watertown stockyards.

A tug and a lighter are pictured alongside the *Venetian.* Her hull is cracked to the deck, beneath the stack. Observe her minimal superstructure. To the right, the Lighthouse Establishment tender *Geranium* repositions wayward buoy # 8. The *Geranium* had checked the buoy's location only hours before the wreck.

Furness Line was founded in the seventies by the energetic Christopher Furness, of West Hartlepool. In 1882 Furness entered the London–Boston trade, succeeding the London firm of Adamson & Ronaldson. Although an attempted immigrant trade from Stockholm to Boston and New York failed, the line successfully operated services to many American and Canadian ports. The Wilson's & Furness-Leyland Line was basically the continuation of Furness's London–Boston service in cooperation with Leyland Line, and the continuation of the separate London–New York trade in cooperation with Wilson Line.[34]

[9.12] 1907. The Warren Line steamer *Sachem,* flying the firm's famous red and white "white diamond" houseflag at her main truck. The hoist of four flags from the jigger truck spell out the *Sachem's* personal signal letters, and indicate that this is a posed photograph. In 1907 Warren Line steamers departed Boston for Liverpool twenty-nine times.[35] In previous years Warren had frequently been the most active transatlantic line serving the port; in 1893 the line effected ninety-nine sailings, seven more than the combined Leyland and Cunard total.[36]

No line better represented Boston's strong and old commercial relations with Liverpool, as it was descended from the famous White Diamond Line of sailing packets established in 1844 by the Bostonian Enoch Train. In 1854 Train failed, to be succeeded immediately by the Boston firm of Warren & Thayer, which took over Train's sailing dates, houseflag, and certain of his ships. Frederick Thayer and George Warren had successively managed Train's Liverpool house. Warren & Thayer was succeeded after several years by George Warren & Company, of Liverpool, and by the outbreak of the Civil War most of Warren's vessels had acquired British registry. The threat of Confederate commerce raiders completed the process.[37]

In 1865 Warren began to supplement his sail service with occasional chartered steamships. In the mid-seventies the firm withdrew from sail, and purchased several steamers—coinciding with Leyland Line's entrance into the Boston–Liverpool cargo trade.

By 1879 the business was prosperous enough for the firm to order its first new steamers. Reflecting its packet line origins, the line continued to carry passengers in addition to freight. Through the eighties and early nineties much of the line's cargo business—the usual Boston trade in cattle, sheep, swine, beef, grain, provisions, apples, and so on [38]— was carried in chartered steamers belonging to the closely allied British & North Atlantic Steam Navigation Company, also of Liverpool.

The decline of Warren Line can likely be traced to the 1894 takeover of Dominion Line by the owners of British & North Atlantic. In 1896 Dominion inaugurated a Liverpool–Boston passenger service; by 1902 all of Warren's chartered British & North Atlantic vessels had been sold or were transferred to Dominion. In 1912 Furness (by that date called Furness, Withy & Company) acquired a controlling interest in Warren, and added the "white diamond" to its growing collection of houseflags.[39]

It is worthy of mention that Furness, Withy still operates the service as the "Furness-Warren Line," and that it is the only British transatlantic line which uses Boston as a terminal port. Two fine new freighters, the *Nova Scotia* and the *Newfoundland,* are employed, with sailings about every two weeks or twenty days to Halifax and Liverpool.

[9.13] The Allan Line's *Hibernian* was one of the earliest "spar deck" steamers on the North Atlantic. Built in 1861, she was lengthened in 1871, and extensively modernized in 1884. She is probably shown sometime in the late eighties, although she remained in service until 1901. The men on the foredeck are busy "catting" the anchor. Notice her bowsprit and figurehead.

The Allan Line was a Glasgow-based firm (with strong ties in Montreal) which was a pioneer in the United Kingdom-Canada steamship business, and contributed greatly to Canadian development. The line's principal winter ports were Halifax and Portland (where the ships connected with the Canadian Grand Trunk Railroad). Sporadic services to Boston occurred in the seventies.[40]

In the early eighties the North American grain and cattle trade was growing, while the costs of steel shipbuilding in Britain were reduced; accordingly, Allan Line built a number of big steamers, too many to be employed to Portland and Canada alone.[41] By 1891 the company was maintaining eight distinct services from Liverpool and Glasgow to various South and North American ports. At one point thirty-seven Allan steamers were operating on the North Atlantic.[42] Boston received a fortnightly service to Glasgow; at Boston, the Allan liners lay at the Hoosac Tunnel Docks, and, later, Mystic Pier One. Most of their inbound cargo was shipped in bond by rail to Canada.

In the nineties transatlantic shipping suffered from the general business depression, and there was a great surplus of tonnage. Rates fell drastically. Two of Allan Line's rivals, Dominion and Beaver Lines, experienced great difficulty—Beaver eventually went into liquidation. Allan Line survived in relative comfort, largely because of the keen management of the Allan family members, who acted as their own underwriters and personally managed the Glasgow, Liverpool, London, Quebec, Montreal, and Boston offices.[43]

[9.14] 1901. The Wilson Line's *Ohio* steams slowly out of Nantasket Roads. An ugly wooden "cattle shed" extends nearly her entire length. Wooden cattle sheds for deck loads were notoriously dangerous affairs. It was not unknown for steamers to lose shed, cattle, and all in winter gales, creating a maximum of suffering for all concerned. The *Ohio* flies the traditional British "pilot jack" from her fore truck — in this instance it signals the pilot schooner standing on the Boston Light station that there is a pilot aboard who wishes to be retrieved. Port of Boston people saw only the relatively pleasant end of the cattle trade.

I did not include this photograph because Wilson was any great power at Boston—Wilson was primarily involved in the Hull-New York and London-New York trades; in 1901 Wilson Line steamers cleared Boston for Hull nineteen times.[44] Rather, it is here because I am intrigued by vessels which are in their dotage and are surviving in an age changed from their own. The *Ohio* is not really so very old —she was built in 1881 as the Monarch Line's *Egyptian Monarch*—but steamer design had advanced greatly in the intervening decades. Old-style running light towers stand forward. The rigging on her fore and mainmast indicates that she was previously bark-rigged. The stains on her house, hull, and stack give her the appearance of a work-weary vessel. Undoubtedly the highly corrosive cattle urine caused relatively rapid deterioration of ships kept long in the trade. In 1904 she will be scrapped.

Aboard ship the cattle swayed in unison, and a loaded steamer was said to begin rolling while still in the harbor.

[9.15] February 1895. The British steamer *Barnstable,* of Middlesboro, lies at Long Wharf. She has just arrived, a week out of Port Antonio, Jamaica, with passengers and bananas. The bitter westerly wind which has covered her with ice still snaps at her flags. Icing conditions usually do not extend far offshore, and the *Barnstable* probably obtained most of her covering in Massachusetts Bay. Its weight has affected her stability, although the unloading of cargo from her starboard side may exaggerate her list. Banana steamers were loath to wait offshore for better conditions, since their cargoes were highly perishable. Bananas were endangered as much by the cold of the North Atlantic as they were by the heat of the tropics. Occasionally whole cargoes arrived spoiled and were taken to sea and dumped.

In 1871 Captain Lorenzo Baker, of Wellfleet, sailed the schooner *Telegraph* from Port Antonio to Long Wharf with the first large cargo of bananas landed at Boston. Baker was intrigued by the possibilities of the trade, although distant Boston was an illogical banana port and his Cape Cod neighbors ridiculed the "monkey food." Shipping bananas in sailing vessels was a highly speculative business, demanding skill and luck—under normal conditions bananas could be unsalable twenty days after harvesting. Initially, Captain Baker sailed bananas in the summer only, and spent winters fishing at home. In 1877, however, Baker moved to Port Antonio to actively encourage banana cultivation. The Boston end of the business was handled by Andrew Preston, a young produce merchant. In 1879 the Standard Steam Navigation Company, of Boston, in which Baker was a partner, introduced the first of two auxiliary steam schooners on the run.[45]

In 1885 Baker, Preston, and associates from the shipping company organized the Boston Fruit Company; formal incorporation was delayed until the end of a five-year trial period. By 1890 Boston Fruit was the most successful—although far from the largest—banana seller in the country. With the 1890 reorganization Baker became both president and tropical manager, while Preston remained as the Boston manager. In the early nineties the firm made modest incursions into the banana markets of New York, Philadelphia, and Baltimore. In 1894 Boston Fruit formed a key alliance with the legendary Minor Keith, a courageous little man from Brooklyn who had become the giant of Central American railroad builders and banana growers. By 1895 the tonnage of bananas entering the port of Boston was surpassed only at New Orleans and New York. In 1899 Boston Fruit became the controlling member of a confederation of twelve banana-growing and shipping companies called the United Fruit Company. Under the direction of Andrew Preston, United Fruit eventually became the largest tropical farm and shipping concern in the world.[46]

Boston Fruit began to charter modern steel steamers in 1888, and owned only one ship outright. When the *Barnstable* and her sister *Brookline* were leased in 1895 they were the premier vessels of the trade; they remained in service for a quarter-century. In 1896 they were joined by the *Beverly* and the *Belvidere,* which were slightly larger and could load 30,000 bunches. In 1903 United Fruit began to build refrigerated ships, and in several decades' time the company's Great White Fleet numbered over a hundred vessels.[47]

Bananas remained a fixture at Long Wharf up to the Second World War. Gilbert Payson described the situation at about the turn of the century:

The United Fruit Co. rented the whole south dock and bananas were everywhere . . .

When one of their big steamers came into the dock with a cargo of bananas, the wharf immediately became the busiest kind of place . . . The banana teamsters had little regard for each other, and none at all for non-banana traffic; so a husky director of traffic was very necessary, and the man who did it, Capt. Geo. M. Dix, Master Mariner, was one of the finest old fellows I ever met. Although a retired seacaptain he never swore, but everyone of the rough-necks on the Wharf respected and obeyed him.[48]

[9.16] 1905. The handsome White Star liner *Arabic* (laid down as Atlantic Transport Line's *Minnewaska*) is backed out of the Charles River by three tugs. White Star liners berthed at the Hoosac Tunnel Docks, Charlestown. Notice her separate small forward house supporting the bridge.

White Star Line (Oceanic Steam Navigation Company) was a Liverpool concern founded in the sixties as an amalgamation of the shipping interests of T. H. Ismay with Liverpool interests in the great Belfast shipbuilding firm of Harland & Wolff. The intention of the alliance was to enter the North Atlantic passenger trade, primarily in competition with Cunard, using advanced vessels of the company's own design and build.[49]

In 1902 White Star was acquired by the International Mercantile Marine Company, a giant American combine created by J. P. Morgan. The I.M.M. attempted to gain control of North Atlantic shipping, and owned or controlled White Star, Red Star, American Line, Leyland, Dominon, Atlantic Transport, and Holland-American Lines.

White Star was the I.M.M.'s prestige line and was expanded at the expense of lesser lines. White Star came to Boston in 1903, having been given Dominion Line's Liverpool-Boston and Mediterranean-Boston services, ships and all.[50]

[9.17 and 9.18] Two unusually good photographs of a big steamer underway. It is 1907, and the White Star liner *Republic* is making knots down the ship channel, bound for Liverpool. The pilot will leave by the pilot ladder, which will be lowered from the open forward side port. The *Republic* was built by Harland & Wolff in 1903 as the Dominion liner *Columbus*, but she was transferred to White Star before she entered service.

In 1907, 131,000 transatlantic passengers were carried by ships entering and clearing Boston—the overwhelming majority were arriving immigrants. Reflecting the rise in Italian immigration, White Star established services from the Mediterranean to Boston and New York. In 1907 White Star landed 21,555 steerage passengers from the Mediterranean at Boston.[51]

The *Republic*'s wireless antennas are seen suspended between her main, mizzen, and jigger masts. On January 23, 1909, while on a voyage from New York to Naples, the *Republic* was rammed by an Italian steamer and sent the first important radio call of distress. Five large liners responded, and a sister, the *Baltic,* received her people and took her in tow. She sank before making port, and, until eclipsed by the White Star liner *Titanic,* was the largest vessel ever lost at sea.[52]

[10] The Navy in the Port

The Boston Navy Yard at Charlestown was established in 1800. Its location at the confluence of the Mystic and the Charles rivers afforded deep-water launching sites with minimal ice problems. It was conveniently located to communities of shipbuilders and related mechanics.

In the pre-Civil War decades the Boston Navy Yard was one of the most complete and active naval complexes on the coast. It possessed a superior dry dock and likely the finest ropewalk in the nation. Shiphouses, launching ways, foundries, smitheries, machine shops, timber sheds and basins, spar sheds, a sail loft, a boat shop, a block shop, and other facilities were provided in the most adaquate manner.

The story of shipbuilding at the Navy Yard is similar to that of commercial shipbuilding at Boston. Although the business of wooden shipbuilding demanded highly skilled labor, capital and plant requirements were relatively modest, and in the era of wooden hulls the vessels of the fleet were constructed at the government's various navy yards. Among the many notable vessels built at Charlestown were the frigates *Hartford*, *Merrimac*, and *Princeton*, and the ships-of-the-line *Independence* and *Vermont*.

Post-Civil War iron and steel shipbuilding, by contrast, entailed complicated new technology, and necessitated vast expenditures for greatly enlarged facilities. Of the fourteen "first raters" carried on the Navy list in 1900 only one was built by a government yard (Norfolk), reflecting the government's failure to undertake the vast job of modernizing most of the navy yards, including Boston. Seven of the first raters were built at Philadelphia by William Cramp, two each were built by private shipbuilders at Chester, Newport News, and San Francisco. The only Boston Navy Yard-built vessels of any rate carried on the 1900 list were one militarily useless wooden steam frigate, one unserviceable wooden sailing frigate, and two wooden sailing ships-of-the-line, spending their last days serving as receiving ships at navy yards. All were retained more through force of habit than for any good reason.

During the Civil War over five thousand men were employed at the Navy Yard helping to build and maintain the vast and motley fleet which effected the great blockade of southern ports. Immediately after the war the yard followed the Navy into a remarkable period of corruption and inactivity. Usually employing about five hundred men, many of them politically connected, the facility spent years accomplishing virtually nothing at great expense. In 1874, in a rare display of initiative, the yard broke up the "74" *Virginia*, which had been laid down in 1818 and had stood on the stocks for over fifty years. In 1879 the commodore commanding the yard was called as a witness before a congressional investigating committee:

Q. Is it not sometimes the case that political influences thrust men on you who are not good workmen?

A. I can't say that they have been thrust on *me*, but I think it is very safe to say that political influence does put a good many men into the navy-yard who are not worth the money the Government pays them. . .

Q. How many men were employed . . . just preceding the election of 1874, on account of the election?

A. By reference to the records, I find that the number so employed, just preceding the election of November 4, 1874, was five hundred and eighty-six in construction department, and a few, about twenty-five, I think, in steam engineering department.[1]

Another witness, a private shipbuilder, marine contractor and surveyor, spoke more freely:

The laborers here don't do anything. I have seen so much of their idleness and inefficiency that I would not pay their board. . . They put in everything—old cripples that are not good for anything. That makes the Navy cost tremendously. It makes me crawl when I go about the yard and see the men loafing. They get hid up out of sight—a pack of loafers that calculate living on the navy yard . . .

Q. Is there a vessel in the yard that is worth anything to the Government?

A. Almost all you have got there are in the hospital, I should say, and hopeless cases. They are not what you require . . .

Q. Is there one of them you think could be put to sea?

A. Not one of them.[2]

Despite the investigation things did not improve immediately. Henry Hall reported in 1882 that four of the yard's six launching ways were occupied by "old style ships which will not be completed."[3] In the early 1900s the yard was redeveloped.

[10.1] A scene at the Boston Navy Yard, Charlestown, probably taken in 1852—thereby making this the oldest photograph (it is a daguerreotype) in the book. A sloop-of-war is being prepared for metaling in Dry Dock Number One, while a rigger tars the mizzen rigging. A sloop-of-war was a small ship-rigged warship carrying guns on her spar deck only. This particular vessel is almost certainly one of the five sloops which were built (one at Boston) in 1839. Being fast and stiff, they were popular vessels, and one of the five, the *Dale*, lasted until 1905.

The sloop's "channels"—the protrusions along the hull which provide a wider base of attachment for the shrouds—are divided by the gunports. The jib-boom is housed alongside the sharply steeved bowsprit. Notice the big foretop, and the ample proportions of her spars. As a general characteristic, small American naval vessels suffered from being over-sparred, over-gunned, and over-canvassed.[4]

Dry Dock Number One was begun in 1827 and completed in 1833. It was designed and constructed by the great Massachusetts engineer Loammi Baldwin. Built of Quincy granite, it was a notable engineering accomplishment and is still in use. The *Constitution* enjoyed first entrance.

[10.2] In 1863 the famed yacht *America* was assigned to duty as a "practice vessel" at the Naval Academy at Newport. She cruised in company with the sloop-of-war *Marion* (built at Boston in 1839), which was also being used for training. The two are pictured at anchor off the Boston Navy Yard, with the old "74" *Ohio* lying beyond. The granite buildings in the center background housed smitheries, a foundry, and machine shops. Three howitzers are mounted on the *America*'s deck. A cadet maintains boat watch astern. Rear Admiral E. H. Leutze, who served on the *America* as a cadet, described the cruise of the summer of '63 many years later:

I was only fifteen years old at the time . . . I remember a quartermaster named Sam Bowles, a middle-aged Gloucester fisherman, who was our coast pilot and really about the only one on board who could handle the *America* well, especially in a gale . . . . A large Number 4 was painted on the mainsail to make the vessel look like a New York Pilot Boat. We cruised on the coast of Maine, looking for a rebel privateer called the *Tacony* . . . .

We had a pretty rough time on the *America* as there were very poor accommodations and no toilet arrangements, and also suffered a good deal of seasickness, especially in a gale off Portland, Maine in which we had to lay to three days. We were all glad when our detail ended and we went back to the *Marion*, who was anything but comfortable herself, as she was very low between decks so that an average sized lad of fifteen could not stand anywhere near straight on the berth deck.[5]

Note the extreme rake of the *America*'s masts; her spindly topmasts; loose-footed, brailed-in foresail; and big forestaysail. The rake was primarily a matter of fashion. Although it did serve to increase the staying effect of the shrouds, in light air the sails would resist winging out. When sailing before a breeze the main boom could not be sheeted out far without fetching up on the rigging. The strain on the headstays was great. When the *America* was rebuilt after the war Donald McKay straightened her masts.

The 74-gun *Ohio* served as a receiving ship at Boston for many decades. Built at the New York Navy Yard, 1817–1820, in her youth she was probably the finest vessel of her rate in the world. She was handsome, a good seaboat, carried her allowances with ease, handled like a frigate, and was a favorite command.[6] She was sold out of the service at Boston in 1883.

[10.3] The screw frigate *Wabash,* serving as a receiving ship, probably in the late seventies. Across the river appear the steeple of Old North Church, the trees on Copp's Hill, and, at far right, the smokestack and round retention building of the large Boston Gas Light Company plant. The *Wabash* is moored outside of the timber basin dike at the Navy Yard. A white awning covers a protective wooden housing.

The *Wabash* was built at the Philadelphia Navy Yard in 1854–55, one of six generally similar vessels. She was equipped with a horizontal twin cylinder engine which was intended to serve as an auxiliary to her sail. As a class, the screw frigates were probably the finest naval vessels in the world, being designed and built at the height of American maritime industry. They were armed with the advanced Dahlgren guns, probably the most effective naval guns then in use, and made an immense contribution in the Civil War.[7]

The 1861 Confederate reconstruction of the screw frigate *Merrimac* into a steam-propelled, armored floating fortress marked the beginning of the monumental naval revolution which rendered the *Wabash* and her kind obsolete. Moving with characteristic deliberation, the Navy kept her at Boston as a receiving ship until about 1900.

Receiving ships were revered navy yard institutions, and no yard would be caught without one. They first originated as the result of eighteenth-century Royal Navy health reforms, and served as halfway stations where newly recruited men were checked for disease and vermin before joining the fleet. A proper late-nineteenth-century receiving ship, on the other hand, was a worthless floating relic which fronted as a dormitory for recruits and transient bluejackets, and provided never-ending repair work for navy yard employees.

Owing, probably, to the fact that one of my great-aunts married Commodore Horatio Bridge USN, my grandparents always cultivated the successive commandants of the First Naval District. I well recall a visit with my grandmother to Admiral and Mrs. Sampson at the Charlestown Navy Yard, in the fall of 1899, because the Admiral sent me on board the old receiving ship U.S.S. *Wabash,* to be measured by the naval tailor for a sailor suit, complete with bell-bottomed trousers.— *Samuel Eliot Morison* [8]

[10.4] A rowing cutter for a warship, probably newly built in the Navy Yard boat shops. The ox drover certainly looks dressed for command.

[10.5] A view of a portion of the interior of the Navy Yard's magnificent ropewalk. When the frigate *Constitution* was virtually rebuilt in Dry Dock Number One from 1927 to 1931 the ropewalk was still able to manufacture the ancient-style four stranded hemp shroud-laid cordage required for her standing rigging—occasionally navy yard conservatism is fortuitous.

[10.6] The "protected cruiser" *Boston* at Boston in 1889. White-gloved marines stand aft. The chains attached to the rudder are apparently for emergency steering.

After the Civil War the Navy sank to a deplorable state. Inordinately corrupt and lethargic, it became a standard of inefficiency. While European powers experimented with advanced warships of iron and steel mounting turreted rifled guns, the only new American construction for almost twenty years consisted of some worthless "coastal defense" monitors, Congress having reverted to one of its periodic revivals of Jeffersonian naval theory.

By 1882 the situation was so blatantly bad that something had to be done, and funds were begrudgingly appropriated for the construction of four modern vessels. The cruisers *Chicago, Atlanta*, and *Boston,* and the dispatch vessel *Dolphin* (really nothing more than a big yacht) eventually resulted. All were built by Roach, on the Delaware. Gone were the days when fleets came from the forests, and the construction of the new vessels overextended the nation's feeble steel shipbuilding and gun-founding resources. The vessels themselves were neither very advanced nor especially successful, but they marked the beginning of the modern Navy. They contributed to the expansion of industry which soon rendered the nation largely independent of European gun and armor manufacturers, and made the Spanish-American War possible.

The *Boston* was a member of Dewey's Pacific squadron and participated in the Battle of Manila Bay. She suffered the greatest damage of any American vessel in that action, receiving a shell which disrupted an ensign's stateroom. The war itself was a curious affair, initiated for a variety of reasons. For the big navy proponents, it proved to be a splendid exercise. Basking in the glow of victory immediately after the war, a naval historian expressed a common sentiment:

By the Civil War we wiped away the curse of human slavery, and disintegrating States were blended into one great nation. With all its horror the effect of that war upon our people was most beneficent. And through the war with Spain we have been reminded that blood is thicker than water, and we have learned that there can be no permanent peace on earth, and no substantial progress in real culture, until the one race that fully comprehends the meaning of Liberty and Justice is dominant beyond dispute.[9]

[10.7] August 1890. For a generation after the Civil War the Grand Army of the Republic constituted a powerful political force. Politicians were eager to entertain at G.A.R. happenings. In the summer of 1890 the National Encampment was held at Boston, and President Harrison arrived aboard the cruiser *Baltimore,* escorted by a sizable naval fleet. Here we see the "protected cruiser" *Atlanta* in the process of firing twenty-one salutes while the President is transported ashore for a day of speech making.

The bluejackets manning the yards will not fall like rows of dominoes because they are supported by lines rigged at waist height. Men, masts, yards, and sails all join in a tableau of ceremonial anachronism. The vessel supporting them is from another age.

[10.8] 1905. The armored cruiser *Maryland* was the first vessel to enter the Navy Yard's new 729-foot granite and concrete dry dock, one of the largest in the world. The addition of the dock greatly increased the yard's value as a repair facility for the fleet. Port of Boston interest groups had long lobbied in Washington for the construction of such a dock, capable of effecting emergency repairs on the largest commercial steamers calling at the port.

The protruding armor plating at the *Maryland*'s waterline shielded engines and boilers. This was supplemented by an arched interior deck which began well below the waterline and rose to cover the machinery. When enemy shells exploded in the exterior armor, the interior shield prevented any further penetration of fragments. Several American battleships built in the nineties, intended primarily to serve as coastal defenders, were fitted with armor belts of 18-inch thickness. The *Maryland*'s Krupp belt was 6 inches at its thickest point.[10]

A vessel of the *Maryland*'s class would normally carry a complement of 880 men. If the sailing navy was the navy of "wooden ships and iron men," the steam navy was composed of "steel ships and steel men." There were probably few more unpleasant locations on earth than in the fireroom, engine room, ammunition hoists, or gun turrets of a coal-burning warship operating under battle conditions in hot weather with compartments closed and the blowers shut down.

[10.9] 1907. The new armored cruiser *Tennessee,* built by Cramp on the Delaware, and the frigate *Constitution,* built at Boston in 1797. The smaller vessel to the left is probably the naval yacht *Scorpion.* Although as individuals the *Constitution* and the *Tennessee* reflect over a century of change, the switch from sail to steam in the Navy did not really get underway until the Civil War.

The *Constitution* was last under sail in the early eighties while serving as a training vessel. She then deteriorated for about fifteen years as a receiving ship, stationed for the most part at Portsmouth Navy Yard. Political pressure brought her back to Boston for her one hundredth birthday in 1897, and inspired substantial and vital repairs in 1906.[11]

The *Scorpion* was formerly the yacht *Sovereign.* Because of the charges of junketing which followed the construction of the dispatch steamer *Dolphin* in the eighties, no additional dispatch vessels were built. Therefore, when the Spanish War was declared, the government was forced to purchase a fleet of yachts at enormously inflated cost.[12] When the wireless made dispatch vessels obsolete the Navy changed their ratings to "fourth raters" or "patrol craft."

Despite their obvious dissimilarities, the *Tennessee* and the *Constitution* had much in common. When new, both were among the finest and most advanced warships in the world. And although one vessel was of steel and steam, and the other of wood and wind, many similar considerations entered into their designs. The design of naval vessels generally evolved separately from the development of merchant vessels, due to the very different service requirements and because they were the products of governmental bureaucracies.[13] An advanced naval vessel often reflected changes in administration quite as much as design innovations.

Despite instances of unnecessary conservatism, it must be recognized that naval vessel design was very difficult, entailing the satisfaction of many conflicting demands. The ideal warship must be fast, seaworthy, maneuverable, and—if sail—weatherly. She must carry her immense weight of guns as high as possible for fighting effectiveness. The characteristics of the guns had direct influence on hull design—some United States battleships built in the nineties, through oversight, were unable to bring their big guns to bear broadside without heeling to a degree which was detrimental to aiming.[14] The ship must have space for stores for a very large crew for a long period. Steamers required extensive bunker space. The *Constitution*'s wooden hull had to support a very heavy rig and a heavy armament, and had to be able to withstand the collisions and shot of battle. The *Tennessee* required a hull capable of supporting guns so powerful that the muzzle gases would splinter a deck; and armor capable of stopping a projectile fired by such a device. A warship must have stability, yet every additional foot of draft decreased her effectiveness in coastal waters. The characteristics of her hull motion greatly affected the accuracy of her fire power.

Given these and other requirements, shaped by a multitude of limitations prescribed by materials, tools, funds, tactics, politics, and so on, it is fair to say that successful vessels, like the *Constitution* and the *Tennessee,* represented sophisticated achievements by talented men. It is ironic in the extreme that throughout history man's weapons have represented the highest state of his technology.

[11] Recreation

Undoubtedly many persons have always enjoyed the sensations of swimming in the sea, floating on the sea, and walking and sitting by the sea. From the beginnings of society there have been aquatic communities whose people spend much of their lives in and on the water. But it is unlikely that there was ever a time previous to the western industrial revolution when large numbers of individuals not necessarily economically dependent on the sea could afford the time and expense of seaside recreation and boating.

Life in industrial America was unquestionably very hard for many classes of workers, involving long hours of hard labor under poor conditions for small wages. The work week was six days, and even in the later decades of the nineteenth century there were employers who considered the "vacation habit" an outgrowth of abnormal and distorted business practice. Mortality rates in big city immigrant slums were very high.

Nevertheless, the dark side of industrialism (combined, in this case, with the failures of Irish and European social practices) should not be overemphasized. The post-Civil War era saw the blooming of amusement parks, resort hotels, public bathing and other such sports, summer cottages, railroad and steamboat excursions, the great bicycle craze, and yachting. Clearly, everyone was not enslaved in a sweatshop. Nor did only the idle rich participate in recreational activities. Amusement parks and steamboat excursions were patronized by the public at large. The use of the automobile only partly explains the fact that today there is demand for only a

small portion of the steamer capacity once serving Nantasket Beach. In the eighties, daily summer train schedules in fine print covered nearly an entire page in the *Transcript*—many people were traveling about. Living conditions for a very considerable portion of the population were evidently more comfortable and relaxed than some social historians have indicated.

Before the Civil War, yachting and resorting of consequence was enjoyed by only a very few. In colonial and federalist times, prosperous merchants maintained gentlemen's farms in the country, combining the traditions of the English manor and the American frontier. In the twenties and the thirties, as Massachusetts turned inland for profit, seaside pleasure became the new fashion. The first local resort and yachting center was the peninsula of Nahant, which received its first summer cottages about 1820, and was host to the first open yacht race in 1845.[1] Not surprisingly, some of the most active early yachtsmen were young ex-China merchants who had turned to railroads for wealth, but who never lost their taste for salt water. Yachts were generally slightly refined versions of the standard local pilot and clipper fishing schooners.

Yachting grew rapidly after the Civil War. The first regular yacht club on Massachusetts Bay was the Boston Yacht Club, organized in 1865. The South Boston and Lynn clubs followed in 1868. The Eastern Yacht Club was formed in 1870 by a group of secessionists from the Boston Yacht Club, and it was very definitely a Boston organization, despite the location of its station at Marblehead.[2] Within the next fifteen years active clubs were established at Hull, Quincy, Dorchester, Charlestown, Chelsea, East Boston, and Winthrop.[3] It is probably accurate to say that Massachusetts Bay was the greatest yachting center in the country. Although Newport and New York undoubtedly claimed more big yachts, Massachusetts Bay was likely home to more owner-sailed yachts and sailing regattas.

Industrial profits supported the design and construction of increasingly sophisticated yachts. The latter decades of the century saw important advances in the development of small-vessel design, and were rewarding years for imaginative naval architects.

[11.1] Swimming, strolling, and bicycling at Marine Park, South Boston, probably in the mid-nineties. Yachts lie at moorings in Dorchester Bay. Thompson's Island is across the water. Swimming and yachting conditions in the harbor were greatly improved by the construction of the great sewer to Moon Island in the eighties. A mile and a half of sewer was tunneled under Dorchester Bay from Old Harbor Point to Squantum. At some points the sewer reached 150 feet beneath sea level and was cut through solid slate and conglomerate rock. Four giant steam pumps were installed at Old Harbor Point. Sewage from a reservoir at Moon Island was released on the ebb tide, and was carried eastward between Long Island and Rainsford Island.[4] In general, considering the state of technology and the size of the population, nineteenth-century public works were of a high order. Much of the sewage which has fouled the harbor and closed South Boston beaches in recent years has resulted from the overloading and disrepair of nineteenth-century sewers.

One of the chief factors in the summer pleasure of Boston is the immense three-decked steamer *Empire State*, of 1,700 tons, with a length of 320 feet, and 80 feet beam, and spacious and beautiful saloons, dining rooms, promenade-decks. . . a hull of almost imperishable live-oak, new boilers, a highly disciplined crew, and a vigilant and veteran captain. The hours of sailing are so arranged that people. . . may breakfast at home, take a sea-voyage of a hundred miles, and have supper at home, all on the same day. . . . So perfect is the discipline maintained on the boat that disturbances are unknown and many parties of ladies and children go out on the excursions without escort, quite secure against annoyance. . . On moonlight evenings the steamer leaves her pier at about eight o'clock, and runs out past Boston Light, and along the front of Nantasket Beach, which is at such times illuminated with bonfires, electric lights, and rockets, and presents a scene of wonderful brilliancy and Oriental weirdness.—*M. F. Sweetser, 1882.*[5]

The very existence of a big steamer employed solely by excursions was a sign of the times, reflecting the growth of the industrial middle class and mass recreation. The domesticated sea voyage and the scenes of Oriental weirdness both competed in the booming recreation industry.

This wonderful photograph, taken as the *Empire State* departed Newburyport, well displays the remarkable shape of the old paddler. The superstructure is practically suspended by a system of stays and spars; a hogging frame gives longitudinal strength to the supporting hull beneath. Sweetser's figure of an eighty-foot beam is perhaps the measurement at the widest point of the overhanging guards; the beam of the actual hull is half that. Built at New York in 1848, the steamer mounts her boilers outboard, forward of the paddle-wheels, in the old fashion intended to lessen the damage caused by explosions. Amidships, the black walking beam pumps steadily away, producing a satisfying frothy wake. The *Empire State* began life with the famous Fall River Line and remained in its employment for twenty-three years. While operating out of Boston she was enrolled at Taunton.

[11.3] The gentleman standing in the window is Captain J. Marshall Phillips, entrepreneur and mariner, master and part owner of the excursion steamer *Empire State*. Captain Phillips was a member of a famous Taunton shipping family which pioneered in the development of big coal schooners. He was managing owner of several notable schooners and master of the superb four-masters *King Philip* and *Pocahontas*.

He was a fine shipmaster of the old school, a driver of men and ships who gloried in racing the *King Philip* at fourteen knots all through a wild night, and yet he was never seen on his quarter-deck dressed other than in his best church-going rig with a diamond pin in his tie. It is said of him that he would stand by and watch a hawser run out through a chock rather than soil his hands to save it.[6]

Despite the quartermaster posed at the wheel, the *Empire State* is apparently lying fast to a wharf, probably during an excursion stopover. It appears that a departing passenger has left her handbag beneath the pilothouse steps. Captain Phillips ran a variety of trips, including tours to Ipswich Bay, Newburyport, the Isles of Shoals, Provincetown, and around Race Point down to Highland Light. Also popular were fishing trips to Stellwagen Bank.

[11.4] The *John Romer*'s passengers disembark at
Pemberton. A narrow gauge railway ran from Pemberton to Nantasket Beach. Once the desolate hunting grounds of the brooding Daniel Webster, the
beach area was rapidly developed after the Civil War
into a resort patronized by the new industrial middle class. According to an 1882 visitor's guide:

Here now appear the flying horses, goat-wagons, and
Punch-and-Judy shows of the city parks. . . there are
all manner of excursions *en masse,* armies of basket-
bearers from Worcester and Berkshire, and even from
farthest Albany; lodges and encampments of mystical
organizations, yearly dwindling societies of veterans of
the Secession War, cohorts of Hibernian merry-makers,
the banded populations of Weymouths and Bridge-
waters and Braintrees without number. . .

Although it has many natural advantages, the embryo
town does not yet compete with Newport or Oak Bluffs
in prosperity, or with Chautauqua or Old Orchard in
tranquil piestic fervors. As the Independent Corps of
Cadets have not been in the habit of encamping here,
the climate remains unspoiled.—*M. F. Sweetser* [7]

The reference to the parties from Albany is especially interesting, for in many respects the capital
of New York was spiritually located in New England. The more recent adoption of Old Orchard
Beach by French Canadians from Quebec is a similar phenomenon.

[11.5] About 1890. Members of a fishing party display some of their catch. The schooner is an old-time shore fisherman (notice the big single headsail) apparently chartered for the day by a social group.

[11.6] 1889. The pilot schooner *Hesper* is trimmed by the fisherman *Fredonia* in a match race. Designed by Edward Burgess, the fleet *Fredonia* was built for Commodore J. M. Forbes of the Eastern Yacht Club, and was used as a yacht this first season. The *Hesper* rarely experienced a defeat and was practically unsurpassable in a blow. On this occasion the pilots allowed that the recent addition of outside ballast had diminished her light air performance. The Commodore had little cause to crow, since he was using a borrowed mainsail from the America's Cup defender *Puritan,* while the *Hesper* made do with working sails.

In 1886 the story had been different. In April much of the Boston fishing fleet was tied up by a strike, and fisherman designer Thomas McManus persuaded Commodore Forbes to put up a cash award and a cup for a race open to working two-masted vessels. Other Bostonians added to the purse. The swift *Hesper* was allowed to compete only on the condition that she would be ineligible to receive the prize money. The course was a respectable one, from Boston Light to Davis Ledge (off Minot's) to Half Way Rock (off Beverly) and back to the start. The *Hesper* won the cup, beating the fastest of the nine fishermen entered by forty minutes.[8] The pilot's great fund of local knowledge, of course, was undoubtedly an important factor.

[11.7] Yachting at Hull, 1887. The sloop *Coyote*, center, displays a stylishly hogged bowsprit. The white sloop astern is clinker-built. The strangest sight to modern eyes is the spectacle of a small boat actually being propelled through the water by means of oars, the world being innocent of any knowledge of the outboard motor.

In 1884 the fleet of the Hull Yacht Club included sixty-four cats; sixty-three sloops; twenty-one cutters; twenty-four schooners; one yawl; and ten steamers. Seventy-five of the sailers were keel boats; eighty-nine had centerboards. The club was founded only four years before.[9] With the ebbing of Hull's social tide, however, the club soon went into a decline and was absorbed into the Boston Yacht Club.

[11.8] A sailing party, about 1890. While in many ways life in the Boston area is better today than it was during the nineteenth century, in respect to sailing in the harbor and adjacent waters we are much the poorer. If these gentlemen were to sail into Boston today, I suspect that the change which would shock them the most would be the terrific increase in the noise level, caused by the nearly ceaseless traffic of jets using Logan International Airport. This noise, more than the lack of shipping, the polluted water, the sprawl of the surrounding cities, the blighted ugliness of the islands, or the acrid pall from the burning refuse barges moored off Calf Island, has changed the character of the harbor. A day spent sailing in the jet age is likely to prove more depressing than refreshing. By contrast, Robert Carter described a yachting visit in the chartered fishing sloop *Helen*, of Swampscott, in 1858:

The wind was northwest, and the day fair and splendid, and not too warm, though it was very hot, I believe, on shore. As we passed Nahant Point we saw a great fleet of vessels coming out of Boston Harbor, spreading their white wings to fly to the uttermost ends of the earth. At 11, however, the wind shifted to the east, and the fog . . . came rolling rapidly in again, involving everything in its blinding embraces. . . As the fog gained on us and grew denser, we ran in, and came to anchor between the island called the Outer Brewster and the island on which Boston-light is situated. . .

Two schooners, yachts from Boston, were fishing and carousing near us, and a party from one of them was on shore on the lighthouse island, making chowder. . . about the middle of the afternoon, the fog clearing away, the Skipper suggested that cunners would be good for supper, and that they could be caught close to the rocky shores of the island near which we were anchored. The Professor and myself accordingly took the dory and pulled to the nearest point of rock, on which the surf was slightly breaking. . .

The sky and sea were so beautiful, and the air was so delicious, the surf broke so splendidly over the many rocky points and ledges which surrounded us, that I fear we prolonged our fishing beyond what the necessities of supper strictly required. . .

When we returned to the sloop, we found the seamen fast asleep. On awakening, and inspecting wind and tide, they decided that we must remain where we were for the present. Refreshing ourselves with lemonade concocted by the Skipper, into which he had put a little whiskey to correct the acidity, we gave ourselves up to the contemplation of a fleet of jellyfish which were sailing by in prodigious numbers. The Professor rigged a dip-net, and caught a variety of specimens.

I spent a good part of the afternoon in watching these sun-squalls, as the Skipper called them, which I think are the loveliest and the strangest of all the productions of the sea. . .

About 6 o'clock the Pilot took the dory and went ashore to the lighthouse in search of milk. As he was returning from this expedition a sudden commotion in the water near the sloop attracted my attention. . .

"A school of bluefish!" exclaimed the Professor excitedly. . . He shouted to the Pilot to make haste with the dory. . . As the dory approached he jumped in, nearly oversetting it in his hurry, and telling the Pilot to row in the direction where the bluefish last showed themselves, threw overboard the jig and rapidly unwound the line . . .

I went below to see what the books said of the animal. Shortly afterward, hearing the Professor alongside, I went on deck. A young man, a stranger, was sitting at the oars. The old Pilot, unable to get any milk at the lighthouse, had gone ashore on the Outer Brewster, on whose green surface he had espied a cow. A young fisherman, resident there, had volunteered to row the dory while the Professor trailed for bluefish, and the Professor, after catching two or three, had run alongside to give me a chance at the sport.[10]

[11.9] The racing catboats *Almira* and *Harbinger,* both of Boston, run down wind on a very damp Glorious Forth, 1890. From Ipswich Bay to Cape Charles the growth of popular yachting coincided with the vigorous heyday of the American catboat. The greatest concentrations of cats were probably in Massachusetts Bay, Cape Cod Bay, Nantucket Sound, Vineyard Sound, Buzzard's Bay, and Narragansett Bay, although many were sailed in the waters of Long Island and New Jersey. In the Massachusetts Bay area the largest fleets were maintained by Boston Harbor clubs.

Cats were built in many styles for many purposes. Yachting models were generally evolved from working cats. Most were under thirty feet, although some brutes used for fishing and party boating were forty feet on deck. In general, they possessed very shoal draft, a huge cockpit, and absolute simplicity of rig. Their large sail area and very wide beam (the *Harbinger* had a waterline length of 27.8 feet and a 13-foot beam) reflected deeply rooted American notions of vessel design which were largely determined by the characteristics of coastal waters.

Keenly competitive catboat racing on Massachusetts Bay was well established in the early seventies, the fastest boats generally being Herreshoff and Pierce products.

The *Harbinger* was designed and built by Hanley at Monument Beach, Cape Cod, in 1889, and was the sensation of that season. Her most dramatic victory was over two crack cutters in a heavy northeast blow—ideal cutter conditions. Thereafter, Hanley cats were the premier cats on the Bay. The *Almira,* completed by Hanley in 1890, was the *Harbinger*'s great rival.[11]

Although cats could be sailed by minimal crews, and were quick in stays, most were afflicted with fierce weather helms, especially when running before a quartering breeze. This vice became excessive when the size of the mainsail was increased for racing, and some racing cats were equipped with bowsprit and headsail to improve their balance. Racers gained speed at the expense of simplicity and ease of handling—two basic catboat virtues. Racing cats became an extreme and dead-ended species.

[11.10] The cat *Koorali,* of Beverly, displays most appealing proportions, marred only by the rather graceless headstay arrangement. Most cats were sailed without any stays, relying on the exaggerated depth from the partners to the step to support the mast. The combination of a beamy hull, possessing the stability of a church, with a heavy mast setting ample sail stepped right in the eyes of the vessel, created considerable torque. In a seaway with a stiff breeze many limber old cats wrinkled their deck canvas in a scandalous fashion.

The *Koorali* was one of the Hanley-built flyers which dominated Massachusetts Bay catboat racing in the nineties.

4208-Koorali

[11.11] I confess to an unreasonable partiality for catboats, and have included this additional catboat photograph despite the knowledge that I have ignored other important and interesting Massachusetts Bay yacht types (no doubt the most notable omission is that of the innovative Forty-Foot Class sloops sailing from Marblehead). But, such as I am, it would have grieved me more not to have presented this view of the cat *Mab,* of Quincy, so obviously a vessel of good intentions and high character. Although her topsides here display the scars of a long summer and a mild case of "nail sickness," the *Mab* enjoyed much status. In the early nineties she was the indisputed queen of the Massachusetts Bay 16-foot catboat class.[12] Her trim form reflected the concentrated rays of the genius of Nat Herreshoff, "the Wizard of Bristol." Despite her racing record she was modestly rigged, and no doubt was charitable toward women and children.

[11.12] Early 1900s. A sloop of the species that only a young boy or an old man could truly love, moored at the entrance of the Little Mystic Channel. No doubt she sails better on one tack than on the other. Presumably, if her people sailed in neckties, everyone sailed in neckties.

Across the channel, two small coasters—the outboard schooner is possibly the *Omaha* of Bucksport, Maine—lie alongside a big half-brig (or is she a bark?) of probable Mediterranean extraction. Hidden behind the sloop's mainsail, a barge discharges at a coal pocket. The big Boston & Maine grain elevator in the background was built in fruitless expectation of winter Canadian grain receipts.

[11.13] The keel schooner yacht *Gitana* was designed by D. J. Lawlor for William F. Weld in 1882. When new, her registered length was 102 feet; four years later she was lengthened to 114.6 feet overall. She is pictured before lengthening. The *Gitana* was the first local schooner rigged with her mainmast stepped nearly amidships, and with a shorter foremast. This soon became the accepted fashion for both yachts and fishermen.[13] The *Gitana* was no slouch, and accounted well for herself in competition.

The two hands on the jibboom are hanking on a jibtopsail. Most yacht professionals were either Scandinavians (usually Norwegian) or State of Mainers (often Deer Islanders). In this particular instance they are likely the latter. Often, yachts with foreign sailors carried a Maine captain. It was maintained in some quarters that a Norwegian crew was preferable to a Deer Island crew for racing, since the Islanders were inclined to regard a tactical command as a suggestion rather than as an order. It was a curious phenomenon that so many Deer Islanders found employment on yachts; many big yachts were admirable vessels, superbly managed, and sailed with great style, yet it was by no means a foregone conclusion that the Deer Island skipper of a miserable little kiln wood schooner would deign to wave as a neighbor who "went yachting" passed him in a lordly gold plater.

[11.14] Aboard the *Gitana,* 1884. Appreciate the elegant binnacle, the exquisite boats, the stalwart crew, the armament, and the last word in *art nouveau* skylights. The pulling boat on the starboard davits has ends which will not quit. No butts appear in the decking, except where it "nibs" into the center "king plank."

The *Gitana*'s original owner, William F. Weld, was a grandson of the great Boston merchant shipowner of the same name. Later, she was owned by Frank McQuesten, son of a successful coastwise lumber shipper. Appropriately, therefore, she was the product not only of a local designer and builder, but also of local shipping fortunes. She was cruised extensively by both owners, sailed often in the Caribbean, and made several voyages to the Mediterranean. In the early nineties she was considered to have sailed more miles than any other American yacht.[14]

[11.15] In the cabin of the *Gitana,* 1884. The only articles which appear to be strictly functional in design are the barometer and the spittoon. I fear that additional comments on my part would be superfluous, so I will point out only the renderings of Weld & Company's famous Flying Black Horse houseflag on the pillow on the settee, and on the lampshade to the left of the piano, to the right of the mantlepiece.

[11.16] 1892. The handsome keel schooner *Œnone* was designed by Edward Burgess for Colonel Hugh Cochrane, a Boston merchant. She was built by William McKie at East Boston in 1888. The Flying Black Horse houseflag snapping in the breeze at the main truck indicates that she is sailing under charter to a member of the Weld family. She is manned by a uniformed crew, and members of the party aft do not have to concern themselves with such matters as sweating-up halyards or horsing-in sheets. In the event that the mainsail requires reefing, a wiry sailor will crawl out to the precarious footropes at the end of the boom to tie the reef points, thereby preserving the Corinthians from danger or indignity. Except for the helmsman, the sailors stand forward of the mainmast until needed. It was common practice to hoist the long spinnaker pole alongside either the foremast or (as here) the mainmast when it was not in use.

[11.17] 1887. The America's Cup defender *Volunteer,* of Boston, gets her anchor in Dorchester Bay for a trial sail. She was a rush job from her very conception, and true to the spirit, riggers are still at work bending her mainsail. A keel-centerboarder, she set nearly 9,300 square feet of canvas. From her first sail forth she was a wonderful success, and, under Captain Henry Haff, handily defeated the challenger *Thistle.* She went on to enjoy an active life, spent mostly as a schooner-rigged cruising yacht. This was a period of remarkable advances in naval architecture, and racing yachts were quickly outclassed by newer boats. While she was campaigning, the *Volunteer* was the pride of New England.

In the background, two three-masted coasting schooners lie at anchor, with sail set, awaiting the tide.

[11.18] 1890. The steam yacht *Corona* lies off the Atlantic Works, East Boston, The bulky gentleman sitting in the wicker chair on the fantail is likely Mr. E. C. Taft, the owner. Steam yachts came under steam vessel inspection statutes, and were required to be manned by a licensed engineer and pilot. In fact, however, licenses were issued for the operation of yachts under one hundred tons with a minimum of examination.[15]

A comparison of the profile of the *Corona* with that of the plumb-stemmed yacht lying beyond her stern illustrates something of the variety of steam yacht design. With no common heritage to fall back on, steamers tended to resemble sailing yachts, naval craft, or commercial vessels. Notice the *Corona*'s ridiculous topmasts, and the bowsprit complete with dolphin striker. No doubt adding to the confusion were the conflicting desires of owners, many of whom were men of recently acquired wealth and taste casting their monies into the great waters for the very first time. Professional crews were a great boon to such yachtsmen.

[11.19] This seemed a suitably pleasant and civilized scene with which to conclude. It was taken about 1890 aboard Frank McQuesten's sloop *Thelma,* sailing off the North Shore. The old gentleman with his knees tucked up is father George McQuesten, Boston lumber shipper and schooner owner. The other party members are likely business associates. A paid hand, probably Norwegian, steers. No apologies are due for the fact that the *Thelma* sailed out of Marblehead, since Marblehead had become the most important center of "Boston" yachting.

Appendices　　Notes　　Index

[Appendix I] Brief Remarks Concerning Several
of the Photographers

Albert S. Southworth and Josiah T. Hawes, partners, were pioneer American photographers. Both men were inspired to enter the infant profession by the excitement surrounding the discovery of the daguerreotype process. Southworth, born a Vermonter, opened a studio in Boston in 1841. Hawes, born in West Virginia and a carpenter by trade, joined him in 1844. Southworth left the business in 1861; Hawes continued into the seventies. The daguerreotypes included in this collection were likely taken by Hawes, who was apparently the more active and imaginative photographer.[1] The largest collection of Southworth & Hawes plates is held by the Metropolitan Museum of Art, New York. Smaller lots are held by the Museum of Modern Art, New York; Museum of Fine Arts, Boston; Mr. Richard Parker, Marblehead, Massachusetts; George Eastman House, Rochester, New York, and Mr. Richard Holman, Holman's Print Shop, Boston.

Nathaniel L. Stebbins was Boston's foremost marine photographer. Born in Meadville, Pennsylvania, in 1847, he became interested in photography in 1882, and soon after entered the profession at Boston. He was always keenly interested in all things maritime. His photographs display great skill, artistry, and fond dedication—he obviously was a man in love with his work. After Stebbins' death in 1922 his collection of over 25,000 negatives passed to an associate, Mr. E. U. Gleason. After Mr. Gleason's death in 1928 the vast majority of the plates were

tragically sold for old glass. Many were carefully peeled for use as window panes. None would have survived but for the quick action of Mr. William S. Appleton, founder of the Society for the Preservation of New England Antiquities, Boston, who rescued over five thousand.[2] It is a chilling experience to thumb through Stebbins' carefully kept photo logs, now held by the Society, and read the descriptions of thousands upon thousands of needlessly destroyed photographs. A smaller lot of Stebbins photographs is held by the Peabody Museum, Salem. Some Stebbins plates may also be included in the collection of the Mariners Museum, Newport News.

Thomas A. Luke was a talented amateur. Oddly, all of his marine photographs appear to have been taken within a relatively short period in the midnineties. At this time he was living at Ashby, Massachusetts, and worked as a mechanic at Fitchburg. He took his photographs on weekends and during vacations. Most of his marine photographs were taken at New York or on the West Coast, and the several Boston scenes included in this collection are barely representative of his notable work.[3] Luke's marine plates are held by the Peabody Museum of Salem.

I wish that I knew more about Baldwin Coolidge since his photographs add much to this collection. Coolidge was apparently a Boston-area civil engineer and amateur photographer who, at some point, became a professional photographer. Although his marine photographs are of great interest and high quality, they constitute a minor portion of his surviving work. In addition to local views, Coolidge photographed a great number of early painted portraits. Most of his marine photographs appear to have been taken in the mid-eighties. Coolidge's plates are held by the Society for the Preservation of New England Antiquities, Boston.

Henry G. Peabody was one of the outstanding pioneer American photographers. Peabody graduated from Dartmouth College in 1876 and then worked in and around Boston as a view and marine photographer. He was employed by the Boston & Maine Railroad as their official photographer and was provided with a specially fitted photographic car. He ranged the New England coast recording the great pre-income tax era of American yachting and published several volumes of fine yachting studies. After his wife's untimely death, Peabody and his only daughter moved to Pasadena, California, where he became a popular stereopticon lecturer. Peabody was selected by the great western photographer William Henry Jackson to produce "outdoor" negatives for the famous Detroit Publishing Company, the largest post card manufacturer in the United States (the remarkable harbor panorama presented in Chapter 2 was produced as a large folding post card). Shortly thereafter Peabody leased the concession at the Grand Canyon to photograph tourists and the canyon. He is best remembered by many for his striking canyon panoramas.[4]

The fine photographs contributed by Mrs. Paul Gring (excepting several taken by Stebbins) were the work of one of her uncles, either George or Frederick McQuesten. Mrs. Gring's grandfather was George B. McQuesten, a prominent Boston lumber shipper.

Only one photograph by Richard Hildebrand is included in this book; nevertheless, I wish to sketch his story, as many of his photographs have been included in museum collections and published in books without proper acknowledgment. Hildebrand photographed ships at Boston from 1908 through March 1960. He was employed by an Atlantic Avenue plumbing and heating supply concern, and spent his lunch hours taking photographs on the waterfront. On Sundays he and his twin brother religiously walked from Castle Island to Chelsea Creek recording ships in the port. Steamers were his main interest; Norwegian steamers were his passion. Saturdays were spent in the Public Library with the Lloyd's Register, copying ships' data ever so neatly on cards to be filed with the plates. In total, Hildebrand took nearly 15,000 negatives; apparently only half have survived, and these have been scattered among various museums and private collections (a number are included in the Alan Dietch Collection now held by the Peabody Museum).[5]

[Appendix II] Sources of Photographs

2.1 Baldwin Coolidge; Society for the Preservation of New England Antiquities (hereafter cited as SPNEA), Boston, plate 1159B.

2.2 SPNEA, copy neg. 7716B.

2.3 Baldwin Coolidge; SPNEA, plate 468A.

2.4 Bostonian Society, Old State House, copy neg. 40.

2.5 Mariners Museum, Newport News, Va., Eldredge Collection.

2.6 Mariners Museum, Eldredge Collection.

2.7 Peabody Museum, Salem, Mass., copy neg. 17455.

2.8 Stereo view; Peabody Museum, copy neg. 17456.

2.9 Peabody Museum, copy neg. 17584.

2.10 Stereo view; SPNEA, copy neg. 7793B.

2.11 Bostonian Society, neg. 1088.

2.12 Nathaniel Stebbins; SPNEA, copy neg. 4534.

2.13 Stereo view; SPNEA, copy neg. 7726B.

2.14 Strawbery Banke, Inc., Portsmouth, N. H., Patch Collection, plate 25.

2.15 SPNEA, copy neg. 7674B.

2.16 Capt. W. J. L. Parker, USCG (Ret.).

2.17 Peabody Museum, copy neg. 10083.

2.18 Nathaniel Stebbins; SPNEA, plate 20945.

2.19 Henry G. Peabody; Library of Congress, Washington, plate LC–D4–15517 left.

2.20 Henry G. Peabody; Library of Congress, LC–D4–15516 left, center, and right.

3.1 Daguerreotype by Southworth & Hawes; Mr. Richard Parker, Marblehead, Mass., and Mr. Beaumont Newhall, Rochester, N.Y.

3.2 Daguerreotype by Southworth & Hawes; Mr. Richard Parker and Mr. Beaumont Newhall.

3.3 J. W. Black; Peabody Museum, Salem, Mass., neg. 2564.

3.4 Peabody Museum, copy neg. 17588.

3.5 Capt. W. J. L. Parker, USCG (Ret.).

3.6 Nathaniel Stebbins; Society for the Preservation of New England Antiquities, Boston, copy neg. 7679B.

3.7 Mrs. Paul Gring, Cambridge, Mass., and Capt. F. E. Bowker, Mystic, Ct.

3.8 Mrs. Paul Gring.

3.9 Peabody Museum, copy neg. 3894.

3.10 Baldwin Coolidge; Hart Nautical Museum, M.I.T., Cambridge, Mass.

3.11 Hart Nautical Museum.

3.12 T. E. Marr; Peabody Museum, neg. 8641.

3.13 T. E. Marr; Peabody Museum, neg. 8640.

3.14 Nathaniel Stebbins; SPNEA, copy neg. 7688B.

3.15 Quincy Historical Society, and Mr. Hobart Holly.

3.16 Mrs. Paul Gring and Capt. F. E. Bowker.

3.17 Baldwin Coolidge; SPNEA, plate 1200B.

3.18 Stereo view; American Antiquarian Society, Worcester, Mass.

3.19 Nathaniel Stebbins; SPNEA, copy neg. 7697B.

3.20 Baldwin Coolidge; SPNEA, plate 127A.

3.21 Stereo view; SPNEA, copy neg. 7725B.

3.22 Probably Henry G. Peabody; Library of Congress, Washington, D.C., plate 04933, Detroit Publishing Collection.

3.23 Nathaniel Stebbins; SPNEA, 15988.

3.24 Peabody Museum, copy neg. 17576.

4.1 Nathaniel Stebbins; Society for the Preservation of New England Antiquities, Boston, copy neg. 7729B.

4.2 Baldwin Coolidge; SPNEA, plate 38C.

4.3 Baldwin Coolidge; SPNEA, plate 42C.

4.4 Nathaniel Stebbins; SPNEA, plate 8748.

4.5 Nathaniel Stebbins; SPNEA, copy neg. 3883.

4.6 Mr. Thomas Lampee, Brookline, Mass., and Mr. Robert Lampee, Tiburon, Calif.

4.7 Nathaniel Stebbins; Peabody Museum, Salem, Mass., plate 2361.
4.8 Nathaniel Stebbins; SPNEA, copy neg. 102.
4.9 Nathaniel Stebbins; SPNEA, plate 3628.
4.10 The Boston Pilots
4.11 Mr. Thomas Lampee, Mr. Robert Lampee.
4.12 Mr. Thomas Lampee, Mr. Robert Lampee.
4.13 Dr. F. Damon; Smithsonian Institution, Washington, D.C., neg. 56913.
4.14 Nathaniel Stebbins; SPNEA, copy neg. 7690B.
4.15 Nathaniel Stebbins; Peabody Museum, copy neg. 17573.
4.16 Nathaniel Stebbins; SPNEA, plate 17953.
4.17 Nathaniel Stebbins; SPNEA, copy neg. 7710B.
4.18 Towing receipt; W. H. Bunting.
4.19 Nathaniel Stebbins; SPNEA, copy neg. 120.
4.20 Peabody Museum, neg. 11626.
4.21 Mrs. Paul Gring, Cambridge, Mass.
4.22 Nathaniel Stebbins; SPNEA, plate 18655.
4.23 Peabody Museum, copy neg. 17575.
4.24 Nathaniel Stebbins; SPNEA, plate 18761.
4.25 Boston Public Library, copy neg. B9135.
4.26 Halliday; SPNEA, plate H1142.
4.27 James Bliss & Co., Dedham, Mass.

5.1 Baldwin Coolidge; Society for the Preservation of New England Antiquities, Boston, plate 557B.
5.2 Nathaniel Stebbins; SPNEA, plate 17929.
5.3 A. Acores; Peabody Museum, Salem, Mass., neg. 10051.
5.4 Smithsonian Institution, Washington, D.C., neg. 44790.
5.5 Baldwin Coolidge; SPNEA, plate 193A.
5.6 Probably W. K. Watkins; SPNEA, copy neg. 7699B.
5.7 Mrs. Paul Gring, Cambridge, Mass.
5.8 A. Acores; Peabody Museum, neg. 9854.
5.9 Smithsonian Institution, neg. 44790E.
5.10 Mrs. Paul Gring.
5.11 Baldwin Coolidge; SPNEA, plate 185A.
5.12 Baldwin Coolidge; SPNEA, plate 166A.
5.13 Baldwin Coolidge; SPNEA, plate 556B.
5.14 Baldwin Coolidge; SPNEA, plate 1186B.
5.15 Nathaniel Stebbins; SPNEA, plate 1551.
5.16 Nathaniel Stebbins; SPNEA, plate 13969.
5.17 Nathaniel Stebbins; SPNEA, copy neg. 7730B.
5.18 Nathaniel Stebbins; SPNEA, plate 19062.
5.19 Nathaniel Stebbins; SPNEA, plate 23188.
5.20 Mrs. Paul Gring, Cambridge, Mass., and Capt. F. E. Bowker, Mystic, Ct.
5.21 A. Acores; Peabody Museum, neg. 10025.

6.1 Bostonian Society, Old State House, neg. 1575.
6.2 Nathaniel Stebbins; Peabody Museum, Salem, Mass., copy neg. 7295.
6.3 Nathaniel Stebbins; Society for the Preservation of New England Antiquities, Boston, copy neg. 7694B.
6.4 Nathaniel Stebbins; SPNEA, plate 15614.
6.5 Baldwin Coolidge; SPNEA, plate 224B.
6.6 Baldwin Coolidge; SPNEA, copy neg. 7715B.
6.7 Peabody Museum, neg. 13316.
6.8 Probably Willard Jackson; Peabody Museum, plate 321.
6.9 Baldwin Coolidge; SPNEA, plate 226B.
6.10 Mrs. Paul Gring, Cambridge, Mass.
6.11 Mrs. Paul Gring.
6.12 Nathaniel Stebbins; Peabody Museum, plate 2349.
6.13 Mrs. Paul Gring.
6.14 Mrs. Paul Gring.
6.15 Mrs. Paul Gring.
6.16 Mrs. Paul Gring.
6.17 Mrs. Paul Gring.
6.18 Baldwin Coolidge; SPNEA, plate 1183.
6.19 Baldwin Coolidge; SPNEA, plate 1184B.
6.20 Nathaniel Stebbins; SPNEA, plate 154.
6.21 Nathaniel Stebbins; SPNEA, copy neg. 111.
6.22 Nathaniel Stebbins; SPNEA, plate 2916.
6.23 Nathaniel Stebbins; Peabody Museum, plate 2347.
6.24 Nathaniel Stebbins; SPNEA, plate 4161.
6.25 Baldwin Coolidge; SPNEA, copy neg. 7712B.
6.26 Capt. W. J. L. Parker, USCG (Ret.).
6.27 Capt. W. J. L. Parker, USCG (Ret.).
6.28 SPNEA, copy neg. 7711B.
6.29 Thomas Luke; Peabody Museum, plate 4872.
6.30 Nathaniel Stebbins; SPNEA, plate 11695.
6.31 Richard E. Hildebrand; Mr. Frank W. Kelly, South Boston.
6.32 Nathaniel Stebbins; SPNEA, plate 14468.
6.33 Nathaniel Stebbins; SPNEA, plate 18147.
6.34 Nathaniel Stebbins; SPNEA, plate 18169.
6.35 Nathaniel Stebbins; SPNEA, plate 19116.

7.1 Nathaniel Stebbins; Society for the Preservation of New England Antiquities, Boston, plate 3220.
7.2 Nathaniel Stebbins; SPNEA, plate 4972.
7.3 Nathaniel Stebbins; SPNEA, plate 17218.
7.4 R. Loren Graham, Swampscott, Mass.
7.5 Leslie R. Jones; *Boston Herald Traveler*
7.6 Nathaniel Stebbins; SPNEA, copy neg. 13688A.
7.7 Nathaniel Stebbins; SPNEA, copy neg. 13927A.
7.8 Nathaniel Stebbins; SPNEA, copy neg. 13928A.
7.9 Nathaniel Stebbins; SPNEA, copy neg. 7731B.

7.10 Stereo view; San Francisco Maritime Museum, Weinstein Collection, I12.19705.
7.11 Stereo view; SPNEA, neg. 7724B.
7.12 Nathaniel Stebbins; SPNEA, copy neg. 4433A.
7.13 Nathaniel Stebbins; SPNEA, plate 754.
7.14 Nathaniel Stebbins; SPNEA, plate 4232.
7.15 Nathaniel Stebbins; SPNEA, plate 18715.
7.16 Josiah Hawes; Mr. Richard Holman, Holman's Print Shop, Boston.
7.17 Nathaniel Stebbins; SPNEA, plate 19071.
7.18 Baldwin Coolidge; SPNEA, plate 1158B.
7.19 Nathaniel Stebbins; SPNEA, plate 6963.
7.20 Nathaniel Stebbins; SPNEA, copy neg. 13854.
7.21 Nathaniel Stebbins; SPNEA, copy neg. 7734B.
7.22 Nathaniel Stebbins; SPNEA, plate 3205.
7.23 Nathaniel Stebbins; SPNEA, plate 13980.
7.24 Nathaniel Stebbins; SPNEA, plate 18722.

8.1 Bostonian Society, Old State House, copy neg. 1031.
8.2 Joseph G. Minot; Peabody Museum, Salem, copy neg. 17454.
8.3 Josiah Hawes; Mr. Richard Holman, Holman's Print Shop, Boston.
8.4 Nathaniel Stebbins; Society for the Preservation of New England Antiquities, Boston, plate 819.
8.5 Nathaniel Stebbins; Peabody Museum, plate 7417.
8.6 Nathaniel Stebbins; SPNEA, plate 1292.
8.7 Nathaniel Stebbins; Peabody Museum, copy neg. 17248.
8.8 Baldwin Coolidge; SPNEA, plate 195A.
8.9 Peabody Museum, neg. 14098.
8.10 Nathaniel Stebbins; SPNEA, plate 2160.
8.11 Nathaniel Stebbins; SPNEA, copy neg. 7732B.
8.12 Nathaniel Stebbins; Peabody Museum, plate 7394.
8.13 Thomas Luke; Peabody Museum, plate 4632.
8.14 Baldwin Coolidge; SPNEA, plate 189A.
8.15 Thomas Luke; Peabody Museum, plate 4649.
8.16 Henry G. Peabody; Peabody Museum, plate 6234.
8.17 Peabody Museum, neg. 6826.
8.18 Mr. Andrew Nesdall, Waban, Mass.
8.19 Mr. Andrew Nesdall.
8.20 Halliday; SPNEA, plate H1208A.
8.21 Thomas Luke; Peabody Museum, plate 4552.
8.22 Nathaniel Stebbins; Peabody Museum, plate 2313.
8.23 Nathaniel Stebbins; Peabody Museum, plate 7338.
8.24 Henry G. Peabody; Peabody Museum, plate 6161.
8.25 Henry G. Peabody; Peabody Museum, plate 6216.
8.26 Nathaniel Stebbins; Peabody Museum, plate 7307.
8.27 Nathaniel Stebbins; Peabody Museum, plate 7372.
8.28 Nathaniel Stebbins; Peabody Museum, plate 7440.

9.1 Daguerreotype by Southworth & Hawes; Mr. Richard Parker, Marblehead, Mass., and Mr. Beaumont Newhall, Rochester, N.Y.
9.2 Peabody Museum, Salem, Mass., copy neg. 1784.
9.3 Nathaniel Stebbins; Society for the Preservation of New England Antiquities, Boston, plate 779.
9.4 Stereo view; Peabody Museum, copy neg. 17587.
9.5 Nathaniel Stebbins; SPNEA, copy neg. 7795B.
9.6 Nathaniel Stebbins; Peabody Museum, neg. 12755.
9.7 Nathaniel Stebbins; Peabody Museum, copy neg. 17574.
9.8 Nathaniel Stebbins; SPNEA, copy neg. 7733B.
9.9 Peabody Museum, neg. 11722.
9.10 Nathaniel Stebbins; SPNEA, plate 15715.
9.11 Nathaniel Stebbins; SPNEA, copy neg. 7692B.
9.12 Nathaniel Stebbins; SPNEA, plate 17954.
9.13 Probably Nathaniel Stebbins; Peabody Museum, neg. 9089.
9.14 Nathaniel Stebbins; SPNEA, plate 12441.
9.15 Nathaniel Stebbins; SPNEA, plate 5334.
9.16 Nathaniel Stebbins; SPNEA, plate 16094.
9.17 Nathaniel Stebbins; SPNEA, plate 17974.
9.18 Nathaniel Stebbins; SPNEA, plate 17973.

10.1 Daguerreotype by Southworth and Hawes; George Eastman House, Rochester, N.Y., neg. 5660.
10.2 Peabody Museum, Salem, Mass., copy neg. 6238.
10.3 Peabody Museum, neg. 16995.
10.4 Stereo view; Society for the Preservation of New England Antiquities, Boston, copy neg. 7607B.
10.5 Stereo view; SPNEA, copy neg. 7723B.
10.6 Nathaniel Stebbins; SPNEA, plate 2797.
10.7 Nathaniel Stebbins; SPNEA, plate 3192.
10.8 Probably Henry G. Peabody; Library of Congress, Washington, Detroit Publishing Collection, plate 70157/22187.
10.9 Nathaniel Stebbins; SPNEA, plate 18143.

11.1 Halliday; Society for the Preservation of New England Antiquities, Boston, plate H1180B.
11.2 Peabody Museum, Salem, copy neg. 9108.
11.3 SPNEA, copy neg. 7709B.
11.4 Stereo view; SPNEA, copy neg. 7720B.
11.5 Mrs. Paul Gring, Cambridge, Mass.

11.6 Nathaniel Stebbins; SPNEA, copy neg. 7693B.

11.7 Nathaniel Stebbins; SPNEA, copy neg. 7685B.

11.8 Mrs. Paul Gring.

11.9 Nathaniel Stebbins; SPNEA, copy neg. 7689B.

11.10 Nathaniel Stebbins; SPNEA, copy neg. 7794B.

11.11 W. B. Jackson; Library of Congress, Washington, plate 70157/5180.

11.12 Edward Spaulding; Mr. Andrew Nesdall, Waban, Mass./Peabody Museum, neg. 11995.

11.13 Baldwin Coolidge; SPNEA, plate 1188B.

11.14 Nathaniel Stebbins; Mrs. Paul Gring.

11.15 Nathaniel Stebbins; Mrs. Paul Gring.

11.16 Nathaniel Stebbins; SPNEA, plate 4122.

11.17 Probably Henry G. Peabody; Library of Congress, plate 70157/4935.

11.18 Nathaniel Stebbins; SPNEA, copy neg. 7696B.

11.19 Mrs. Paul Gring.

Notes

This book has been annotated as a convenience for readers who wish to pursue topics to greater depth, and as a mark of my appreciation for the efforts of those writers before me whose careful notes have helped me so very much. Nevertheless, the notes in this book are by no means complete, and in many instances the recorded source is only the principal source among several used to construct a passage or page.

SOME PRELIMINARY CONSIDERATIONS

1. Thomas Morton (C. F. Adams, ed.) *The New English Canaan of Thomas Morton* (Boston, The Prince Society, 1883), p. 209.

CHAPTER 1: A SHORT HISTORY OF THE PORT OF BOSTON

1. Benjamin A. Gould, *Boston Harbor* (Boston, City Council, 1863), 6.

2. Samuel Eliot Morison, *The Maritime History of Massachusetts, 1783–1860* (Boston, Houghton Mifflin, 1921).

3. John Winthrop, ed. James Savage, *The History of New England from 1630 to 1649* (Boston, Thomas West, 1826), 31.

4. Edward Randolph, ed. Robert Toppan, *Edward Randolph* (Boston, the Prince Society, 1898), 69.

5. Hamilton A. Hill, *The Trade and Commerce of Boston, 1630 to 1890* (Boston, Damrell & Upham, 1895), 36.

6. Bernard Bailyn and Lotte Bailyn, *Massachusetts Shipping, 1697–1714* (Cambridge, Harvard University Press, 1959), 21.

7. Ralph Davis, *The Rise of the English Shipping Industry in the Seventeenth and Eighteenth Centuries* (London, Macmillan, 1962), 68.

8. Bailyn, *Massachusetts Shipping,* 28.

9. Morison, *Maritime History,* 22.

10. *Ibid.,* 26.

11. *Ibid.,* 28–29.

12. *Ibid.,* 29.

13. *Ibid.,* 85–86.

14. *Ibid.,* chaps. V–VI.

15. *Ibid.,* 154–155.

16. Hill, *Trade and Commerce,* 90.

17. Morison, *Maritime History,* chap. XIII.

18. *Ibid.,* 189.

19. *Ibid.,* 191.

20. George R. Taylor, *The Transportation Revolution, 1815–1860* (New York, Rinehart, 1951), 18.

21. Morison, *Maritime History,* 206.

22. *Ibid.,* 106.

23. *Ibid.,* 257.

24. *Ibid.,* 97.

25. Richard Henry Dana, *Two Years Before the Mast* (Boston, Houghton Mifflin, 1868), 386–387.

26. *Ibid.,* 252–253.

27. Morison, *Maritime History,* 269–271.

28. *Ibid.,* 280–283.

29. Hill, *Trade and Commerce,* 127.

30. *Annual Report of the Commissioner of Navigation, 1910* (Washington, Government Printing Office, 1910), 210–212.

31. U.S. Document 204, 21st Cong., 2nd sess., 1830–31, Senate Documents, vol. II, 280.

32. Edward C. Kirkland, *Men, Cities, and Transportation* (Cambridge, Harvard University Press, 1948), I, 7.

33. *Ibid.,* 6–11.

34. Carl C. Cutler, *Queens of the Western Ocean* (Annapolis, United States Naval Institute, 1961), 415–547.

35. Robert G. Albion, *The Rise of New York Port,*

1815–1860 (New York, Scribner's, 1939), 126–129; Kirkland, *Men, Cities and Transportation* I, 13–14.

36. Kirkland, *Men, Cities, and Transportation* I, 15–17.

37. *Ibid.*, 17–18.

38. *Ibid.*, 11.

39. Albion, *New York Port*, chap. VI.

40. *Ibid.*, chap. V.

41. *Ibid.*, 241.

42. *Ibid.*, 241–252.

43. U.S. Document 379, 26th Cong., 2nd sess., 1840–41, Senate Documents, vol. V, 294.

U.S. Document 604, 31st Cong., 2nd sess., 1850–51, House Executive Documents, vol. VIII, no. 15.

44. *Boston Shipping List*, September 9, 1843.

45. *Ibid.*, April 18, 1843.

46. *Ibid.*, September 18, 1850.

47. *Ibid.*, January 1, 1851.

48. Cutler, *Queens*, 444–457.

49. John G. B. Hutchins, *The American Maritime Industries and Public Policy, 1789–1914* (Cambridge, Harvard University Press, 1941), 259.

50. Hutchins, *Maritime Industries*, 266.

51. Morison, *Maritime History*, 333.

52. Howard I. Chapelle, *The Search for Speed Under Sail, 1700–1855* (New York, W. W. Norton, 1967), 398–400.

53. R. H. Thornton, *British Shipping* (Cambridge, Cambridge Univ. Press, 1959), 43.

54. *Third Annual Report of the Boston Board of Trade*, 1856 (Boston, 1856), 84–85.

55. Hutchins, *Maritime Industries*, 259.

56. *Ibid.*, 426–429.

57. *Ibid.*, 285.

58. *Ibid.*, 316–317.

59. *Ibid.*, 323.

60. *Ibid.*, 324.

61. U.S. Document 825, 34th Cong., 1st and 2nd sess., 1855–56, Senate Executive Documents, vol. XVI, 348.

U.S. Document 1458, 41st Cong., 3rd sess., 1870–71, House Executive Documents, vol. X, 748.

62. Hutchins, *Maritime Industries*, 377–378.

63. Stephen Salsbury, *The State, the Investor, and the Railroad* (Cambridge, Harvard University Press, 1967), 1.

64. Kirkland, *Men, Cities, and Transportation*, J, 81–84.

65. Kirkland, *Men, Cities, and Transportation*, I, 97.

66. Salsbury, *The State*, 132.

67. Kirkland, *Men, Cities, and Transportation*, I, 126.

68. Arthur M. Johnson and Barry E. Supple, *Boston Capitalists and Western Railroads* (Cambridge, Harvard University Press, 1967), 41; Kirkland, *Men, Cities, and Transportation*, I, 126

69. Kirkland, *Men, Cities, and Transportation*, I, 153.

70. *Ibid.*, 366–367; Hill, *Trade and Commerce*, 156–157.

71. Kirkland, *Men, Cities, and Transportation*, I, 370.

72. *Ibid.*, 381.

73. George P. Baker, *The Formation of the New England Railroad Systems* (Cambridge, Harvard University Press, 1949), 145–176.

74. Kirkland, *Men, Cities, and Transportation*, I, 430.

75. *Ibid.*

76. Baker, *Railroad Systems*, 71–99.

77. Kirkland, *Men, Cities, and Transportation*, II, 78–79.

78. *Ibid.*, 103–104.

79. *Ibid.*, 527–528.

80. *Ibid.*, I, 503.

81. *Ibid.*, 506.

82. *Ibid.*, 507.

83. *Ibid.*

84. *Ibid.*, 508–509.

85. *Ibid.*, 511.

86. *Ibid.*, 514.

87. Edwin J. Clapp, *The Port of Boston* (New Haven, Yale University Press, 1916), 88.

88. Kirkland, *Men, Cities, and Transportation*, I, 518–519.

89. *Ibid.*, 523–525.

90. Hill, *Trade and Commerce*, 161.

91. *Eleventh Annual Report of the Boston Chamber of Commerce, 1896* (Boston, 1897), 165–166.

92. *Boston Shipping List*, January 4, 1871. Boston *Commercial and Shipping List*, January 3, 1885.

93. Kirkland, *Men, Cities, and Transportation*, I, 524.

94. *Ibid.*

95. *Report of the State Board on Docks and Terminal Facilities* (Boston, 1897), 104–105.

96. *Statistical Abstract of the United States, 1900* (Washington, Government Printing Office, 1901), 447.

97. *Report of the State Board*, 75.

98. *Statistical Abstract, 1900*, 3.

99. *Manufacturing*, pt. 1, vol. 4, Eleventh Census, 1890 (Washington, Government Printing Office, 1895), 6.

100. *Ibid.*

101. *Boston Shipping List*, January 4, 1871; Boston *Commercial and Shipping List*, January 3, 1885; *Fifteenth Annual Report of the Boston Chamber of Commerce, 1900* (Boston, 1901), 171.

102. U.S. Document 2947, 52nd Cong., 1st sess., 1891–92, 1026, 1058.

103. William A. Baker, *A History of the Boston*

Marine Society (Boston, Boston Marine Society, 1968), 248.

104. *Eleventh Annual Report of the Boston Board of Trade, Merchants' Exchange,* 1864 (Boston, 1865), 66

105. *Fifteenth Annual Report of the Boston Chamber of Commerce, 1900* (Boston, 1901), 223.

106. Salsbury, *The State*, 8.

107. Johnson and Supple, *Boston Capitalists*, 24–32.

108. *Ibid.*, 107–126.

109. *Ibid.*, 51–54.

110. *Ibid.*, 24.

111. *Ibid.*, 82.

112. *Ibid.*, 56.

113. *Ibid.*

114. *Boston Evening Transcript*, November 17, 1897.

115. Johnson and Supple, *Boston Capitalists*, 205.

116. Morison, *Maritime History*, 369.

117. Albion, *New York Port*, 405.

118. Hill, *Trade and Commerce*, 149.

119. *Hearings Before The Merchant Marine Commission* (Washington, Government Printing Office, 1904), 501.

120. *Ibid.*, 238.

121. Kirkland, *Men, Cities, and Transportation,* II, 463.

122. *The Port of Boston,* Shawmut Series Number 227 (Boston, National Shawmut Bank, 1923), 30.

123. Shawmut Series 227, 36.

124. Clapp, *The Port of Boston*, 115.

125. *Ibid.*, 114.

126. *Ibid.*, chap. IX.

127. *Ibid.*, 126.

128. *Statistical Abstract of the United States, 1969* 90th ed. (Washington, Government Printing Office, 1969), 578.

129. W.P.A. Writers' Program, *Boston Looks Seaward* (Boston, Bruce Humphries, 1941), 228.

CHAPTER 2: SOME WATERFRONT VIEWS

1. M. F. Willoughby, *Lighthouses of New England* (Boston, T. O. Metcalf, 1920), 142.

2. *Savannah and Boston* (Boston, 1865), 14.

3. Harold Murdock, *1872* (Boston, Houghton Mifflin, 1909), 160.

4. Col. Frank Forbes, "The Old Wharves of Boston," *Proceedings of the Bostonian Society,* January 15, 1952, p. 26.

5. William A. Fairburn, *Merchant Sail* (Center Lovell, Fairburn Marine Educational Foundation, 1945–1955), 3145.

6. Ralph Eastman, *Pilots and Pilot Boats of Boston Harbor* (Boston, Second Bank-State Street Trust Co.,

1956), 71; statements of Mr. Thomas Lampee, Brookline, Mass.

7. Z. William Hauk, *T Wharf* (Boston, Alden-Hauk, 1952), 88–89.

8. Shubael Bell, *Bostonian Society Publications* 2nd ser., III, 30–32.

9. Forbes, "Old Wharves," 29.

10. Edward Chase Kirkland, *Men, Cities and Transportation,* 2 vols. (Cambridge, Harvard University Press, 1948), II, 156.

11. Forbes, "Old Wharves," 30.

12. *Ibid.*, 32.

13. Josiah Quincy, *Atlantic Avenue* (Boston, 1873), 10–11.

14. Letter from Edward C. Kirkland.

15. Edwin J. Clapp, *The Port of Boston* (New Haven, Yale University Press, 1916), 331.

16. *Boston's Growth* (Boston, State Street Trust Co., 1910), 41–42, 46.

17. R. G. F. Candage, Master Mariner, *Boston Harbor* (Boston, 1881), 19.

See also Benjamin A. Gould, *Boston Harbor* (Boston, Farwell, 1863).

18. *Annual Report of the Boston Chamber of Commerce, 1881* (Boston, 1889), 132.

19. *Seventeenth Annual Report of the Boston Chamber of Commerce, 1902* (Boston, 1903), 185.

20. Timothy T. Sawyer, *Old Charlestown* (Boston, J. H. West, 1902), 286, 406–407.

21. *Twenty-ninth Annual Report of the Boston Board of Trade, Merchants' Exchange,* 1882 (Boston, 1883), 62.

22. Clapp, *The Port of Boston*, 29.

23. *Ibid.*, 36.

24. *Boston's Growth*, 43.

25. George B. Goode and Others, *The Fisheries and Fishery Industries of the United States* (Washington, Government Printing Office, 1887), sect. ii, 201.

CHAPTER 3: SHIPBUILDING AND REPAIRING

1. William A. Fairburn, *Merchant Sail* (Center Lovell, Fairburn Marine Educational Foundation, 1945–1955), 2905.

2. Fairburn, *Merchant Sail*, 2949.

3. *Ibid.*, 2912.

4. *Second Annual Report of the Boston Board of Trade* (Boston, 1856), 61–62.

5. Henry Hall, *Report on the Shipbuilding Industries of the United States* in U.S. Census Office, Tenth Census, 1880, census reports, vol. 8 (Washington, Government Printing Office, 1884), 110.

6. Hall, *Shipbuilding*, 110.

7. Robert G. Albion, *The Rise of New York Port,*

1815–1860 (New York, Scribner's, 1939), 406.

8. U.S. Document 960, House Executive Documents, vol. 14, 35th Cong., 1st sess. (Washington, Government Printing Office, 1858), 624.

9. Edward Chase Kirkland, *Men, Cities and Transportation* (Cambridge, Harvard University Press, 1948), II, 198.

10. U.S. Document 1458, House Executive Documents, vol. 10, 41st Cong., 3rd sess. (Washington, Government Printing Office, 1871), 769–770.

11. Hall, *Shipbuilding*, 111.

12. W.P.A. Writer's Project, *Boston Looks Seaward* (Boston, Bruce Humphries, 1941), 200.

13. Howard I. Chapelle, *The Search for Speed under Sail, 1700–1855* (New York, W. W. Norton, 1967), 359.

14. *The Champion of the Seas Times* (Mystic, Marine Historical Association, 1952), 2.

15. John Lyman, "Donald McKay's Ships and Their Owners," *Log Chips*, August 1950, p. 2.

16. Richard C. McKay, *Some Famous Sailing Ships and Their Builder Donald McKay* (New York, Putnam, 1931), 10; Fairburn, *Merchant Sail*, 2945.

17. Robert K. Cheney, *Maritime History of the Merrimac—Shipbuilding* (Newburyport, Mass., Newburyport Press, 1964), 142, 277–292.

Hall, *Shipbuilding*, 86.

Statements of Capt. W. J. L. Parker, USCG (Ret.).

18. Fairburn, *Merchant Sail*, 2972.

19. *Ibid.*

20. Capt. W. J. Moore, *Down Easter Captain* (Ilfracombe, Devon, Arthur Stockwell, 1967), 128.

21. Fairburn, *Merchant Sail*, 2970.

22. *Ibid.*, 2969.

23. Hall, *Shipbuilding*, 200; also an untitled manuscript at the Hart Nautical Museum, Cambridge, Mass.

24. Lucius Beebe, *The Big Spenders* (Garden City, Doubleday, 1966), 379.

25. *Hearings Before the Merchant Marine Commission* (Washington, Government Printing Office, 1904), I, 668.

26. Thomas Walton, *Steel Ships: Their Construction and Maintenance* (London, Charles Griffin, 1926), 214–233.

27. Hall, *Shipbuilding*, 201.

28. John H. Morrison, *History of American Navigation* (New York, W. F. Sametz, 1903), 405.

29. Statement of Mr. Albert Barnes, The Mariners Museum, Newport News, Va.

30. *A Testimonial to Charles J. Paine and Edward Burgess from the City of Boston for their Successful Defence of the America's Cup* (Boston, Boston City Council, 1887), 71.

CHAPTER 4: SOME USEFUL VESSELS AND INSTITUTIONS OF THE PORT

1. M. F. Willoughby, *Lighthouses of New England* (Boston, T. O. Metcalf, 1920), 193–194.

2. Sumner I. Kimball, *Joshua James* (Boston, American Unitarian Association, 1909), 76.

3. Kimball, *James*, 5.

4. Sumner I. Kimball, *Organization and Methods of the United States Life-Saving Service* (Washington, Government Printing Office, 1890), 17–18.

5. Edouard Stackpole and James Kleinschmidt, *Small Craft at Mystic Seaport* (Mystic, Marine Historical Association, 1959), 74–75.

6. Kimball, *Organization*, 22.

7. Kimball, *James*, 50–75.

8. *Ibid.*, 85–94.

9. *Ibid.*, 97–100.

10. Capt. Stephen H. Evans, *The United States Coast Guard 1790–1915* (Annapolis, United States Naval Institute, 1945), 32.

11. Arnold B. Johnson, *The Modern Light-House Service* (Washington, Government Printing Office, 1889), 44–46; George R. Putnam, *Lighthouses and Lightships* (Boston, Houghton Mifflin, 1917), 214–225.

12. Ralph Eastman, *Pilots and Pilot Boats of Boston Harbor* (Boston, Second Bank-State Street Trust Co., 1956), 10–11.

13. *Thirtieth Annual Report of the Boston Board of Trade, Merchants' Exchange*, 1883 (Boston, 1884), 39.

14. Howard I. Chapelle, *The National Watercraft Collection*, United States National Museum Bulletin 219 (Washington, Government Printing Office, 1960), 91.

15. Charles I. Lampee, "Memories of Cruises on Boston Pilot Boats of Long Ago," *Nautical Research Journal*, 10: 57–58 (Spring 1959)

16. *Thirtieth Annual Report,* 39.

17. Statement of Mr. Thomas Lampee, Brookline, Mass.

18. Lampee, "Memories," 47.

19. *Ibid.*, 56.

20. *A Brief History of the Boston Floating Hospital* (Boston, a B.F.H. pamphlet, 1906).

21. *Twenty-ninth Annual Report of the Boston Board of Trade, Merchants' Exchange*, 1882 (Boston, 1883), 32.

22. Robert Greenhalgh Albion, *The Rise of New York Port, 1815–1860* (New York, Scribner's, 1939), 147.

23. *The Boston Globe*, August 13, 1900.

24. Boston City Document #11, 1894, 9.

25. Boston City Document #26, 1871, 261–262.

26. *Ibid.*, 263.

27. (Boston) *Sunday Herald,* October 31, 1920; Boston City Document #26, 141.

28. M. F. Sweetser, *King's Handbook of Boston Harbor* (Cambridge, Moses King, 1882), 21.

29. Samuel E. Morison, *The Maritime History of Massachusetts, 1793–1860* (Boston, Houghton Mifflin, 1921), 244.

30. Sweetser, *King's,* 219.

31. *Seventeenth Annual Report of the Boston Port and Seamen's Aid Society* (Boston, 1884).

32. J. P. Goldberg, *The Maritime Story* (Cambridge, Harvard University Press, 1958), 12; John B. Hutchins, *The American Maritime Industries and Public Policy, 1789–1914* (Cambridge, Harvard University Press, 1941), 429–430.

33. *Report of the Commissioner of Navigation, 1886* (Washington, Government Printing Office, 1887), 330.

34. W.P.A. Writers' Project, *Boston Looks Seaward* (Boston, Bruce Humphries, 1941), 169–170.

CHAPTER 5: FISHING

1. Raymond McFarland, *A History of the New England Fisheries* (New York, University of Pennsylvania, D. Appelton & Co., agents, 1911), 22.

2. Lorenzo Sabine, *The Principal Fisheries of the American Seas* (Washington, D.C., 1853), 7.

3. McFarland, *A History,* 26.

4. H. P. Beck, *The American Indian As a Sea-Fighter in Colonial Times* (Mystic, Marine Historical Association, 1959), 16–17.

5. McFarland, *A History,* 39.

6. *Ibid.*

7. George B. Goode et al. *The Fisheries and Fishery Industries of the United States* (Washington, Government Printing Office, 1887), sect. ii, 186–213.

8. Sabine, *American Seas,* 190.

9. McFarland, *A History,* 193.

10. *Ibid.,* 189.

11. *Ibid.,* 287.

12. *Ibid.,* 201.

13. See any *Annual Report of the Commissioner of Navigation* after 1885.

14. Goode, *The Fisheries,* sect. ii, 189.

15. *Ibid.,* 190.

16. *Ibid.,* 189.

17. *Ibid.,* 137.

18. *Ibid.,* 184.

19. *Boston Evening Transcript,* December 27, 1879.

20. *Eleventh Annual Report of the Boston Fish Bureau* (Boston, 1886), 19.

21. *Thirty-Third Annual Report of the Boston Fish Bureau* (Boston, 1908), 5.

22. *Fisheries of the United States, 1908,* Census Report (Washington, Government Printing Office, 1911), 153.

23. *Thirty-Third Annual Report,* 15.

24. *Ibid.*

25. Wesley George Pierce, *Goin' Fishin', The Story of the Deep-Sea Fisherman of New England* (Salem, Marine Research Society, 1934), 69–70.

26. *Ibid.,* 63.

27. James B. Connolly, *Fishermen of the Banks* (London, Faber and Gwyer, 1928), 26.

28. W.P.A. Writer's Project, *Boston Looks Seaward* (Boston, Bruce Humphries, 1941), 185.

29. Gilbert R. Payson, "Long Wharf and the Old Waterfront, History and Reminiscences," *Proceedings of the Bostonian Society,* January 17, 1928, pp. 38–39.

30. Goode, *The Fisheries,* sect. iv, 6.

31. *Ibid.,* 15.

32. *Ibid.,* sect. v, vol. I, no. 6, pp. 247–248; sect. iv, 20.

33. 1908 Census, 153.

34. Goode, *The Fisheries,* sect. iv, 103.

35. *Ibid.,* 8.

36. Pierce, *Goin' Fishin',* 149.

37. McFarland, *A History,* 210.

38. Goode, *The Fisheries,* sect. v, vol. I, pp. 490–491.

39. *Ibid.,* 240.

40. Statement of Mr. Albert M. Barnes, Mariners Museum, Newport News, Va.

41. Goode, *The Fisheries,* sect. v, vol. I, pp. 234–240.

42. McFarland, *A History,* 261.

43. *Thirteenth Annual Report of the Boston Fish Bureau* (Boston, 1888), 22.

44. Goode, *The Fisheries,* sect. v, vol. I, p. 248.

45. *Twenty-Third Annual Report of the Boston Fish Bureau* (Boston, 1898), 4.

46. Goode, *The Fisheries,* sect. v, vol. I, pp. 3–89.

47. *Ibid.,* sect. iv, 58.

48. *Ibid.,* 109–110.

49. Howard I. Chapelle, *The National Watercraft Collection,* United States National Museum Bulletin 219 (Washington, Government Printing Office, 1960), 224.

50. Pierce, *Goin' Fishin',* 199–201.

51. B. B. Crowninshield, *Fore-and-Afters* (Boston, Houghton Mifflin, 1940), 14–15.

52. Chapelle, *Watercraft,* 226.

53. *Ibid.,* 172.

54. Crowninshield, *Fore-and-Afters,* 17.

CHAPTER 6: COASTAL SAIL

1. *Annual Report of the Commissioner of Navigation, 1910* (Washington, Government Printing Office, 1910), 210–212.

2. *Statistical Abstract of the United States, 1914*

(Washington, Government Printing Office, 1915), table 217, 299.

3. *Statistical Abstract*, 299.

4. Howard I. Chapelle, *The National Watercraft Collection*, United States National Museum Bulletin 219 (Washington, Government Printing Office, 1960), 40.

5. Lt. W. J. Lewis Parker, *The Great Coal Schooners of New England, 1870–1909* (Mystic, Marine Historical Association, 1948), 28–29.

6. John Lyman, "Three-Masted Schooners Built on the East Coast," *Log Chips*, 3: 56–58 (April 1953).

7. Parker, *Coal Schooners*, 30.

8. Charles S. Morgan, "New England Coasting Schooners," *The American Neptune*, January 1963, 23: 6.

9. Parker, *Coal Schooners*, 15.

10. John Lyman, "Three-Masted Schooners," January 1951; January and May 1952, and "Four-Masted Schooners Built on the East Coast," *Log Chips*, 1: 17–18 (September 1948).

11. John G. B. Hutchins, *The American Maritime Industries and Public Policy, 1789–1914* (Cambridge, Harvard University Press, 1941), 557.

12. *Eleventh Annual Report of the Boston Board of Trade, Merchants' Exchange 1864* (Boston, 1865), 66.

13. *Twenty-Seventh Annual Report of the Boston Board of Trade, Merchants' Exchange 1880* (Boston, 1881), 98–99.

14. Hutchins, *Maritime Industries*, 546.

15. *Fifteenth Annual Report of the Boston Chamber of Commerce, 1900* (Boston, 1901), 223.

16. *Ibid.*, 171.

17. B. B. Crowninshield, *Fore-and-Afters* (Boston, Houghton Mifflin, 1940), 33.

18. Boston *Commercial and Shipping List*, January, July 1885.

19. *Ibid.*, January 3, 1885.

20. George S. Wasson and Lincoln Colcord, *Sailing Days on the Penobscot* (Salem, Marine Research Society, 1932), 194–204.

21. Boston *Commercial and Shipping List*, July 18, 1885.

22. *The Photographic History of the Civil War*, vol. IV (New York, Review of Reviews, 1911), 334.

23. William Bronson, *Still Flying and Nailed to the Mast* (New York, Doubleday, 1960), 99; see also Samuel Eliot Morison, *One Boy's Boston 1887–1901* (Boston, Houghton Mifflin, 1962), 21–26.

24. Howard I. Chapelle, *The History of American Sailing Ships* (New York, W. W. Norton, 1935), 301.

25. Robert Carter, *A Summer Cruise on the New England Coast* (Boston, Crosby & Nichols, 1964), 109.

26. Crowninshield, *Fore-and-Afters*, 31.

John F. Leavitt, *Wake of the Coasters*, Middletown, Wesleyan Univ. Press, 1970, p. 151.

27. Boston *Commercial and Shipping List*, July 1860.

28. Capt. Alfred Green, *Jottings From a Cruise* (Seattle, Kelly, 1944), 142–143.

29. Statement of Capt. W. J. L. Parker, USCG (Ret.).

30. Frederick S. Laurence, *Coasting Passage* (Arlington, Mass., C. S. Morgan, 1950), 34.

31. Edward C. Kirkland, *Industry Comes of Age* (New York, Holt, Rinehart & Winston, 1961), 139–140.

32. Parker, *Coal Schooners*, 14–15.

33. J. W. Somerville, "West Indian Hurricane," *The American Neptune*, 6: 133 (April 1946).

34. Parker, *Coal Schooners*, 15–16.

35. *Ibid.*, 16.

36. *Ibid.*, 18.

37. Lyman, "Four-Masted Schooners," 17–18.

38. *Report of the Commissioner of Navigation, 1886* (Washington, Government Printing Office, 1887), 331.

39. Capt. W. J. Moore, *Down Easter Captain* (Ilfracombe, Arthur H. Stockwell, 1967), 98.

40. Crowninshield, *Fore-and-Afters*, 35.

41. *Ibid.*, 35–36.

42. Parker, *Coal Schooners*, 35–36.

43. *Ibid.*, 23.

44. Morgan, *Coasting Schooners*, 17.

45. "The Sailor's Graveyard," *The New England Fisheries*, July 1918.

46. Statement of Mr. John Clement, Litchfield, N.H.

47. A. E. Averill, "A Maine Boy at Sea in the Eighties," *The American Neptune*, 10: 204–205 (July 1950).

48. Crowninshield, *Fore-and-Afters*, 53.

49. Hutchins, *Maritime Industries*, 379.

50. William A. Fairburn, *Merchant Sail* (Center Lovell, Fairburn Marine Educational Foundation, 1945–1955), 2616–2617.

51. Parker, *Coal Schooners*, 77.

52. *Seventeenth Annual Report of the Boston Chamber of Commerce 1902* (Boston, 1903), 232.

53. Parker, *Coal Schooners*, 90.

54. *Ibid.*, 91.

55. *Ibid.*

56. *Ibid.*, 64.

57. *Ibid.*, 65.

58. Statement of Capt. W. J. L. Parker, USCG, (Ret.).

59. *Boston Evening Transcript*, November 28, 1888.

60. *Hearings before the Merchant Marine Commission* (Washington, Government Printing Office, 1904), I, 405–406.

61. Laurence, *Coasting Passage*, 14.

CHAPTER 7: COASTAL STEAM

1. *Boston Shipping List*, January 1, 1851.

2. *Ibid*, January 2, 1861.

3. Boston *Commercial and Shipping List*, January 1, 1881.

4. *Fifteenth Annual Report of the Boston Chamber of Commerce 1900* (Boston, 1901), 171.

5. *Fifteenth Annual Report*, 163, 171.

6. *Report of the State Board on Docks and Terminal Facilities* (Boston, 1897), 75.

7. John B. Hutchins, *The American Maritime Industries and Public Policy, 1789–1914* (Cambridge, Harvard University Press, 1941), 565–566.

8. John H. White, *American Locomotives, An Engineering History, 1830–1880* (Baltimore, Md., Johns Hopkins Press, 1968), 74.

9. Francis B. C. Bradlee, *Some Account of Steam Navigation in New England* (Salem, Essex Institute, 1920), 84.

10. Bradlee, *Some Account*, 86.

11. *Ibid.*, 129–130.

12. Edward C. Kirkland, *Men, Cities, and Transportation* (Cambridge, Harvard University Press, 1948), II, 175–176.

13. *Ibid.*, 130.

14. Thomas H. Eames, "The Wreck of the Steamer *Portland*" in John M. Richardson's *Steamboat Lore of the Penobscot* (Augusta, Me., Augusta Journal Print Shop, 1941), 147; *Boston Evening Transcript*, November 30, 1898.

15. George S. Wasson and Lincoln Colcord, *Sailing Days on the Penobscot* (Salem, Marine Research Society, 1932), 66–67.

16. M. F. Sweetser, *King's Handbook of Boston Harbor* (Cambridge, Moses King, 1882), 274.

17. Howard S. Buck, an excerpt from *The Old City of Bangor; A Confession* (Chicago, privately printed, 1934), reprinted in *Steamboat Bill of Facts*, no. 12 (December 1943), 214.

18. Richardson, *Steamboat Lore*, 26.

19. N. Hawkins, *New Catechism of the Steam Engine, with Chapters on Gas, Oil, and Hot Air Engines* (New York, T. Audel, 1900) 389–393.

20. David Plowden, *Farewell to Steam* (Brattleboro, Vt., Stephen Greene, 1966), 89.

21. T. C. Purdy, *Report on Steam Navigation in the United States,* a Tenth Census Report (Washington, Government Printing Office, 1884), 34.

22. Kirkland, *Men, Cities, and Transportation*, II, 129.

23. Statement of Capt. W. J. L. Parker, USCG (Ret.).

24. Erik Heyl, "The Neptune Quintuplets," *Steamboat Bill of Facts,* no. 40 (March 1951), 2–5.

25. C. P. Pittee, "The Gloucester Steamboats," *The American Neptune,* 12: 288–293 (October 1952).

26. Bradlee, *Some Account*, 43.

27. Heyl, "Quintuplets," 4; Bradlee, *Some Account*, 135. For differing accounts see Purdy, *Report*, 10; and *Twenty-Seventh Annual Report of the Boston Board of Trade, Merchants' Exchange 1880* (Boston, 1881), 46. I suspect that the accuracy of the latter account suffers from an excess of local pride.

28. *Twenty-Seventh Annual Report,* 46.

29. Kirkland, *Men, Cities, and Transportation*, II, 183.

30. Dumas Malone, ed., *Dictionary of American Biography* (New York, Scribner's, 1934), XIII, 239–241.

31. Bradlee, *Some Account*, 137.

32. Malone, *Dictionary*, 241.

33. Edmund F. Gray, "A Brief History of the Boston & Philadelphia Steamship Co.," *Steamboat Bill of Facts,* no. 49 (March 1954), 6.

34. Kirkland, *Men, Cities, and Transportation*, II, 171.

35. Thomas Main and Thomas Brown, *The Marine Steam Engine* (Philadelphia, Henry Carey Baird, 1865), 138–139.

36. Hutchins, *Maritime Industries*, 568–569.

37. William B. Taylor, "A Short History of the Merchants' & Miners' Transportation Co.," pt. III, *Steamboat Bill of Facts,* no. 41 (March 1952), 7.

38. Taylor, "Merchants' & Miners'," pt. II, *Steamboat Bill,* no. 40 (December 1951), 84.

39. *Ibid.*, pt. IV, *Steamboat Bill,* no. 42 (June 1952), 36.

40. George A. Hough, Jr., *Disaster on Devil's Bridge* (Mystic, Marine Historical Association, 1963), 19–21.

41. Kirkland, *Men, Cities, and Transportation*, II, 179–181.

42. Hough, *Disaster on Devil's Bridge*, 19–21.

43. *Ibid.*, 19, 123.

44. *Hearings before the Merchant Marine Commission* (Washington, Government Printing Office, 1904), I, 407.

45. Kirkland, *Men, Cities, and Transportation*, II, 176.

46. Howard I. Chapelle, *The National Watercraft Collection,* United States Museum Bulletin 219 (Washington, Government Printing Office, 1960), 150.

47. W. J. Alward, "Our Coastwise Caravans," *Harper's Monthly Magazine,* 119: 404 (August 1909).

48. *Hearings before Merchant Marine Commission.*

49. *Ibid.*, 48.

50. *Ibid.*, 50.

51. Kirkland, *Men, Cities, and Transportation*, II, 70.

52. Alward, "Caravans," 408.

53. *Eighteenth Annual Report of the Boston Chamber of Commerce, 1903* (Boston, 1904), 186.

54. *Ibid.*, 240–241.

55. Lt. W. J. Lewis Parker, *The Great Coal Schooners of New England, 1870–1909* (Mystic, Marine Historical Association, 1948), 92.

56. *Ibid.*, 93.

57. *Ibid.*, 99.

58. *Ibid.*, 101.

CHAPTER 8: DEEP-WATER SAIL

1. *Boston Shipping List*, July 4, 1855.

2. *Ibid.*, July 3, 1875.

3. Boston *Commercial and Shipping List*, July 4, 1885.

4. U.S. Document 1102, House Executive Documents, vol. 11, 36th Cong., 2nd sess. (Washington, Government Printing Office, 1861), 650.

5. U.S. Document 1458, House Executive Documents, vol. 10, 41st Cong., 3rd sess. (Washington, Government Printing Office, 1871), 748.

6. U.S. Document 1966, House Executive Documents, vol. 16, 46th Cong., 3rd sess. (Washington, Government Printing Office, 1881), 838.

7. U.S. Document 2853, House Executive Documents, vol. 23, 51st Cong., 2nd sess. (Washington, Government Printing Office, 1891), 938.

8. Frank Thober, "Square-Riggers Built in the United States since 1870," *Log Chips*, 2 (March, May, July 1952); 3 (September 1952; January, April, July 1953; October 1954).

9. Frank Thober, "Square-Riggers," *Log Chips*, 2 (March, May 1952).

10. William W. Bates, *American Marine* (Boston, Houghton Mifflin, 1893), 255.

11. Frederick C. Mathews, *American Merchant Ships* (Salem, Marine Research Society, 1931), ser. ii, 159–168.

12. *Twenty-Seventh Annual Report of the Boston Board of Trade, Merchants' Exchange, 1880* (Boston, 1881), 97.

13. U.S. Document 1512, House Executive Documents, vol. 9, 42nd Cong., 2nd sess. (Washington, Government Printing Office, 1872), 716.

14. *Annual Report of the Boston Chamber of Commerce for the year 1890* (Boston, 1891), 135.

15. *Ibid.*

16. *Third Annual Report of the Boston Board of Trade, Merchants' Exchange, 1856* (Boston, 1857),

104; Hamilton A. Hill, *The Trade and Commerce of Boston, 1630–1890* (Boston, Damrell & Upham, 1895), 152.

17. Capt. W. J. Moore, *Down Easter Captain* (Ilfracombe, Arthur H. Stockwell, 1967), 29.

18. Henry Hall, *The Ice Industry of the United States* (Washington, Government Printing Office, 1881), 3, from the Tenth Census.

19. U.S. Document 1458, 224.

20. *Sixteenth Annual Report of the Boston Board of Trade, Merchants' Exchange 1869* (Boston, 1870) 140.

21. William H. Rowe, *The Maritime History of Maine* (New York, W.W. Norton, 1948) 260.

22. George G. Putnam, *Salem Vessels and Their Voyages* (Salem, Essex Institute, 1924, 1925), ser. iii, 60.

23. *Ibid.*, ser. iii, 61.

24. *Ibid.*, 72.

25. *Ibid.*, 19–21, 25.

26. *Ibid.*, 49, 151–152.

27. *Ibid.*, ser. ii, 121.

28. *Ibid.*, ser. iii, 73.

29. *Ibid.*, ser. i, 4.

30. *Ibid.*, ser. iii, 67–71.

31. James A. Finn, "Twilight of a Merchant House," *Yankees Under Sail* (Dublin, Yankee, 1968) 26–35.

For a personal account by a Brewer & Co. master, see *Down Easter Captain*, listed above.

32. L. Vernon Briggs, *Around Cape Horn to Honolulu on the Bark Amy Turner, 1880* (Boston, Chas. Lauriat, 1926), 15.

33. For a remarkable first-hand account of the coolie trade see H. C. de Mierre, *The Long Voyage* (New York, Walker, 1963).

34. Bates, *American Marine*, 232–264.

35. J. A. Fincham, *A Treatise on the Masting of Ships and Mast Making* (London, Whittaker, 1843), 217.

36. *Annual Report of the United States Life-Saving Service, Fiscal 1903* (Washington, Government Printing Office, 1904), 29–32.

37. Basil Lubbock, *The Down Easters* (Glasgow, Brown, Son, & Ferguson, 1929), 30–32.

38. Mathews, *Merchant Ships*, ser. ii, 159–168.

39. Isabel Anderson, *Under the Black Horse Flag* (Boston, Houghton Mifflin, 1926), 36–37.

40. John G. B. Hutchins, *The American Maritime Industries and Public Policy, 1787–1914* (Cambridge, Harvard University Press, 1941), 428.

41. Samuel E. Morison, *One Boy's Boston, 1887–1901* (Boston, Houghton Mifflin, 1962), 36.

42. Briggs, *Amy Turner*, 22–24.

43. Statements of Capt. W. J. L. Parker, USCG (Ret.).

44. *Hearings Before the Merchant Marine Commission* (Washington, Government Printing Office, 1904), I, 526–527.

45. *Ibid.*, 411–417.

46. Frederick W. Wallace, *In The Wake of the Wind-Ships* (New York, Geo. Sully, 1927), 269.

47. Basil Lubbock, *The Last of the Windjammers* (Glasgow, Brown, Son & Ferguson, 1929), 21–24.

48. *The Boston Globe*, February 18, 1900.

49. *Report of the Boston Chamber of Commerce for 1910* (Boston, 1910), 136.

50. *Annual Report of the Commissioner of Navigation, 1906* (Washington, Government Printing Office, 1907) 233.

51. *The Boston Globe*, April 29, 1900.

52. Alan Villiers, *The Way of a Ship* (New York, Scribners', 1953), 147.

CHAPTER 9: DEEP-WATER STEAM

1. *Eleventh Annual Report of the Boston Chamber of Commerce 1896* (Boston, 1897), 165–166.

2. *Report of the State Board on Docks and Terminal Facilities* (Boston, 1897), 110–111.

3. *Ibid.*, 111.

4. *Annual Report of the Commissioner of Navigation, 1885.* (Washington, Government Printing Office, 1885), 46–47.

5. *Annual Report of the Commissioner of Navigation, 1887.* (Washington, Government Printing Office, 1887), 15.

6. *Annual Report of the Commissioner of Navigation, 1900.* (Washington, Government Printing Office, 1900), 25.

7. *Ibid.*, 125.

8. *Twenty-ninth Annual Report of the Boston Board of Trade, Merchants' Exchange 1882* (Boston, 1883), 33.

9. Robert Greenhalgh Albion, *The Rise of New York Port, 1815–1860* (New York, Scribner's 1939), 325.

10. Robert K. Cheney, *Maritime History of the Merrimac-Shipbuilding* (Newburyport, Newburyport Press, 1964), 80–84. Cheney maintained that the *Ontario* made three trips.

11. Hamilton A. Hill, *The Trade and Commerce of Boston, 1630 to 1890* (Boston, Damrell & Upham, 1895), 161.

12. *Report of State Board,* 104–105.

13. *Ibid.*, 143–144.

14. *The Port of Boston, U.S.A.* (Boston, a pamphlet from the Directors of the Port of Boston, 1914), x, xi.

15. Samuel E. Morison, *The Maritime History of Massachusetts, 1783–1860* (Boston, Houghton Mifflin, 1921), 298.

16. Carl Cutler, *Queens of the Western Ocean* (Annapolis, United States Naval Institute, 1961), 236.

17. C. R. Vernon Gibbs, *Passenger Liners of the Western Ocean* (London, Staples, 1952), 49.

18. Henry Fry, *The History of North Atlantic Steam Navigation* (London, Sampson, Low, Marston, 1896), 66, 90, 284.

19. C. D. Kunhardt, *Steam Yachts and Launches: Their Machinery and Management* (New York, Field and Stream, 1887), 26.

20. Eng. Captain Edgar C. Smith, *A Short History of Naval and Marine Engineering* (Cambridge, Cambridge University Press, 1938), 129–130.

21. *Ibid.*, 174.

22. N. R. P. Bonsor, *North Atlantic Seaway* (Prescot, Lancashire: T. Stephenson & Sons, 1955), 21–22.

23. U.S. Document 2299, House Executive Documents, vol. 19, 48th Cong. (Washington, Government Printing Office, 1885), 819, 826.

24. Fry, *North Atlantic Steam*, 105.

25. See Sir James Bisset's *Tramps and Ladies* (U.K.: Angus & Robertson, 1959) for a deck officer's account of service aboard some early Cunarders.

26. B. Martell, "On Causes of Unseaworthiness in Merchant Steamers," *Transactions of the Institute of Naval Architects*, 21: 10–11, 41 (1880).

27. Martell, "Causes of Unseaworthiness," 19.

28. Fry, *North Atlantic Steam*, 265–266.

29. *Nineteenth Annual Report of the Boston Chamber of Commerce, 1904* (Boston, 1905), 60, 123.

30. *Tenth Annual Report of the Boston Chamber of Commerce, 1895* (Boston, 1896), 134–135.

31. Plimsol, Samuel, *Cattle Ships* (London, 1890).

32. Bonsor, *Seaway*, 332–336.

33. Information from the *Boston Evening Transcript* and *The Boston Globe* during the week following the wreck. In fairness to the pilot, who was a respected mariner of long experience, it should be remembered that the version of the events leading up to the wreck as reported in the newspapers was based largely on hearsay. Mr. Thomas Lampee, of Brookline, whose grandfathers were both pilots, recalls that the accident was a very sore point of conversation for many years afterward.

34. Bonsor, *Seaway*, 349–357.

35. *Twenty-Second Annual Report of the Boston Chamber of Commerce 1907* (Boston, 1908), 53.

36. *Tenth Annual Report*, B.C.C. 148.

37. Bonsor, *Seaway*, 226; Cutler, *Queens*, 308, 373; Hill, *Trade and Commerce of Boston*, 145, 160.

38. *Report of State Board*, 108–109, consisting of the complete list of Warren Line exports from Boston for 1895.

39. Bonsor, *Seaway*, 228–230.

40. *Ibid.*, 83–96.

41. Fry, *North Atlantic Steam*, 153.

42. Bonsor, *Seaway*, 91.

43. Fry, *North Atlantic Steam*, 158.

44. *Sixteenth Annual Report of the Boston Chamber of Commerce 1901* (Boston, 1902), 181.

45. Charles M. Wilson, *Empire in Green and Gold* (Henry Holt, 1947), 18–35.

46. *Ibid.*, 69–109.

47. *Ibid.*, 77–85, 135–148.

48. Gilbert R. Payson, "Long Wharf and the Old Waterfront, History and Reminiscences," *Proceedings of the Bostonian Society* (January 17, 1928), 38.

49. Gibbs, *Passenger Liners*, 184–185.

50. Bonsor, *Seaway*, 259.

51. *Twenty-Second Annual Report of the Boston Chamber of Commerce*, 42.

52. Gibbs, *Passenger Liners*, 269.

CHAPTER 10: THE NAVY IN THE PORT

1. U.S. Document 1703, House Miscellaneous Documents, vol. 6, 44th Cong., 1st sess., 1875–1876 (Washington, Government Printing Office, 1876), 5.

2. *Ibid.*, 209–210.

3. Henry Hall, *Report on the Shipbuilding Industries of the United States* in vol. 8, Tenth Census Reports, 1880 (Washington, Government Printing Office, 1884), 235–236.

4. Howard I. Chapelle, *The History of the American Sailing Navy* (New York, W. W. Norton, 1949), 366.

5. J. C. Bruzek, "The U.S. Schooner Yacht America," *United States Naval Institute Proceedings* (September 1967), 180.

6. Chapelle, *Sailing Navy*, 314.

7. Frank M. Bennet, *The Steam Navy of the United States* (Philadelphia, Warren, 1896), 141–150.

John R. Spears, *The History of Our Navy* (New York, Scribner's, 1899), IV, 15–25.

8. Samuel Eliot Morison, *One Boy's Boston, 1887–1901* (Boston, Houghton Mifflin, 1962), 54.

9. Spears, *Our Navy*, V, 493.

10. Fred T. Jane, *Fighting Ships* (London, Sampson, Low, Marston, 1915), 171, 175.

11. Thomas P. Horgan, *Old Ironsides* (Boston, Burdette, 1963), 63.

12. Spears, *Our Navy*, V, 76.

13. Chapelle, *Sailing Navy*, 17, 371.

14. Spears, *Our Navy*, V, 119.

CHAPTER 11: RECREATION

1. Samuel E. Morison, *The Maritime History of Massachusetts, 1783–1860* (Boston, Houghton Mifflin, 1921), 247.

2. Harry Brown, *The History of American Yachts and Yachtsmen* (New York, Spirit of the Times Publishing Co., 1901), 38–39.

3. J. D. J. Kelley, *American Yachts, Their Clubs and Races* (New York, Scribner's, 1884), 106.

4. M. F. Sweetser, *King's Handbook of Boston Harbor* (Cambridge, Moses King, 1882), 106.

5. Sweetser, *King's Handbook*, 257–260.

6. W. J. L. Parker, *The Great Coal Schooners of New England, 1870–1909* (Mystic, Marine Historical Association, 1948), 23.

7. Sweetser, *King's Handbook*, 64–66; sequence of paragraphs reversed.

8. Statements of Mr. Thomas Lampee, Brookline, Mass.; Ralph Eastman, *Pilots and Pilot Boats of Boston Harbor* (Boston, Second Bank-State Street Trust Co., 1956), 48–49.

9. Kelley, *American Yachts*, 359.

10. Robert Carter, *A Summer Cruise on the New England Coast* (Boston, Crosby & Nichols, 1864), 28–33.

11. Henry G. Peabody, *Representative American Yachts* (Boston, H. G. Peabody—Heliotype Press, 1893), 23.

12. Peabody, *American Yachts*, 23.

13. B. B. Crowninshield, *Fore-and-Afters* (Boston, Houghton Mifflin, 1940), 69.

14. Peabody, *American Yachts*, 10.

15. C. D. Kunhardt, *Steam Yachts and Launches; Their Machinery and Management* (New York, Forest and Stream, 1887), 108.

APPENDIX I

1. Beaumont Newhall, *The Daguerreotype in America* (New York, Duell, Sloan & Pierce), 1961.

2. E. Florence Addison, "Nathaniel L. Stebbins, Marine Photographer," *Old Time New England*, 41: 2 (1950), 30–33.

3. Statement of Andrew Nesdall, Waban, Mass.

4. Letter from Robert Weinstein, Los Angeles, Calif.

5. Letter from Frank Kelly, South Boston, Mass.

Index

Index